pre-intermediate

teacher's book

Innovations

a course in natural English

Hugh Dellar and Andrew Walkley
with Richard Moore

United Kingdom • United States • Australia • Canada • Mexico • Singapore • Spain

Innovations Pre-intermediate
Teacher's Book
Dellar/Walkley/Moore

Publisher: *Christopher Wenger*
Series Editor: *Jimmie Hill*
Director of Development: *Anita Raducanu*
Director of Marketing: *Amy Mabley*
Editorial Manager: *Howard Middle / HM ELT Services*
Intl. Marketing Manager: *Eric Bredenberg*
Editor: *Lydia Kacelnik*
Copy Editor: *Process ELT (www.process-elt.com)*
Production Management: *Process ELT*

Printed in Singapore.
1 2 3 4 5 6 09 08 07 06 05 04

Sr. Print Buyer: *Mary Beth Hennebury*
Associate Marketing Manager: *Laura Needham*
Cover/Text Designer: *Studio Image & Photographic Art (www.studio-image.com)*

Printer: *Seng Lee Press*

For more information, contact Thomson Learning, High Holborn House, 50/51 Bedford Row, London WC1R 4LR United Kingdom or Thomson Heinle, 25 Thomson Place, Boston, Massachusetts 02210 USA. You can visit our Web site at: www.heinle.com

ISBN: 0-7593-9624-8
Teacher's Book

Contents

Introduction		4
Unit 1	**Where are you from?**	10
Unit 2	**Likes and dislikes**	16
Unit 3	**Have you got … ?**	21
Unit 4	**Times and dates**	26
Review: Units 1–4		32
Unit 5	**Buying things**	34
Unit 6	**How are you?**	40
Unit 7	**School and studying**	46
Unit 8	**Work and jobs**	52
Review: Units 5–8		59
Unit 9	**Eating out**	61
Unit 10	**Family**	68
Unit 11	**Getting around**	74
Unit 12	**Free time**	81
Review: Units 9–12		88
Unit 13	**Places to stay**	90
Unit 14	**What was it like?**	96
Unit 15	**What's on?**	102
Unit 16	**Telephoning**	107
Review: Units 13–16		114
Unit 17	**Accidents**	116
Unit 18	**Problems**	123
Unit 19	**Money**	130
Unit 20	**Society**	136
Review: Units 17–20		143

Introduction

Innovations, first published in 2000, was originally created to provide intermediate to high-intermediate students with interesting models of natural spoken English to motivate them beyond the intermediate plateau. *Innovations* has now been expanded and developed into a new series for teachers looking for a fresh approach to teaching young adults (*Elementary* (publication in 2005), *Pre-intermediate*, *Intermediate*, *Upper-intermediate*). It is based on a language-rich, lexical/grammatical syllabus that starts with the kinds of conversations learners want to have.

What's so innovative about *Innovations*?

Innovations Pre-intermediate, like the rest of the series, sets out to maximise students' ability to speak English with confidence and to help them begin to understand natural spoken English. It does this not simply by providing students with plenty of opportunities to use language in personal, creative and communicative contexts, but more importantly, by providing a predominantly spoken model of English. The English presented in the whole *Innovations* series is the English commonly used in everyday life by fluent, educated speakers. The series syllabus is designed to meet students' communicative needs and is therefore quite compatible with the objectives and 'can do' statements of the Common European Framework (CEF). At all levels, the prime concern is with what students will be able to *say* afterwards. As a result, the starting point for the syllabus is not the usual list of tense-based structures, but rather the typical kinds of conversations students want to be able to have in English. What is then presented and practised is the language (vocabulary and grammar) to have those conversations. However, writing is not neglected, and it is a strong feature of the Workbook.

How does *Innovations Pre-intermediate* fit in with the rest of the series?

At the elementary level students learn to use some of the most common questions they will be asked and a limited number of typical replies. In doing so, they cover a lot of basic grammar and vocabulary in specific contexts. *Innovations Pre-intermediate* recycles much of this language and builds on it by providing longer models of conversations for students to copy and practise. The additional listening sections help students' receptive understanding. The Coursebook also uses a wide range of topics to introduce new vocabulary and broaden the areas students are able to talk about, while a balance is maintained between functional and interactional English. Grammar is taught in small chunks, with several features focused on more than once in different contexts so that over a period of time students gain a fuller experience of how grammar is used. Through this constant recycling and expanding of their English, students are provided with a very solid basis for the conversations they most need and want to have. It brings students to a level where they can meet the challenge of intermediate-level English, with its more concentrated work on vocabulary and grammar.

In conjunction with *Innovations Intermediate, Innovations Pre-intermediate* will take students to the level of the Preliminary English Test (PET), and through (CEF) Level B1.

Organisation

Innovations Pre-intermediate is divided into twenty units. Each unit is further divided into three two-page sections, all of which provide self-contained and coherent lessons of 60–90 minutes. However, teachers may wish to vary the order in which they teach these elements as they see fit.

The first two-page section of each unit contains a short model conversation which students learn. This practises pronunciation and helps develop their conversational confidence. They can then go on and have longer conversations. Many courses miss out this essential first stage of learning short conversations. The vocabulary and grammar tasks in this section are tightly focused on the model and allow students to vary and personalise the conversation.

The second two-page section focuses on reading. The reading sections contain a broad variety of texts and tasks to develop students' receptive reading skills. They are carefully graded to allow students and teachers to get the maximum benefit from them. The majority of the texts are also recorded on the Audio CDs/cassettes. Within these sections, the activities focus on topic vocabulary and useful lexis from the texts. Aspects of grammar are also presented and practised. These presentation texts often provide examples of language usage that go beyond the context of the unit, as a way of giving the class variety and showing how language can have a broader usage.

Finally, the third two-page section gives students further listening practice in the form of one or two extended dialogues or a number of short dialogues. The listening tasks aim to give students the valuable skills practice they need at this stage, but again, there are useful language tasks to go with them.

Writing sections feature in all the odd-numbered units of the Workbook. These start with a 'Key word' section, which deals with common problems regarding linkers in writing (*however, although*, *because* and *because of*, etc.). This is then followed by a model of a typical text students may need to write in real life or for exams like PET and First Certificate in English (FCE). Students are then given a similar text to write as a task. In addition to the writing tasks in the Workbook, a number of activities in the Coursebook have a writing element.

There are five **Review** units with exercises to test and revise what students have learnt.

The **Tapescript** at the back of the Coursebook features all the conversations, listening texts and most of the pronunciation exercises that appear on the Audio CDs/cassettes.

The **Grammar commentary** at the back of the Coursebook provides students with general learning advice and more detailed information on individual grammar points.

The **Expression organiser** at the back of the Coursebook allows students to record and translate some of the most important expressions in each unit.

Other components

The Coursebook is complemented by a set of three Audio CDs/two Audio cassettes, a Workbook, this Teacher's Book, and a separate, photocopiable Teacher's Resource Book. There is also support in the form of a website with useful links, and the test-creating CD-ROM Exam View® Pro.

- **Audio CDs/cassettes**

  The Audio CDs/cassettes contain recordings of all the dialogues and reading texts, pronunciation exercises and those lexical exercises where the stress and intonation are particularly important.

- **Workbook**

  The Workbook can be used for self-study, but any of the exercises may be done either in class or as homework. In addition, the Workbook contains the writing tasks. It closely follows the contents of the Coursebook to provide the full support and revision students need at this level, but with some additional benefits. For example, we use the conversations in the Coursebook to gently introduce students to the kind of cloze test they will encounter in exams like PET and FCE. There are also some additional language exercises to expand students' vocabulary, and language notes that actually teach students useful items of grammar and lexis. Teachers may choose to use the Workbook or decide that there is sufficient exercise material in the Coursebook. If teachers choose not to use the Workbook as part of the course, it is a good idea to recommend it to students as additional practice.

- **Teacher's Resource Book**

  The Teacher's Resource Book provides forty photocopiable activities and games which closely support the material in the Coursebook.

- **ExamView® Pro**

  This unique CD-ROM contains a bank of test items for each unit that teachers can modify and customise. It is simple and quick to use and provides unit-by-unit tests for those teachers that require them.

- **Web materials**

  Teachers can visit the publisher's website: www.heinle.com. This includes a list of links that provide an extension to the topics and content of each unit, together with exercises for students to complete.

Getting the most out of *Innovations*

This Teacher's Book provides plenty of detailed advice on how to get the most out of *Innovations Pre-intermediate*. However, there are some general points to make about the special features you will find in the Coursebook. These features are highlighted in the next section.

Features of Innovations

Conversation

The first section of each unit is based on a short conversation. These conversations are good examples of typical conversations that people have about everyday topics, and contain many commonly-used expressions. In fact, one of the aims is to get students to memorise a lot of this language. There are memorisation activities in several of the units and these activities could be adapted and used for other units. For example, in **Making plans** on page 26 students use a skeleton of notes to help them remember the conversation. You could use this technique with any of the other conversations by writing the skeleton on the board and then asking students to use the notes to have the conversation in pairs. After students have become used to this technique, you could ask them to make their own set of notes based on the completed conversation.

When using the conversation in class, play the recording once so that students can answer the gist questions. Then play the recording again and ask them to try to fill in each of the gaps as they listen. They should then compare their answers with a partner. Play the recording a third time, but this time pause after each gap. Elicit the missing words and maybe write the complete expression on the board. Model the pronunciation and get students to practise saying it. Play the recording through one more time with students following the completed script.

Many of the conversations have been 'sound scripted' in the **Tapescript** at the back of the Coursebook. Here, stressed words have been capitalised and pauses have been clearly marked. This helps students get used to the way language is 'chunked' – where speakers pause, and more importantly, where they do not pause – and to the rhythm of spoken English. Students listen to the recording while reading the sound script. Then ask them to use the script to read the conversation aloud in pairs, focusing on the phrasing and stress.

Much of the language presented and explored in the unit appears in the conversation, so students get to see and hear it in meaningful contexts. For example, in **Making friends** on page 8, Danko is talking about his home town of Split and says *There are lots of lovely people there.* Expressions with *there's / there are* is the focus of a later **Using grammar** activity on page 12.

Reading

The second part of each unit is based on a reading text. These texts are derived from authentic articles, but have been re-written to include maximally useful vocabulary and collocations. The texts are all related to the topic of the unit and are designed to elicit some kind of personal response from students.

Encourage students to read the whole text through without worrying too much about any words they don't know – ask them to put their pens down for a minute and relax! One good way of ensuring they do this is to play the recording of the reading while students follow the text in silence. If you feel the recording is too fast for your students, read it yourself at a pace they can cope with. This also gives students the opportunity to hear how the text is spoken. Important vocabulary is focused on later, and students need to gain confidence in their ability to understand most – if not all – of a text. Encourage students to focus on the many words they *do* know!

With both the reading and listening texts, you could simply ask students: *Do you have any questions about the text?* Note that this is a different question to *Are there any words which you don't know?* because it allows students to ask about anything. They can ask about words they *do* know, but which may appear with a new meaning or in a new collocation; they can ask about whole expressions; they can ask about the content; they can even ask you what *you* think. Encouraging students to ask questions is a good way to encourage them to notice language. It can also help to create a good relationship between you and your students.

Most reading texts are followed by a comprehension task and activities that focus on particular lexical items or collocations within the text. Encourage students to re-read the text and notice how these items are used within the texts. There are also speaking activities where students have the opportunity to react personally to the text and to extend the discussion on a related theme. These can either be done in pairs or in small groups.

Listening

The third part of the unit is based on a listening text, either a single conversation or a series of conversations, related to the overall topic of the unit. Unlike the conversations in the first section of the unit, they give students the opportunity for more extended listening practice. Again, remind students that they don't need to understand everything. You may need to play the recording a couple of times. Finish up by asking students to listen and read along with the tapescript at the back of the Coursebook.

Each listening is usually accompanied by pre-listening and post-listening speaking tasks that help students prepare for and react to the content of the conversations. There are also activities that exploit useful vocabulary and grammar appearing in the conversations.

Using vocabulary

Throughout *Innovations Pre-intermediate* there are sections explicitly dealing with vocabulary. These sections focus on expressions and collocations both related to the topic of the unit and based on language appearing in the conversations or readings. As you go through the answers, you can also get students to repeat the key language for pronunciation and ask the kind of questions mentioned in **Noticing surrounding language** on page 8. The teaching notes for each activity give examples of specific questions to ask. The vocabulary exercises are usually followed by opportunities for students to use some of the language in short speaking tasks.

Key words

There are several **Key word** sections throughout *Innovations Pre-intermediate* that focus on useful expressions containing very common words like *get*, *die*, and *sort out*. It might be a good idea for students to devote a page in their notebooks to each of these key words. They can record the expressions from the activity and then add to their list whenever they notice more examples.

Using grammar

Each unit contains at least one section dealing with a particular grammatical structure. These structures range from the traditional tense-based structures like the past simple to other structures like using *not enough* and *too*. The structures are always given in meaningful contexts, and students see how they can use the language themselves. Give students the basic patterns for the structure and encourage them to record examples from the exercises in their notebooks. Again, there are speaking tasks linked to the particular structure. Reference is always made to the corresponding section in the **Grammar commentary**.

Grammar commentary

The **Grammar commentary** starts on page 165 of the Coursebook, with two pages outlining the basic approach to grammar taken in the course. Ask students to read these pages early on in the course and discuss questions that arise from it. The grammar points that follow refer to the **Using grammar** sections within the units. As a rule, you can ask students to read the **Grammar commentary** as a way to review the language after they have worked on the activities. However, in some cases you might want students to come up with a guideline or 'rule' themselves and then compare it to the explanation in the **Grammar commentary** before working on the exercises. The **Grammar commentary** is another good source of useful examples for students to record.

Pronunciation

As *Innovations Pre-intermediate* places such an emphasis on spoken English, pronunciation is given a high priority throughout. There are activities practising things like stress, linking and contractions in most units. There are also several activities in each of the **Review** units which focus on stress patterns, and some individual sounds and consonant clusters that many students find difficult. The recording provides students with models and they should be encouraged to repeat the examples several times chorally and individually, until they can say them naturally. Of course, you could also model the examples yourself.

Speaking activities

There are speaking tasks throughout the Coursebook. These are intended both as a way of encouraging students to use some of the new language they have met in personalised ways, and also as an opportunity for students to relax and enjoy talking to each other! Whenever possible, try to introduce these speaking tasks by talking about yourself and encouraging the class to ask you questions. This serves as a model of what you are asking students to do and is another good source of language input. Also, students generally like finding out more about their teachers.

You may wish to use these discussion periods as a chance to monitor students' spoken performance and to gather student errors to focus on later, or as a chance to listen for gaps in students' vocabularies which can later be addressed. A good way to give feedback on these sections is to re-tell what one or two students said. Re-telling what students say – sometimes called reformulation – is a good technique because it allows even the weakest students to share their experiences and ideas with the whole class without the pressure of performing in front of them. It's quicker — there are no painful pauses — and maintains the pace of the lesson. Finally, it allows you to correct and introduce useful new language in a way which acknowledges that the student has successfully conveyed his/her meaning. You can write some of this new language on the board if you like, but it is not strictly necessary.

Real English

The **Real English** notes throughout the Coursebook refer to a particular piece of language – a word, expression or grammatical structure – that appears in one of the tasks. The notes contain features of everyday English which many more traditional coursebooks overlook, and so it is important to draw students' attention to the explanations and examples. Add more examples or ask a few related questions to exploit the notes further, if you wish.

Review units

After every four units there is a **Review**, which gives students the chance to re-visit and consolidate language they have studied. Most of the activities involve pair or small group work and so are best done in class. Each **Review** contains several activities focusing on the grammar and vocabulary from the previous four units as well as a section on pronunciation. There are also **What can you remember?** and **Look back and check** activities, where students repeat and recall information they have learned. Repeating activities, perhaps unsurprisingly, often leads to better student performance the second time round, and you may want to do these activities more regularly as a quick way of revising things. You could use the **Vocabulary quizzes** with the whole class divided into two or more teams. Award points and score them as if they were real quizzes.

Tapescript

The **Tapescript** starts on page 148 and features all of the conversations from the listening sections as well as sound scripts of several of the conversations.

Language strips

The language strips at the beginning of each unit contain expressions from the unit which students may have difficulty with. Using the strips before starting the unit gives you the chance to pre-teach some of the expressions that students will encounter, as well as a way of previewing the topic of the unit. You could start off by having a short task where students quickly look through the strip to find expressions that fit certain criteria, for example, those they have heard before, or those they could use about themselves. The teaching notes contain specific tasks that you can set for each unit. You can then follow up by asking students to share their ideas in groups. This lets students help each other with some of the more difficult expressions.

Another technique is to ask students to choose a couple of expressions that look interesting and find out what they mean by looking in their dictionary and then share their ideas in small groups. You may need to give some guidance about how students can do this. For example: for *Have you got a light?* in **Unit 1**, tell students to look at the phrases at the end of the dictionary entry for the key word, in this case, *light*. If students are studying in an English-speaking country, you could also encourage them to go out and ask people about the expressions. The notes for each unit also give definitions and examples for some of the more idiomatic expressions.

The language strips are also useful as a source of five-minute filler activities, between more substantial activities or at the end of a lesson, and used in this way, serve to recycle some of the language. Again, there are specific suggestions in the notes for each unit, but the following are some general ideas which can be used for most of the strips:

1. Ask students to find the expressions which are responses to two or three questions or remarks you write on the board.
2. Copy some of the expressions onto an overhead transparency, leaving some gaps. Ask students to complete the expressions before opening their Coursebooks, and then compare their answers with the strip.
3. Ask students to identify expressions which contain language which has occurred in an earlier unit, such as a tense or key word like *get*.
4. Ask students to discuss what words such as *it, this* or *there* could refer to.
5. Ask students to sort the expressions in different ways:
   a. positive vs. negative expressions.
   b. formal vs. informal expressions.
   c. those which are more likely to be used by men/women.
   d. those more likely to be used by young/older people.
   e. remarks which initiate a conversation vs. responses.
   f. (perhaps most importantly) those they would like to use themselves vs. expressions they would not feel comfortable using.

Noticing surrounding language

Although all the activities have a primary focus, for example, a particular grammar structure or a listening task, all the language is presented in natural contexts. This means that the surrounding language is just as important as the language being explicitly focused on. If the exercise concerns the present perfect, do not miss the opportunity to point out other surrounding common words and expressions at the same time. One of the most important ways students will improve on their own is if they notice more. Turn 'noticing' into a major classroom activity. In order to do this, you need to not only explain meaning, but also ask students questions such as:

What other things can you … ?

What other things can you describe as … ?

What's the opposite of … ?

What's the positive/negative way of saying … ?

If you do … , what would you do next/what happened before?

Where would you … ?

What do you use a … for?

What would you reply if someone said … ?

Plus more specific questions like:

What was the verb that came before … ?

What was the preposition after … ?

The aim of these questions is to generate useful language connected to the word or expression in the exercise and also for students to get an idea of the limits of collocation and differences with their own first language (LI). Questions like these are better than simply explaining, for three reasons. Firstly, they allow you to check whether students have understood what you have explained. Secondly, they are more engaging for students as you are involving them in the teaching process and accessing their current knowledge. Thirdly, they provide opportunities for students to extend their knowledge by introducing new language. In some ways, the questions are also convenient for you as a teacher, because students provide meanings in attempting answers and you can then provide the actual language by correcting any mistakes or re-stating what they said in more natural English. This new language can also be put on the board, ideally in the form of whole expressions as you would use them in speech.

You may also like to follow up a section of teaching like this by asking students to briefly personalise any new vocabulary you put on the board. For example, you could ask:

Do you know or have you heard about anyone who … ?

Do you know or have you heard about anyone who has … ?

When's the last time you … ? Where? What happened?

Can you use any of these words/expressions to describe things in your life?

Which is the most useful word/expression?

Which word/expression do you like the most?

You could put students into pairs to do this kind of exercise for five or ten minutes. This is a good way of breaking up the lesson and getting away from the Coursebook for a moment. It also encourages students to get to know each other better, and unlike supplementary materials, requires little planning and no fighting with the photocopier!

The teacher's notes suggest specific questions you can ask about language in the texts and there are also good examples of these kinds of questions in the **Vocabulary quizzes** in the **Review** units. It may take a little time for both you and your students to get used to this style of teaching, but it is worth persisting with it, as it produces a dynamic and language-rich classroom.

Recording language

It is a good idea to help students organise a notebook to record the language they meet. Early on in the course talk about recording this language in an organised way and suggest a notebook divided into several sections:

- a section organised alphabetically, containing not only the target words but associated collocations and phrases
- a section organised around themes such as describing people, work, films etc.
- a section organised around 'delexical' verbs and nouns such as *get, take, point, thing*
- a section for phrasal verbs and idioms
- a section for grammatical patterns and structures such as the present perfect and *have to …*

Also, talk about what should be recorded. Instead of just isolated words, encourage the recording of complete expressions, collocations, and even question/response exchanges. The Coursebook is a great resource of useful contextualised language that can be transferred directly to students' notebooks. Ask students to translate these larger expressions and idioms into an equivalent in their own language.

1 Where are you from?

Unit overview

General topic
Meeting people for the first time, talking and asking about where people are from.
Starting a conversation, making friends.

Conversation
Two people meet for the first time.

Reading
Three people explain why they moved to London.

Language input
- Conversation starters: *Do you know anyone here?*
- Past simple: *We decided to move because we didn't like the area.*
- *There is/there are: There's so much to see and do in London.*
- Expressions with *miss* and *lose*: *I missed my train, I got lost on the way here.*

Language strip

You can use the language strip as a way to lead in to the unit. Get students to quickly look through the strip and ask them to predict the theme of the unit. Then ask if they can find any expressions they have actually used themselves. Explain that in this unit they will learn expressions for starting conversations and talking about where people are from. Use the language strip later on in this unit for a small group task. Here are some possibilities:

- Students choose expressions that are questions (e.g. *Where are you from again?*) and come up with a possible response (e.g. *I'm from Belgium*). Then they choose expressions that are responses (e.g. *Oh, I've been there*) and come up with possible prompts (e.g. *Actually, I'm from Ankara*).
- Students discuss examples of what *it* or *there* is referring to in several of the expressions.
- Students choose three or four expressions from the list and – if necessary – change them to be true about themselves (e.g. *I really miss my town*). They can then talk about their choices.

You might need to explain some of the following expressions:

- If you ask someone for *a light*, you are asking them to lend you some matches or a lighter to light a cigarette. *Have you got a light?* can often be used as a way to start a conversation with someone you don't know.
- If you ask someone *Where are you from again?* you are implying that they have probably told you but you have forgotten. It can also be used to be slightly less direct when you have already been speaking to someone for a short time, even if the person hasn't already told you where they are from.
- If you say a place is *right up in the north,* you are emphasising that it is located in the far north of an area, for example a country. You can also use *down* with *south.* For example: *It's way down in the south.*
- If you ask someone if they come from somewhere *originally*, you are asking if they were born and/or grew up there. For example: *A: Are you originally from here? B: Actually, I grew up in a small town about 50 km away.*
- If you *grow up bilingual*, you have two first languages. Bilingual people often use one language with their family or friends and another at school/work.

Remind students to record any of the expressions they like in their notebooks and to take note when they see similar expressions throughout the unit.

Lead in

If this is the first time the class have been together, you could do some small 'getting to know you' activity before even opening the Coursebook. For example, you could give students the task of finding out three interesting things about any three of their classmates. After the activity is over, ask students to tell you some of the expressions they used. You could write them on the board and check that everybody understands them. You can then lead in to the first task (**1 Starting a conversation**) by explaining that students will now see several more ways in English of starting a conversation with someone they don't know.

Conversation

1 Starting a conversation

Before asking students to answer the two discussion questions, talk about how you yourself would answer them. This not only helps students get to know you, but also provides them with a model of how to answer. You may want to write some useful expressions on the board. For example:
I'm very sociable.
I'm a bit quiet.
I usually don't make the first move.
I'm a good listener.

Students can work on the two matching tasks individually or in pairs. Go through the answers and model the pronunciation. Get students to practise this along with you.

Answers

1. d. 2. a. 3. b. 4. c. 5. g. 6. h. 7. f. 8. e.

For further practice tell students to close their Coursebooks. Say each conversation starter and ask students to try to remember the matching response. Then divide the class into pairs and get them to take turns doing the same. This will give you another chance to monitor their pronunciation.

To generate some related language, ask students for variations of some of the responses. For example:
*What would you say if the answer to **1** was yes? (Actually, yes. But I think that one's free.)*

You may need to explain that in **d** *go ahead* means 'OK'. Give students some other examples when you can use this expression:
A: Do you mind if I answer the phone?
B: No. Go ahead.

Point out the expression *Take a seat.* You might want to add a couple of other related expressions with *seat:*
I'm afraid that seat's taken.
Can you save my seat?

Remind students to record any of the expressions they like from this task in their notebooks.

The final task provides an opportunity to talk about some related cultural issues. Talk about some of the typical sentence starters you use or know about. You could also talk about regional variations and differences based on age or gender. Go over the example responses and then get students in small groups to talk about these questions. Ask these groups to report back to the class as a whole.

As a follow up, ask pairs of students to write a dialogue based on the photo on page 8. They can then role-play the conversations to each other or to the class.

2 Making friends

This dialogue exposes students to much of the language focused on in this unit. Introduce the task by reading the instructions aloud. Suggest that students initially cover the conversation and remind them that they don't need to understand everything. To help them prepare for the listening task, you might want to elicit what kind of information they would expect to hear. Ask students to share their answers in pairs.

Answers

1. I'm sorry
2. Whereabouts exactly
3. have you been here in Britain?
4. going back
5. take some exams in
6. the main reason

Play the recording for the class. Next, let students read the dialogue as you play the recording again. Then ask them, in pairs, to fill in the first two or three gaps from memory before you play the recording again, this time with pauses so that they can check and fill in the missing words. Do this two or three gaps at a time until the end. Play the recording through one more time with students following the script.

Follow up by getting students to read the conversation in pairs. Then ask them to underline any expressions they find useful, particularly those they think they might use. Encourage them to transfer these into their notebooks. You might want to point out the following:
What's your name again?
I've heard of it but I've never been there.
What do you do back home?
That's the main reason I'm here.

Follow up by asking students to share with you their ideas for famous people from different countries. You don't need to limit examples to people and countries, though. Ask students what their hometown or region is famous for too. Write some phrases on the board to help. For example:
... is the most famous person right now.
Most people have heard of ... .
My town's claim to fame is that ... grew up there.

3 Where are you from? Whereabouts?

Introduce the task and get students to work either individually or in pairs. Then read the conversations one or more times so they can check their answers. Ask students to listen to how the expressions are said, in particular the intonation.

Answers

Conversation 1
So where are you from?
France.
Oh right. Whereabouts exactly?
Grenoble. It's in the south-east. Do you know it?
No. What's it like?
It's OK. It's quite a big city, but it's a nice place to live.

Conversation 2
So where are you from originally?
Oh, a place just near Blackpool.
Oh, yes. Whereabouts exactly?
St Anne's. Do you know it?
Yes, I do, actually. My grandparents lived there!

Conversation 3
So do you live near here?
Not that far. Haringey.
Haringey? Whereabouts exactly?
Allison Road. It's just past the shops where the church is. Do you know it?
Yes, yes. I used to live in Hewitt Road!

Conversation 1: 1.f. 2. b. 3.d. 4. c. 5. e. 6. a.
Conversation 2: 1. b. 2. d. 3. c. 4. e. 5. a.
Conversation 3: 1. d. 2. a. 3. b. 4. e. 5. c.

Follow up by getting pairs of students to practise reading the conversation and underline any useful phrases. In particular you may want to point out some of the location expressions (e.g. *It's in the south-east, a place just near … , Not that far, It's just past …*). You could also ask students to change parts of the conversations so that they are true about themselves.

In checking the answers to the three questions at the end, you may need to explain that Blackpool is a town by the sea in the north-west of England and that Haringey is an area of north London.

Answers

a. Conversations 2 and 3
b. Conversation 2
c. Conversation 1

4 Pronunciation: getting the stress right

This task helps students in the pronunciation of English by focusing on phrasing – speaking in groups of words – and stress. It is important to explain to students that getting this right can really help them be understood better. Bear in mind that stress is often conveyed by a combination of a slightly higher pitch, a lengthening of the syllable and a clearer and slightly louder articulation. Read the directions and play the recording once or twice while students just listen. Then play the recording again, stopping after each sentence, so students can repeat. Finally, you can get students to practise saying the sentences in pairs before they match the sentences to the places on the map. Before students describe the location of the cities at the bottom of page 9, go over and practise some of the location expressions in sentences **1–7**:
on the south/north-east coast
right in the centre of (England)
just outside (London)
in the south-west/north-west of (England)
right up in the north of (Scotland)

Answers

1. Brighton 2. Birmingham 3. Scarborough
4. St Albans 5. Bath 6. Inverness
7. the Lake District

Possible answers:
Cornwall is an area in the south-west of England.
Leeds is a city in the north-east of England.
Swansea is a city on the south coast of Wales.
Warwick is a small city right in the centre of England.
Manchester is a big city in the north-west of England.

Students may want to know the difference between a town and a city. Although the difference usually has to do with size and political/economic importance, in Britain a city traditionally has a cathedral whereas a town doesn't.

5 Practice

Before getting students to work on their own dialogues in pairs, model an example yourself with a student. Try to keep the conversation going and encourage students to do so too. Write expressions on the board that are different from the ones you used, and ask two students to model a conversation. Encourage them as they go along. Use this task to get students moving around, asking each other about where they live. Ask them to report back at the end.

Reading

1 Geography quiz

This task can act as a fun way to introduce the reading text (**I'm not from here originally**). Read aloud the names of the countries in the box so that students can hear the pronunciation. Then go over the expressions. Point out the useful word *somewhere* and write some relevant example expressions on the board. For example:

It's somewhere in the south of Asia.
It's somewhere in the middle of the Pacific.
It's somewhere near Belgium.

Extend the activity by asking students to share any knowledge they have about these countries. For example: What are the capital cities? Who played in the World Cup finals? Have any been in the news recently?

Answers

Albania is in Europe on the Adriatic coast, next to Greece and Serbia.
Bangladesh is in Asia, next to India.
Cuba is an island in the Caribbean, south of Florida.
Denmark is in Europe, north of Germany.
Ecuador is in South America, just north of Peru.
Japan is in Asia, near China and Korea.
Luxembourg is a small country in Europe next to Belgium, France and Germany.
Nicaragua is in Central America, between Costa Rica and Honduras.
Oman is in the Middle East, on the Persian Gulf.
Somalia is in East Africa, next to Ethiopia.
Tunisia is in North Africa, next to Algeria.
Wales is next to England.

2 Before you read

You can ask students to think of reasons why people move from one country/city to another. Students can do this activity either in pairs or small groups, or they can do it together as a class. You may want to list all the reasons on the board before students read the article (**I'm not from here originally**).

3 While you read (I'm not from here originally)

Point out the title of the article. Ask students what they think it means (*The person wasn't born/and or didn't grow up in the place*). Then ask students if they can find a similar expression in the language strip on page 8 (*Do you come from Berlin originally?*).

The initial purpose for reading is for students to find out why the three people came to London. Remind them not to worry about understanding everything. Ask them to check their answers with a partner when they have finished reading.

Answers

Faten came to London because her husband is from there.
Hung came to London as a refugee.
Ian came to London to look for work.

4 Comprehension

In pairs, students can try to remember the answers to these questions and then, as a class, confirm by checking in the article.

Answers

1. Ian 2. Faten and Hung 4. Hung 5. Faten's
6. Faten's children (and perhaps Hung's children too)

Talk about **Real English: refugee**. Explain the difference between a *refugee* and an *immigrant*.

5 Word check

In this task students focus on several useful expressions from the article (**I'm not from here originally**). Ask pairs of students to recall as many of the missing words as they can before they search the article. The expressions are in the same order as they appear in the text. Students can check their answers against the article once they have finished the exercise.

Answers

1. got 2. used 3. miss 4. ago 5. support
6. saved 7. closed 8. lost 9. unemployment
10. during

Provide more practice with these expressions by asking follow-up questions while checking students' answers. For example:
Is anyone here married? When did you get married? Was it a religious ceremony? Where did you get married?
What things do you miss from your country/home town?
Is anyone saving up for something special? What?
Why do you think the factory closed down in **7**? *What other things can 'close down'? (a theatre, a bar)*
What are some other reasons that you might lose you job?

6 Speaking

Introduce this activity by briefly talking about the three questions yourself. Encourage students to ask you follow-up questions. Write any useful expressions on the board. This serves as a model for when students do the activity themselves. You might want to feed in some additional questions to keep the discussion going. For example:
What are some advantages/disadvantages of being bilingual/married to someone from a different country?
What would you miss most if you lived in another country?

As students discuss in pairs or in small groups, go around the class and monitor. Give feedback when and if needed.

7 Using grammar: past simple

One way to introduce this section on the past simple is to ask students to find six or seven expressions in the article on page 10 (**I'm not from here originally**) that include a verb in the past simple. You can then read through the guidelines on forming the past simple tense together as a class. Make sure students hear the examples at least a couple of times.

Get students to work individually or in pairs to complete the list of verbs with irregular forms. Practise the pronunciation as you go over the answers. Because these verbs are so common, you might suggest that students allocate one page in their notebooks for each of these verbs and record example expressions containing the verb as they come across them.

Answers

buy bring come find get grow up have
know leave lose make say tell take go

Now get students to complete the task individually or in pairs. When you go through the answers, you could encourage students to think of possible responses to some of the statements/questions. For example in **2**: *So did you find a job? Why did you lose your job? Do you miss Bolton?*

You might need to explain that Bolton is a town in the north-west of England.

Answers

1. moved, got 2. left, lost
3. moved, died, wanted 4, decided, didn't like
5. didn't feel 6. hated, didn't have
7. did (you) move 8. did (they) leave

For further practice ask students to test each other in pairs. Student A reads each sentence but says *blank* for the missing word. Student B – with the Coursebook closed – repeats the sentence but includes the missing word. When students have finished, they can swap roles. To finish, ask students to look back through the activity and choose a couple of expressions to record in their notebooks. Remind them to record complete expressions and not just individual words. Encourage them to include a translation in their own language too. You can refer students to G1 of the **Grammar commentary** on page 165, which they can read either in class or as homework.

8 Speaking

Give students a few minutes to think about the questions before getting them in small groups to discuss. Write some patterns and expressions on the board to help:

(We) moved/left because (my father got a job.)
(We) moved/left because of (the crime.)
(We) moved/left to (get away from the city.)
(We) moved/left when (my sister) was born.
They've lived there their whole life.
That's a perfectly good reason.

Listening

1 Meeting people

First read the choices **a–f** as a class, answering any questions. Then give students a minute or two to think before they explain their choices to a partner. Make sure they understand that they can choose more than one alternative. Obviously, the answers will vary according to gender. If students are studying abroad, it might also be worth talking about what is considered appropriate, inadvisable or a bit forward in that particular country.

2 Before you listen

This task sets the scene for the listening task. You can discuss these questions as a class or get students to discuss them in pairs. Write some words on the board to help:
a tourist, a camera, a bag, country lane, sinister-looking

3 While you listen

Tell students that they are going to listen to a conversation between the two people in the picture. They should listen to see if their predictions were right. Play the recording once and then get students to discuss the answers to questions **1–4** in pairs. Play the recording again if necessary. You might then get students to follow the script on page 148 as you play it one more time. Ask them to underline and/or ask about any expressions they find interesting.

Answers

1. George and Norman Bates.
2. George is from Washington and Norman is from Burlington.
3. Washington is a dangerous place at night. Burlington has some crime too.

4 Using grammar: *there's / there are*

Read the first three examples and go over the guidelines with the class. You might want to explain that a noun is uncountable when it is used in such a way that is has no plural form. Often this is the case when we are talking about substances or abstract concepts like *crime* or *unemployment*. You shouldn't go into this in too much detail, however, as it is a very complex area and you may risk confusing your students. It would be wrong, for example, to say *crime* is always uncountable because in many contexts it is countable.

Get students to look at the next four examples and then complete sentences **1–8**. They can then compare their answers. You may need to point out that in **4** *people* is a plural noun.

Answers

1. There's 2. There are 3. There are 4. there are
5. There are 6. There's 7. There are
8. there's, There's, there are

Follow up by asking students to suggest places that might fit the descriptions in **1–8**. For example: *I could be about Hong Kong. It's got a great transport system.* Encourage students to look back through the task again and to record any expressions they find useful. You may want to point out the following:

it's good for (shopping)
it's not safe at night
there's not much to do
but that's about it

You can refer students to G2 of the **Grammar commentary** on page 165, which they can read either in class or as homework. Also talk about **Real English: There's a lot of …** on page 13. Point out that students will hear these forms being used, even though some people consider them 'wrong'.

5 Pronunciation: weak forms

You can either play the recording initially to check the answers to **4 Using grammar: *there's / there are*** or, if you have already gone over the answers, as a way to focus on the pronunciation of the contractions *there's/there're*. Play the recording, stopping after each sentence so students can repeat. Then get them to practise asking each other *What's it like there?* and answering with the completed sentences.

6 Practice

Model this activity yourself first. For example, talk about where you grew up, went to college, spent your last holiday. Get students to ask you follow-up questions as a way to encourage them to do the same when they work with their partner. Suggest that they record three or four personalised examples with *there's/there're* from this activity in their notebooks.

7 Key words: *miss* and *lose*

Some students confuse these two words. It's a good idea to focus on contextualised examples like the ones in the activity. Point out that *miss* can express a feeling of sadness because you can no longer do or have something, as in **4**: *I really miss going to the beach*, or it can mean that you failed to do something as in **6–8**. As you go through the answers, ask follow-up questions when possible. For example:

*What else could you have lost in **1**? (my PDA, notebook)*
*How can you change **5** to make it the opposite? (He's really overweight … he's put on a lot of weight … he used to be thin.)*

Answers

1. my address book 2. on my way 3. 2–1
4. the beach 5. weight 6. the class 7. the end
8. my train

For the second task you could get students to test each other in pairs. Point out that we say *miss the bus/train* but usually *miss my flight*.

Answers

1. lost 2. miss 3. miss 4. lost, missed

8 Speaking

Read the patterns aloud to the class and then give students a few minutes to think before getting them to discuss in pairs or small groups. You can also talk about your own answers either beforehand or afterwards. You might want to wrap up with a feedback session where you focus on some problem areas and maybe also some examples of successful communication.

Follow-up

Get students in pairs to write a dialogue between two people meeting for the first time. Either let students decide on the context themselves or suggest one (e.g. a lost tourist and a local, a student in a big city feeling lonely meets someone on a bus etc.). Encourage them to look back through this unit and find expressions to use. They can then role-play the conversation to other groups.

2 Likes and dislikes

Unit overview

General topic
Talking about likes and dislikes, friends and family, music, going out.

Conversation
Two people talk about the music they like and dislike.

Reading
Is it true that people these days think friends are more important than family?

Language input
- Expressions for describing likes and dislikes: *Yes, I love it, No I can't stand him.*
- Expressions for talking and asking about family and best friends: *I usually get on really well with my younger sister, How do you know each other?*
- Expressions with *go*: *How did it go? I went on my own.*
- Expressions with *too*: *I'm too tired to cook tonight, He talks too much.*

Language strip

You can use the language strip as a way to lead in to the unit. Ask students to quickly look through the strip and find any expressions they have actually used themselves or that are true for them. Ask them to share their findings with a partner or with the whole class. Explain that in this unit they will learn about ways to talk about likes and dislikes. Encourage them to choose a couple of expressions in the strip that look interesting and to find out more about them.

Use the language strip later on in this unit for a small group task. Here are some possibilities:
- Students sort the expressions into those that express a positive feeling (e.g. *I love anything by Mark Smith*), a negative feeling (e.g. *I can't stand traditional folk music*), and a middle-of-the-road feeling (e.g. *She's OK, I suppose*).
- Students sort the expressions into those that are connected with likes and dislikes (e.g. *I like anything with Jackie Chan in*) and those connected with relationships (*He sounds really nice*).
- Students choose three or four expressions from the list and change them so that they are true about themselves (e.g. *I like anything with Nicole Kidman in*). They can then share and talk about their choices.

You might need to explain some of the following expressions:
- If you *can't stand* something or someone, you really don't like them. For example: *I can't stand the way he talks.*
- If you use *I suppose*, you are showing that you are a bit uncertain about something. For example: *Do you know when the film starts? 8:00, I suppose.*
- If you *ring* someone, you call them on the phone. You can also use the expression *give someone a ring*. For example: *Give me a ring later this week and we'll arrange to go out.*

Remind students to record any of the expressions they like in their notebooks and to take note when they see similar expressions throughout the unit.

Lead in

You could lead in to this unit by talking about music. Ask students if they like listening to music, who their favourite singers/bands are, who is currently popular in their countries, if they go out to see bands, if they buy many CDs etc. You can also elicit a list of different styles of music (e.g. *hip-hop, new age, techno* etc.) and write them on the board. This leads in nicely to the first activity.

Conversation

1 Speaking

Focus students' attention on the photographs on page 14 and ask them to suggest the kind of music style in each picture **A–G**. Encourage them to give reasons for their choices. You can help by giving them phrases like:
I think it's … because of the hairstyle/the clothes/ instruments.
I know it's (jazz) because that's (Miles Davis).

Answers
classical C country F folk D heavy metal E
jazz B punk A soul G

If possible, play some examples of these styles of music to help students if they are unfamiliar with any of them. You might need to explain that *punk* is a style of rock music that originated in the UK in the middle to late seventies, that *folk music* is a label that tends to be applied to the traditional music of a country and that *soul* originated from black communities in America in the sixties and is a mix of gospel, blues and jazz.

Answers

Some musicians in each genre:
classical: Alfred Brendel country: Loretta Lynn
folk: Joan Baez heavy metal: Metallica
jazz: Louis Armstrong punk: Sex Pistols
soul: Ike and Tina Turner

2 Likes and dislikes

Explain the listening task to students. Tell them to just listen for the styles Ken and Joyce like: they don't have to understand everything they hear. Play the recording, making sure that students cover the text first. Get them to discuss their answers in pairs. Remind them to keep the text covered as they do this.

Answers

Ken likes jazz and probably opera.
Joyce likes jazz, pop and Latin music. (Tito Lopez was a Mexican actor and acid jazz musician.)

Next, let students read the dialogue as you play the recording again. Then ask them, in pairs, to fill in the first two or three gaps from memory before you play the recording again, this time with pauses so that they can check and fill in the missing words. Do this two or three gaps at a time until the end. Play the recording through one more time with students following the script.

Answers

1. hate it 2. thinking of 3. what kind of
4. I prefer 5. heard of her

Ask students to practise reading the conversation using the tapescript on page 148. Get them to do this a couple of times to practise the stress and phrasing. One technique you could use is to ask students to read a short phrase, look up at their partner and say it without looking back down at the Coursebook. This tends to force them to say the group of words together.

Give students a few minutes to look back through the conversation and underline any expressions they find useful, particularly those that express a like or dislike. Encourage them to transfer these into their notebooks. You might want to point out some of the following expressions:
I can't sit still
that kind of music (as a way to avoid repeating the same word)
I'll (lend you a CD) if you like

3 Answering questions

In this activity students focus on different ways to respond to the question *Do you like … ?* They can work individually or in pairs. Explain that *Why do you ask?* is a common expression used to find out the reason why someone asked you something. You could give the class some other examples too. For example:
A: Did you go out last night?
B: Yes, why do ask?
A: Your eyes are all bloodshot and you look tired.

When we don't want to give a reason, we can use the expression *No reason. I just wondered,* as in **f**. Also highlight the pattern in the responses **a–d**: *I'm thinking of* … . In English this is a common way of being tentative. You might also point out some of the modifiers used in several of the conversations: *I quite liked, a bit boring, really boring.*

If students don't know, Coldplay are a British guitar band. Point out that we usually think of a band as plural and so we use *are, were, they* etc.

When students have completed **1–6**, they should match them to the endings **a–f** in the second task. Play the recording once or twice so students can check their answers.

Answers

1. Yes I love it.
2. Yes, they're OK.
3. It's OK, I suppose.
4. No, not really.
5. No, I can't stand him.
6. I've never heard of it.

1. c. 2. a. 3. b. 4. f. 5. d. 6. e.

Next, get students to practise the conversations, paying attention to the stress and intonation. Now play the recording of the sentences, pausing after each one to allow students to repeat. Point out the difference in intonation for the two OKs. Ask which one expresses a more positive feeling (**2**). As a follow-up, ask students to look back and find those expressions that express strong opinions (e.g. *Yes, I love it*) and those that express a weaker opinion (*It's OK, I suppose*).

4 Practice

Introduce this task by getting individual students to ask you the questions first. Use *Why do you ask?* to prompt them for a reason. Then get students to work individually, writing their own responses. Encourage them to get up and wander around the classroom, asking different people. Teach the expressions *we share the same interests, we like the same things, we've got totally opposite tastes* and ask students to report back on what they found out about their classmates.

5 Vocabulary: *What kind?*

This is a useful vocabulary building exercise. Students can complete this individually and then work with a partner, checking their answers and adding one more item to each list. As you go through the answers, ask what each list has in common to practise phrases like *things you read/collect/watch* etc. This is then reinforced in **6 Practice**.

Answers

1. traditional folk music 2. fashion magazines
3. old coins 4. nature programmes
5. e-mails to friends 6. anything by Steven Spielberg

Draw students' attention to the expressions with *anything*. Write some of the patterns on the board:
anything on (politics)
anything to do with ('Star Wars')
anything with (Chow Yun Fat) in
anything by (Steven Spielberg)

Ask students to think of other people and things besides those in the Coursebook. You can then ask questions (e.g. *What kind of films/music do you like?*) and get students to reply using these patterns (e.g. *Anything by Martin Scorsese*). There are also two more variations of this pattern in **6 Practice** (*anything you can dance to, anything about* ...). You may need to explain that Chow Yun Fat is an actor from Hong Kong.

To give students further practice talking about likes and dislikes, write some example questions on the board. For example:
Do you like 'Friends'/sitcoms?
Do you like collecting things like coins?
What do you think of science fiction?

Then get students in pairs or small groups to ask each other.

6 Practice

Students can work on this individually or in pairs. As you go through the answers, ask individual students the same questions (e.g. *So Claude. What kind of things do you listen to?*). This gives students a more controlled practice before the slightly freer personalisation task at the end.

Answers

1. listen to 2. watch 3. go and see 4. collect
5. write 6. read

Once they have finished the exercise, students have a conversation with a partner about something they are interested in.

Reading

1 Introduction

The first reading text introduces the topic of best friends and family. Explain to students that they should read to find out what the professor's opinion is. Then get them to discuss in small groups or as a class whether they agree with it. Point out that they can talk about the situation in their country, not just that in Britain.

2 Vocabulary

The focus here is on useful phrases that students will see again in the main reading text on page 17 (**Family or friends**). Get students to match the beginnings and endings of the sentences and go through the answers. You can then ask students to test each other, with one person reading the beginning of each sentence and their partner giving the ending, without looking at the Coursebook.

Answers

1. c. 2. h. 3. a. 4. f. 5. g. 6. d. 7. e. 8. b.

Ask students to change any of these expressions, if necessary, to make several that are true for them. Demonstrate by doing this yourself. For example:
All my family support Arsenal, but I support Tottenham.
I chat on the phone a lot with my mum.
I'd never go shopping with my sister because she spends hours in one shop and never buys anything.

Try to add details to expand on the basic expression. Students can then do the same in small groups.

Note that a lot of these expressions use common verbs like *get*, *take* and *go*. You might want to suggest that students have a page in their notebooks devoted to expressions with *get* or *take* etc.

Talk about **Real English: my brother and I**. You might want to use this as an opportunity to talk about how language is continuously changing and that it is very difficult to come up with a set of black and white rules governing its use.

3 While you read

Explain the reading task and let students compare their answers in pairs. Then either read the text or play the recording while students follow along. As they do so, ask them to underline complete expressions they think might be useful for their own situation or that they are curious about. There are a lot here, but some worth pointing out are:

I've known her since I was at school.
We get on really well.
I see her a lot.
We do lots of things together.
We like similar kinds of music.
We just found we had a lot of other things in common.
We're still friends …

Answers

Katy, Damien and Edna tend to agree with Professor Morris while Charlotte and Graham don't, and for John it isn't true that he has a lot in common with his best friend. As for Ron, is a dog a friend or part of the family?

4 Comprehension

This is a fun way for students to react to the reading text. Go over the two sentence starters, letting students hear how they are pronounced, and point out the expressions with *sound.* Students have already met *sound* while talking about music (*All his songs sound the same*). Explain that we can also use *sound* when we are giving an opinion about something we have read as well as heard. Get students to work with a partner and then ask them to share their ideas with the whole class.

5 Speaking

The focus here is on some useful expressions for asking about best friends. Students will probably work out that the word with the capital letter starts the question. To reinforce these expressions, tell students to close their Coursebooks and then say the first two or three words of the question to see if they can remember the complete question. You might need to explain that *How do you know each other?* is another way of asking how you met.

Answers

1. What does she do?
2. How do you know each other?
3. How long have you known each other?
4. Do you go out together much?

To help students prepare for talking about their best friends, tell them to look back for some useful expressions in the article. Then talk about your best friend to the whole class. Encourage students to ask you questions. They can then talk to each other in small groups or wander around chatting to several people. Finish up by asking if anyone found out anything interesting.

For further practice with likes and dislikes ask students in pairs to look at the people in the photographs on page 17 and imagine what kinds of things they like doing together, if they have much in common etc. Students can then share their ideas with another group.

Listening

1 Key word: *go*

Lead in to this exercise by asking students to recall or find any expressions with *go* that they have met so far in this unit (e.g. *operas go on too long, she went with her son*). Explain that English has hundreds of common expressions that use common verbs like *go, get, take* etc. Encourage students to record those they find useful and/or interesting. Find the first few expressions together as a class until students get the hang of it.

Answers

It went really well.
It went badly.
I went on my own.
I went with a friend.
I'm going swimming later.
Are you going on holiday in the summer?
Do you want to go for a walk?
I'm going back home on Tuesday.
I'm going out later.
How's it going?
Prices have gone up a lot recently.
How did it go?
The meeting went on for hours.
I went round to a friend's house.
Go on.
There you go.
I'm just going to the toilet.
Sure, go ahead.
I went shopping.
He's just gone to get a newspaper.
Go to bed early.

Take this opportunity to stress that students should record complete expressions, along with a translation of the expression. Illustrate this by asking how students would translate *go* in their own language. The answer should be that it depends on how it is used (i.e. in what expression). Even in English we can't say what verbs like *go, take or do* mean exactly.

2 Pronunciation: stress

Read the explanation to the class and remind students how words are stressed in English: a combination of being said longer, higher, clearer and louder. Play the recording once all the way through while students listen. Then play it again, stopping after each expression so that students can repeat, following the same stress patterns.

3 Listening

The listening task allows students to hear several of the expressions in context. You might want to play the recording once so students can just listen. Then play it again so they can focus on listening for the expressions. Get them to compare their answers in pairs. Then play the recording again so they can answer questions **1–3**.

Answers

1. Tina is Mario's former teacher. Hugh is Tina's boyfriend.
2. He likes going clubbing and doesn't get enough sleep.
3. Hugh doesn't want Tina to know that he met Mario at the club.

4 Speaking

Introduce this speaking task by answering one of the questions yourself (or by talking about someone you know). When you have finished, ask students if they can remember any useful expressions you used, and then write them on the board. Then get students to discuss the questions in small groups.

Talk about **Real English: How did it go?** Practise these questions with the class, focusing on the pronunciation. For example:
I heard you went out on a blind date last night. How did it go?
Has anyone seen (a current film)? So how was it?)

5 Using grammar: *too*

This is sometimes a confusing word for students. In this activity they are encouraged to form a guideline on the usage of *too* from looking at some examples. Start off by asking students to talk about when they were too tired to do something. Then ask them to look at the two examples and match the follow-up comments. They should see that *too* is used when we are expressing something negative: we can't do it or don't like it.

Answers

1. b.   2. a.

Reinforce this by asking students to complete sentences **1–6**. As you go though the answers, take the opportunity to ask follow-up questions. For example:
When were you allowed to stay out all night?
At what age are you old enough to stay out all night?
What other adjectives can you use to describe drinks? (It's too cold/too strong/too sweet.)
What do you want to do when you've had a really long day?

Answers

1. young   2. hot   3. tired   4. busy   5. old   6. late

Elicit the pattern *too (adjective) to (verb)* and write it on the board. Then get students to complete the sentences **a–d**.

Too can also be used in adverbial expressions and *too much* is quite common. Students can complete the task individually and then compare their answers with a partner. Then ask them to think of other possible negative results. Get them to practise reading the conversations aloud. You could then follow up by asking if anyone in the class knows someone who *talks too much*, *talks too quickly* etc. or talk about some people you know. Again, you could use any of the photographs in the unit to generate more examples. Refer students to G3 of the **Grammar commentary** on page 165, which they can read either in class or as homework.

Answers

1. d.   2. c.   3. f.   4. e.   5. a.   6. b.

Possible alternative bad results:

1. She's always running out of breath.
2. I'm not going to invite him over to dinner.
3. She never really thinks about it.
4. I can never concentrate.
5. And now I have indigestion.
6. No-one can get a word in edgewise.

Follow-up

Bring in some music to class, preferably a variety of styles. Play them to students and then get them in small groups to talk about what they think about each one and explain why. You can also use this as a way to give more practice with *too* by teaching expressions like the following:
it's too loud for me
it's too repetitive
there are too many guitars
his voice is too low

3 Have you got ...?

Unit overview

General topic
Talking about and asking for things.

Conversation
Paul cuts his finger and Steven finds a plaster, and something else!

Reading
Four people explain why they don't have certain things.

Listening
Seven people answer questions about what they have got.

Language input

- Describing where things are: *I think there are some in the top drawer.*
- Questions with *have you got ... ?: Have you got any brothers or sisters?*
- Expressions for talking about houses: *I think it's got three bedrooms, It's a bit cramped.*
- Expressions with *I'm thinking of ... : I'm thinking of getting a new car.*
- Reference words: *Why don't you get rid of it and get a new one? These ones are a bit big on me.*

Language strip

You can use the language strip as a way to lead in to the unit. Ask students to quickly look through the strip to find any expressions they have heard or seen before. Ask if they can find any they have actually used themselves or that they might use in the future. Explain that in this unit they will learn ways of asking and talking about things. Encourage them to choose a couple of expressions in the strip that look interesting and to find out more about them. You might need to explain some of the following expressions:

- *Plasters* are what you use to cover small cuts.
- If you are an *only child*, you haven't got any brothers or sisters.
- If you ask someone *Have you got time for something?* you are usually inviting them to join you in doing something social. For example: *Have you got time for a chat/a drink/a quick game of squash?* If students have learnt that drinks are usually 'uncountable', they might ask about *a coffee* and wonder why there is an article. Explain that this is the more common way of saying *a cup of coffee*. Give some more examples: *Do you want to go for a beer? There's a tea on the table for you.*
- If you ask someone *Have you got the time on you?* you are asking them to tell you the time.

Remind students to record any expressions they like in their notebooks and to take note when they see similar expressions throughout the unit.

Use the language strip later on in this unit for a small group task. Here are some possibilities:

- Students make several three- or four-part conversations using expressions from the strip. For example:
  A: *Have you got a thermometer?*
  B: *There's one in the bathroom.*
  A: *Whereabouts?*
  B: *It's on the shelf.*
- Students discuss what *some*, *it* or *one* could be referring to in several of the expressions.

Lead in

For this unit you could just start off with the first activity.

Conversation

1 Explaining where things are

Start off by focusing students' attention on the photos on page 20. First ask if they know what the objects are called in English. Then put the following patterns on the board:
You might ask for a/some ... if you'd ...
You might ask for a/some ... because you wanted to ...

Ask students to use these patterns in answering the first question. For example:
You might ask for a screwdriver if your glasses were broken.

Read the instructions for the listening task aloud. Tell students to listen for the answers to the two questions. Play the recording, making sure that students cover the text. Get them to discuss the answers in pairs. Remind students to keep the text covered as they do this. Check their answers by asking if they remember where the plasters were (*in the cupboard, by the bath*).

Answers

Steven asks if Paul has any plasters because Paul cut his finger on a nail.

Play the recording again and ask students to try to fill in each of the gaps as they listen. They should then compare their answers with a partner. Play the recording a third time, but this time pause after each gap. Elicit the missing words and maybe write the complete expression on the board. Model the pronunciation and get students to practise saying it. Play the recording through one more time with students following the tapescript on page 149.

Answers

1. cut my finger 2. any plasters 3. in the bathroom
4. by the bath 5. on the floor 6. they're not mine

Finish up by asking the class what they think Steven found in the bathroom. The suggestions will possibly include things that a woman, not a man, would have (e.g. stockings).

You might need to explain the following expression: If you *run something under the tap*, you put it under the tap and turn the water on.

2 Using grammar: questions with *have you got … ?*

Have got is very common in spoken English as an alternative to *have* in a lot of contexts. Write *Have you got a … ?* and *Have you got any … ?* on the board. Ask students to suggest several nouns for each pattern. Then suggest a few 'uncountable' nouns like *sugar* and get students to ask the appropriate question. Then ask them to complete the exercise individually or in pairs.

Play the recording so students can check their answers. They may have alternative answers, so invite students to suggest them. Discuss these together as a class. You may need to explain that in English *scissors* is plural and we often say *a pair of scissors*. Ask students for other nouns like this (e.g. *trousers, knickers*).

Answers

1. Have you got a cloth?
2. Have you got a plaster?
3. Have you got a pen?
4. Have you got any scissors / a pair of scissors?
5. Have you got a screwdriver?
6. Have you got any correction fluid?

Get pairs of students to practise reading the conversation on page 149, paying attention to stress and phrasing. Refer students to G4 of the **Grammar commentary** on page 165, which they can read either in class or as homework.

3 Practice

Before students work on this in pairs, make sure they know what the things in the box are. You could ask the same question as in **1 Explaining where things are**. You could also point out a couple of patterns from the previous activity:
I've just (cut myself/met an old friend).
I just need to (open this plug/change this word here).

Model the first item with one student. For example:
A: *Have you got a stapler? I just need to put this report together.*
B: *Yes, there's one in my drawer.*

Get students to change roles and repeat the activity.

4 Speaking

One way to introduce this task is to say a list of objects and get students to tell you where they think they are kept. For example:
A: *First aid kit, shampoo, toothpaste, eye liner …*
B: *In the cabinet in the bathroom.*

You don't have to limit yourself to any of the places in **1–5**. Give students a few minutes to think about what they want to say and help them with any vocabulary. You could follow up by asking pairs of students to write a more extended dialogue, like the one between Steven and Paul, using any of the places listed here and any of the objects in **3 Practice**.

5 Talking about people's houses

A good contextualised example of using *have got* is when we are talking about houses. Start off by asking students to suggest things a decent house should have (e.g. *a couple of bedrooms, a modern kitchen, a nice garden, a nice view* etc.). Then get students to complete the three conversations.

Answers

Conversation 1: the country, bedrooms, garden
Conversation 2: modern, lounge, bathroom, cramped
Conversation 3: floor, building, balcony, lift

As you go through the answers, encourage students to record complete expressions that they find useful in their notebooks. Also ask follow-up questions to extend students' practice with the vocabulary. For example:
What could you say for the opposite of 'They've got a really big house in the country'? (a really small house in the city)
What else do you do in the lounge? (watch TV, chat)
What would you like your flat to look out over? (a river, the beach)

Talk about **Real English: a three-bedroom house**. As extra practice, ask students further questions:
Where are you living at the moment?
What's the house you grew up in like?

Get them to give answers like the examples.

Before students discuss the last two questions in pairs or small groups, talk about these questions yourself, encouraging students to ask you more questions. Then ask them to recall any useful expressions you used. Write these on the board to help when students talk themselves.

Reading

1 Before you read

Focus students' attention on the photos of the four people on page 22 and explain what each of them hasn't got. Encourage students to share their initial reactions. For example: *I'm surprised Andrew doesn't have a watch. I thought teachers always had watches.*

Then get students to try and guess what the people's reasons are for not having these things before they actually read the text (*I haven't got one!*).

2 Jigsaw reading

Divide the class into two groups and get group A to read the text on page 22 and group B to read the text on page 23. Remind students that they are reading to find out the reasons: they don't have to understand everything in the texts.

3 Information exchange

When students have found the answer for **2 Jigsaw reading**, ask them to talk to someone else in their group and check their answers. Encourage them to remember the reasons rather than just reading the answer straight from the text. When everyone is ready, create new pairs: one person from group A and one person from group B. Again, encourage students to try to remember rather than simply reading.

Answers

Amparo hasn't got a mobile phone because she hates them. She doesn't want people ringing her all the time and she doesn't like the way people answer their phones in the middle of a conversation.

Muriel and her husband haven't got any children because they can't have any. Anyway, Muriel is happy they don't because you have to spend a lot of money on your kids and you have less time to go out.

Andrew hasn't got a watch because they feel uncomfortable on him. When he used to wear a watch, he always ended up losing it. He thinks he doesn't need one because he can always look at a clock or ask someone the time.

Boris used to have a TV, but his nephew broke it. He found that he could do without it and spent more time doing other things that were more useful.

4 Language work

The focus here is on several useful expressions from the texts. Students can stay in the same pairs as in **3 Information exchange** or form new pairs (one person from group A, one person from group B). Tell students to read the texts again and underline the expressions they find interesting.

Answers

Andrew says: It's actually a good way of starting conversations with people.

Amparo says: Personally, I sometimes want to get away from the hospital, my kids and my mother and be on my own.

Boris says: So when my sister offered to buy me a new TV and DVD for my birthday, I said I didn't want one.

Amparo says: Sometimes when I talk to patients and their relatives, their phone rings and they answer it.

Muriel says: They don't get enough sleep because the baby wakes them up in the middle of the night.

Muriel says: Sometimes Liam gets upset when people ask, 'Have you got any kids?', but I don't.

Boris says: I used to have one, but one day my three-year-old nephew poured water down the back of it and the TV exploded.

Andrew says: I don't wear my wedding ring because it feels uncomfortable and I don't want to lose it like I lost all those watches.

Ask students further questions to extend their practice with these expressions. For example:
What do you do when you want to get away from people?
What do you say in your own language when you answer the phone? How about in English?
What other reasons are there for not getting enough sleep?
Can you remember other good ways of starting a conversation from Unit 1?

Wrap up by asking students for their reaction to each person in the reading texts. You could write some expressions on the board to help. For example:
Personally, I agree with (Andrew).
I think (Muriel)'s got a good point.
Yes, but it can be useful if you've got (kids).
I don't think I could live without (a TV).

5 Speaking

Use these discussion questions to practise some more expressions with *get*. Go through each one. Explain that if you *get rid of something*, you don't want it any more, so you do something like throw it away (e.g. *I've decided to get rid of my old TV and get one of those flat-screen ones).* After students have finished discussing, get them to ask you questions **1–4**.

6 Using grammar: *I'm thinking of …*

Using the continuous form of the verb is one way we can make things tentative. Contrast the expression *I'm thinking of getting* with *I think I'll get.* Ask which one shows greater certainty. Some students may wonder why *think* is used in the continuous form. When it means 'to have in mind', like here, rather than 'to have an opinion about', it is often used in the continuous form.

Students can work individually on the matching task and then test each other in pairs.

> **Answers**
>
> 1. h. 2. b. 3. g. 4. a. 5. e. 6. c. 7. f. 8. d.

Here are some more questions to ask about some of the language in this activity:

What other forms of transport can we 'take'? (the tube, the train, a taxi)

What else can 'break down'? (the washing machine, talks)

Besides 'rent', what other things can we 'waste money on'? (cigarettes, petrol)

Which other verbs apart from 'find' can we use with 'job'? (lose, get)

Refer students to G5 of the **Grammar commentary** on page 165, which they can read either in class or as homework.

Listening

1 Speaking

Practise the pronunciation of these questions first with the whole class. Then write up some follow-up questions on the board. For example: *What make? What in? What's it like? How is it? How old?* Model a conversation with a student. Encourage students to ask follow-up questions. For example:

S: *Have you got a computer at home?*
T: *Yeah. I have, actually.*
S: *Really? What make?*
T: *I've got a Toshiba laptop.*
S: *What's it like?*
T: *Not bad. It's getting a bit old, though.*

2 While you listen

Explain the task and play the recording. Get pairs of students to compare their answers and share what they remember. As you go through the answers, ask students what they remember about each conversation.

> **Answers**
>
> 1. e. 2. d. 3. a. 4. g. 5. c. 6. f. 7. b.

3 Word check

Although there is one word missing in each part, remind students to focus on and record the complete expression. Get students to work individually or in pairs, completing as many as they can from memory. Then play the recording so they can check their answers. Play the recording again while students read the tapescript on pages 149–150. Ask them to underline any expressions they find interesting or that they want to ask you about. Explain any expressions and then ask pairs of students to practise reading some of the conversations.

> **Answers**
>
> 1. upset, round 2. borrow, press
> 3. licence, transport 4. in, job 5. crashes, rid
> 6. keen, feed 7. work, imagine

Follow up by asking students to discuss questions **1–3** in small groups. You may need to explain that if you are *keen on* something, you like it. You could also teach the informal expression *keen on someone* to mean you are *attracted to someone*. For example:
I think Bob's a bit keen on Teri.

4 Using grammar: reference words

Point out to students that using reference words helps them sound more natural. It stops them having to keep repeating main nouns. The use of *one(s)* is quite common. Read the extract aloud and see if students can remember what the two people are talking about.

> **Answers**
>
> a computer

Ask students to underline the examples of *one* in the extract and then go through the explanation. Explain that *one(s)* is often useful in the context of comparing. Read the four examples, letting students hear how each one is said before getting them to complete the four conversations.

> **Answers**
>
> 1. one 2. ones, ones, ones 3. one
> 4. ones, ones, ones

Get students to practise reading the conversations in pairs. You might also point out the expression *that reminds me* as a useful discourse marker. You could also compare how we use *enough*, as in *I don't think they're big enough* in **4**, with how we use *too*, which was covered in the previous unit.

Talk about **Real English: I can imagine**. You might want to get students to practise the expression by reading the examples aloud.

5 Practice

Lead in to the speaking task by making sure students know what the pictures on page 25 are of. You could also revise some of the 'likes and dislikes' expressions from **Unit 2**. Write up some non-committal expressions too, if necessary. For example:
Neither, really.
They both look good/OK to me.

Make sure students know that *trousers* is a plural noun, i.e. *I prefer those ones.*

6 Further practice

Students can work on the matching task individually or in pairs. Play the recording once so they can check their answers.

Answers

1. g. 2. c. 3. d. 4. e. 5. f. 6. h. 7. b. 8. a.

Point out the use of *a bit* to soften negative adjectives and *I don't really like* as a softer way of saying *I don't like*. Ask a few questions like *What do you think of English food/the coffee from the machine/my clothes?* and get students to respond with negative comments using *a bit* or *I don't really like*.

Play the recording a second time, this time focusing on the stress patterns. Pause after each one and get students to underline the stress. Play the recording a third time, stopping after each one so students can repeat. You can then get pairs of students to test each other, with one person reading the beginnings and the other person, with their Coursebook closed, trying to remember the endings. To wrap up, you might want to ask students to discuss what they think the people are actually talking about.

7 Speaking

This activity gives students a chance to practise some of the language they have met in this unit. Give students a few minutes to think about what they want to say. You might want to give them some ideas by talking about some of the questions first. Try to use expressions students might find useful. For example:
I find it difficult throwing anything out. I've got piles of stuff sitting in the garage. My wife keeps telling me to get rid of it all but I think one day something in there might come in useful.

You might want to wrap up with a feedback session where you focus on some problem areas and maybe also some examples of successful communication.

Follow-up

Ask students to role-play a conversation between a seller and a buyer; they could be selling/buying something like a house or a car. This gives students a chance to re-use some of the language from the unit as they talk and ask about what the house/car etc. has got (e.g. *it's got leather seats*), and allows them to make comparisons (e.g. *I prefer the one with the sunroof*). Go around helping with vocabulary and ask students to perform their role plays to other groups or to the whole class.

4 Times and dates

Unit overview

General topic
Talking about times and dates, special days, and arrangements.

Conversation
Syd and Emily talk about going to a party.

Reading
Six people explain what days are special are for them.

Listening
Six people talk about the last time they did something.

Language input

- Expressions for telling the time: *It's just gone three, It must be around four.*
- Expressions for making arrangements: *Do you want to come? How about eleven at my house?*
- Present continuous for making arrangements: *I'm going to a party later, A friend's coming over to play computer games later.*
- Expressions with *hope*: *I hope you like it, I hope the weather is OK.*
- Time expressions: *ages ago, the other day, the day after tomorrow.*
- Expressions for talking about feelings about the future: *I'm really looking forward to it.*

Language strip

You can use the language strip as a way to lead in to the unit. Ask students to quickly look through the strip and find any expressions they have actually heard or seen before, and any they think they could use in the future. Explain that in this unit they will learn expressions for talking about time, special days, and arrangements. Encourage them to choose a couple of expressions in the strip that look interesting and to find out more about them.

You might need to explain some of the following expressions:

- You use *It's just gone* (+ a time) to say that it is a minute or two past the time. For example: *It's just gone seven, It's just gone half past two.*
- If you use *Shall we say* (+ a time), you are suggesting a time to meet. For example: *What time do you want to meet? Shall we say 6:30?*
- If you say *our anniversary*, you usually mean the date on which you got married, or sometimes, when you started dating. For example: *We're going out for our anniversary*. You say *the anniversary of* when you want to talk about the date an event in the past is remembered or celebrated. For example: *the anniversary of the birth of Martin Luther King Jr.*
- If you say *the other day*, you mean an unspecified day in the past, usually just a few days ago. For example: *A: When did you get your hair cut? B: Just the other day.*

Remind students to record the expressions they like in their notebooks and to take note when they see similar expressions throughout the unit.

Use the language strip later on in this unit for a small group task. Here are some possibilities:

- Students find those expressions connected to the future (e.g. *I'm going out for dinner later*), those connected to the past (e.g. *When was the last time you went to the doctor's?*) and those connected to the present (e.g. *It's our anniversary*).
- Students choose expressions that are questions (e.g. *What time does the film start?*) and come up with a possible answer (e.g. *7:30, I think*). Then they choose expressions that are responses (e.g. *It's just gone ten to seven*) and come up with possible prompts (e.g. *Have you got the time on you?*).

Lead in

Lead in by talking about time with the class. Here are some possible questions:
Do you ever ask people you don't know for the time? In your own language? In English?
Has a stranger ever asked you for the time in English? What did you say? What happened?

You can then explain that in the first activity students will practise typical ways of telling people what the time is.

Conversation

1 Do you know what the time is?

You could start off by asking a few students what the time is. Use a couple of different ways. For example:
Min, do you know what the time is?
How about you, Lee, what time do you make it?

Then focus students' attention on the pictures of the clocks and explain the matching task. Students can work individually or in pairs. Check their answers by asking individual students to say the expressions. Then get the whole class to repeat so you have a chance to work on pronunciation, particularly how the *o* in *o'clock* is reduced to /ə/ and *to* is pronounced /tə/ before a number.

Answers

1. e.   2. c.   3. d.   4. a.   5. g.   6. b.   7. h.   8. f.

You could now ask students to sort the expressions into two groups: those that give an exact answer (2., 3., 5., 7.) and those that are approximate (1., 4., 6., 8.).

Before getting students to work on the second task in pairs, you could write up a couple of other ways of asking for the time. For example:
Have you got the time on you?
What time do you make it?

Students can then use these alternatives if they wish.

Answers

Possible answers:

a. It's just before 12 o'clock.
b. It's a quarter to four.
c. It's almost two o'clock.
d. It's 11:25.
e. It's just after half past seven.

Talk about **Real English: half past nine.** You might want to ask students to look at the clocks again and tell you the time without mentioning the hour. For example: *It's three minutes to, It's five past.* Point out that in these expressions *to* is not reduced to /tə/.

2 Making plans

Explain the situation and ask students to look at the conversation by themselves before discussing with a partner. They should be able to guess the topic fairly easily. You could also ask if anyone wants to guess what phrases were used. A strong confident class could spend perhaps five minutes doing this in pairs. Play the recording once all the way through while students listen. You might want to ask a few comprehension questions. For example:
What kind of party is it?
Where are they going to meet up first?
Where does Emily have to go now?

Play the recording again and get students to follow the tapescript on page 150. To practise some of the useful language in the conversation, ask questions like these:
Do you like being the first one at parties?
Do you prefer meeting up with a friend before going to a party or do you usually go on your own?
How else can you complete this expression 'Have you got time for a …'? (a drink, a chat, game of tennis)

Put students into pairs and ask them to practise reading both roles. Explain the next task and allow them enough time to prepare. Point out that this exercise will help their fluency. Remind them to use the notes on page 26 to help them remember. You might want to get them to practise the conversation a second time with a different partner.

Introduce the discussion questions at the end by talking about a personal experience (or about that of someone you know). For example:
This friend of mine worked for a music magazine and she used to get into concerts for free. Actually, sometimes she pretends she still works for the magazine, just to see if she can get in without paying. Sometimes it works too!

3 Making arrangements

Lead in by asking students what kind of social activities they might make arrangements with their friends for (e.g. *having a coffee, going out to dinner, going and seeing a film*). Then explain that in this activity they will practise ways of inviting someone to do something and making an arrangement for a time and place to meet. As students work on the matching task, either alone or in pairs, ask them to notice the patterns that are being used. You could then write the basic pattern of the conversation on the board and ask students to complete it with their own example in their notebooks. For example:
A: I'm/We're + -ing … . Do you want to come?
B: Yes. OK. What time?
A: Well, … , so how about … ?

Answers

1. how about outside here at a quarter past twelve?
2. how about nine in front of Victoria coach station?
3. how about half past nine at my house?
4. how about 11 a.m. at my house?
5. how about around seven at Tom's diner?

Before students practise the conversations in pairs, model the first one so they can hear the intonation and stress of the patterns. You might want to give a couple of alternative endings. For example:
That sounds great/good.
Great. See you there/then.

Talk about **Real English: Shall we say … ?** Some students might wonder about the use of *shall*. Although in some uses it is quite formal, *shall* is fairly common as a way of making and asking about suggestions. You might want to teach one or two other examples:
Shall we go?
Shall I go first?
What shall we do?

For some extra vocabulary work, ask students to go back and find expressions using *go* (e.g. *We're going on a trip, We're going in the car, We could go and have a coffee* etc.) Ask follow-up questions too. For example:
Where are some places you would go on a trip to from here?

What other expressions do you know that use 'go' to talk about how you get somewhere? (go by bus/by train/on foot)

What do you like to go and do after class/work etc.?

4 Using grammar: present continuous for arrangements

Ask students if they noticed that the opening sentences in **3 Making arrangements** had something in common. Students should be able to come up with something like 'they all have an *-ing* form', if not the actual name of the tense. Go over the explanation of the use of the present continuous for making future arrangements. Also, check that students know how the tense is formed. Write several gapped expressions on the board and get students to complete them. For example:
I'm busy on Friday, but I … doing anything on Saturday.

… you doing anything tomorrow?

What time … you meeting her?

Sorry, but my boyfriend … coming over tonight.

Point out that the present continuous used in this way is usually accompanied by a time expression. Then get students to go back and underline all the examples in **3 Making arrangements**, including any time expressions. Point out that typically we say the contracted forms: *I'm, We're, He's/She's* etc. Get students to practise the pronunciation of these forms when giving their answers.

Answers

1. I'm going shopping later.
2. We're going on a trip to Oxford on Sunday.
3. I'm going to a party later.
4. We're going for a picnic on Saturday.
   We're going in the car, so … .
5. I'm going to the cinema tonight to see *The Beast.*

Students can practise the *-ing* form by completing sentences **1–12**.

Answers

1. 'm meeting	5. 'm going	9. 'm going
2. 'm going	6. 'm having	10. 'm going
3. 're coming	7. 're having	11. 'm going
4. 'm going	8. 'm meeting	12. 're having

There are a lot of useful phrases in this activity and you should encourage students to record the ones they find useful in their notebooks. You might want to point out and explain the following: *a friend of mine, coming over, a week on Friday.*

Here are some additional questions to ask students as you go through the answers:
What things would you take if you went for a picnic?
Have you ever had parties at work?
Where do you usually get your hair cut?
Do you ever have barbecues?
What kind of food do you usually barbecue?

Finish by getting pairs of students to talk about any arrangements using the expressions (or slight variations) from the activity. For example:
A friend of mine's coming over to play cards tonight.

Refer students to G7 of the **Grammar commentary** on page 166, which they can read either in class or as homework.

5 Practice

Model the example conversations with a couple of students first. Point out that when we decline an invitation, we usually explain why we can't come, often using the present continuous. Get pairs of students to practise several conversations like this. You might want to ask them to repeat the activity with a different partner.

Reading

1 Special days

Lead in by telling the class when one or two of the more personalised days from the list are. For example:
My mum and dad's wedding anniversary is in two days. I know that because it's the same day as my birthday. Not the same year, by the way. I was born two years later.

Before getting pairs of students to talk about the days, go over the expressions, making sure they understand the time expressions. Remind them that these phrases are useful when they can't or don't want to be exact.

Follow up by discussing how, or if, students celebrate these days. If you are from a different country from your students, talk about how these days are celebrated in your country. You could use the photographs of cards on page 29 to continue the discussion. Ask questions like:
Are celebrations getting too commercialised?
Do you/we have cards for all kinds of situations and every kind of relationship in your/our countries?
When do you send cards?
What kind of cards do you like to send?
What kind do you like to receive? Do you like funny ones?
Do you like ones with paintings?

Talk about **Real English: December 25th** with the class and get them to practise saying the dates. If appropriate, you can also turn this into a culture sharing discussion by getting small groups to talk about days with special names. Students may ask about *Boxing Day*. Traditionally, this was when domestic servants had the day off and they received presents in a box from their employers. Other days with names include Ash Wednesday, Good Friday, Easter Monday, May Day and Halloween.

2 While you read

Prepare for the reading task by eliciting examples of occasions people might consider special (e.g. *a wedding day, the birth of someone, the first day at school, getting a driving licence*). On the board write *(Date) is special for me. That's the day (I) …* . Then ask students to complete it using some of the examples (e.g. *June 5th is special for me. That's the day I passed my driving test*). This is a good way to revise the past tense. Then ask students to read the article (**Special days**) to see if any of their suggestions were mentioned. You could also play the recording, using it as a listening task first, and then get students to read the article. Remind students that they don't need to understand everything.

3 After you read

In this activity students discuss what they remember with a partner. When they have finished, they can re-read the text to find out about anything they missed. You can also read aloud or play the recording as students underline the expressions. Here are some that you might want to point out:

It's the anniversary of the day
I'll never forget that day
It's a big day for me
return the favour
I'll never forget those dates as long as I live

Answers

14th June was the day Ian stopped smoking.

Murdo likes June 21st because it's the longest day of the year and it never gets really dark.

December 8th is special for Allison because that's when John Lennon was shot.

Shinji likes March 14th, known as White Day, because in Japan that's when women receive presents from men.

Maria's special day is 25th April, Liberation Day, which commemorates the end of the Second World War in Italy.

Nick's special days are 5th December, when his son was born, and 10th December, when his daughter was born.

Demonstrate the final task by writing a date that is special to you on the board and talk about it. Encourage students to ask you further questions. Ask them to do the same when they talk with their partners. You might want to get students to wander around and talk to several people. Finish up by inviting some students to report back on what they found out.

4 Using grammar: present simple with *hope*

In this activity, students practise expressions with *hope*. Introduce the task by asking them to remember why Shinji said Japanese women give small chocolates to lots of men on Valentine's Day. (*They hope they will get bigger, better presents in return on White Day.*) Explain that if we *hope* something is true, we want, and think it's possible, that something will happen. Go through the two examples with students and perhaps introduce a few more. For example:

I hope the bus isn't late tomorrow.
I hope the film starts soon.

Students can complete conversations **1–8** individually or in pairs. Ask individual students to tell you the answers and work on the pronunciation of the *hope* phrases. Then get pairs of students to practise reading the conversations. Encourage them to record expressions from this activity in their notebooks.

Answers

1. you get the job
2. you pass
3. the weather is OK
4. you like it
5. we meet again sometime
6. you get better soon
7. it doesn't cost too much
8. it isn't that bad

The memorisation task helps reinforce this grammatical pattern and you may want to follow up with a more extended practice by asking students to come up with their own mini conversations using the expressions in the box. Get pairs or small groups of students to share what they come up with for the three personalised sentences. You could teach a couple of follow-up questions too. For example:

Why's that?
Do you think it/you will?

Refer students to G8 of the **Grammar commentary** on page 166, which they can read either in class or as homework.

Listening

1 Using grammar: time expressions

In this activity students sort time expressions into those referring to the past and those referring to the future. Students can work on this individually before checking their answers with a partner. When you go through the answers, make sure students understand the use of some of the less obvious expressions like *ages ago, the other day/week* and *a week (from) today*. Ask questions like *Hand in your homework a week from today. So what day is that?*

Answers

1: a., b., e., f., k., l., m., n.
2: c., d., g., h., i., j.

The future expressions in order:
2. the day after tomorrow
3. a week today
4. in a few weeks' time
5. in a couple of months

Refer students to G9 of the **Grammar commentary** on page 166, which they can read either in class or as homework.

2 Pronunciation: linking

This kind of linking is sometimes difficult for students to produce. Get students to mark the linking first and then play the recording right the way through. Play the recording again, this time stopping after each phrase so that students can repeat. If they are having problems, you can use the technique of adding one syllable at a time starting from the end: i.e. *go, ago, sago, gesago, agesago.*

Answers

weeks_ago
in_a couple_of
ages_ago
when_I was_a
in_a minute_or two
(day_after is linked with a /j/ sound and in_1999 is linked with a slightly lengthened /n/)

Tell students to practise the phrases they have just heard by talking about themselves to a partner.

Talk about **Real English: in a few weeks' time.** Practise the examples by asking *When are you going to have your next cup of coffee/cigarette/test/dentist's appointment/big exam etc.?*

3 Before you listen

Here students can practise using some of the expressions from **1 Using grammar: time expressions**. Encourage them to use linking when possible. Model the eight questions with the class first, explaining any expressions (e.g. *a day off school*) if necessary. Then get individual students to ask you the questions. Try using a variety of expressions in your answers. Encourage students to ask you follow-up questions.

4 Listening

Play the recording and get pairs of students to compare their answers. Play the recording a second time so they can check.
1. f. 2. e. 3. d. 4. b. 5. a. 6. c.

5 Comprehension check

Let students spend a few minutes on this before playing the recording again. You might also want to ask them to follow the tapescript on page 150 as you play it for a final time. Explain that a *department store* is a big shop that sells lots of different things, such as furniture, clothes, cooking stuff etc.

Answers

Conversation 1:	I'd like it cut a little bit please.
Conversation 2:	There's a sale on at the department store in the High Street
Conversation 3:	He's going to tell me I have to have a tooth taken out.
Conversation 4:	I'm really looking forward to going away.
Conversation 5:	I'm a bit nervous about their visit.
Conversation 6:	It was nearly twenty years ago, just before I left school.

6 Speaking

Get pairs of students or small groups to talk about these discussion questions. Then get them to ask you. **1** provides a great opportunity to work on the vocabulary of hairdressing. It might be a good idea to let students ask about the expressions they want to learn, rather than overwhelming them with vocabulary.

7 Feelings about the future

In this activity students practise the expressions *I'm (not) looking forward to* and *I'm dreading* while also revising some of the language from the unit. Here are some examples of additional questions to ask as you go through the answers to the two matching tasks:
What would you wear to a job interview?

What other kinds of appointment can you have? (doctor's, optician's)

How many weeks is 'a couple'? What could you use if it was shorter? Longer?

Answers

1\. d. 2. a. 3. c. 4. b. 5. g. 6. e. 7. h. 8. f.

8 Free practice

Check that students understand that *I'm really looking forward to it* expresses a positive feeling. Explain that *I'm not really looking forward to it* expresses a 'softened' negative feeling.

Answers

Answers could vary depending on the individual but the most probable responses are:
I'm really looking forward to it: 4,. 6,. 7.
I'm not really looking forward to it: 1., 2., 5., 8.
3\. could go either way.

Model the two conversations and then get students to ask several people in the class. Point out another *hope* expression: *I hope you have a good time.*

Follow-up

Tell students to write down on a piece of paper five activities they would enjoy inviting a friend to do (e.g. *playing tennis, seeing a film, going for a hike, going for a drink*). They should now go around the class asking other students to join them. They should arrange a time and place to meet. They should each make a note of these arrangements (e.g. *tennis with Juan, Saturday, 11 a.m., tennis courts*). Remind students that if they have already made an arrangement, they should explain why they can't come. Finish up by asking who made the most arrangements.

Review: Units 1-4

Most of these exercises should be done in pairs or small groups.

1 Act or draw

Get students to read through the list individually first. Then ask them in turns to draw or act out the five words or expressions they have chosen. Next, they should ask their partner about any of the words or expressions they are not sure of.

2 Tenses

Answers

1. didn't
2. are growing up
3. bought it
4. Do you like, I've never heard
5. do
6. 'm thinking
7. are you doing, 'm meeting
8. the other day
9. 'm going
10. you like it

3 Grammar

Answers

1. in, on 2. it, off 3. a, one 4. any, some
5. on, in 6. Do, do 7. too 8. ones

4 Questions and answers

Answers

1. c. 2. e. 3. a. 4. b. 5. d. 6. f. 7. j. 8. g.
9. h. 10. i.

5 What can you remember?

When students have finished working in groups of four, invite a few students to tell you what they remember.

6 Verb collocations

Answers

1. join 2. cut 3. save 4. share 5. stop 6. do
7. waste 8. make 9. collect 10. support

Examples of other collocations
1. a club 2. a slice of bread 3. a penalty
4. a book 5. laughing 6. something else 7. food
8. a phone call 9. paintings 10. the Labour Party

7 Look back and check

Ask students to choose one of the activities. You could then get them to do the other one on another day. For extra practice, ask students who chose **a.** to write a small conversation containing three of the *go* expressions.

8 Expressions

Answers

1. love 2. idea 3. round 4. rather 5. stand
6. say 7. keen 8. great 9. believe 10. live

9 Vocabulary quiz

Answers

1. Have you got a light?
2. Fail an exam.
3. A job.
4. Miss a class.
5. No.
6. Possible answer: You could get a speeding ticket.
7. You pay.
8. Possible answer: A pair of scissors/a knife.
9. Possible answer: A button.
10. There isn't enough room. There are too many things/people.
11. Sad.
12. Possible answer: A car, a train.
13. 9:03.
14. Possible answer: A birthday, getting a new job, your team winning a competition.
15. 31st December.
16. Possible answer: A dentist's appointment, a driving test.

Pronunciation

Go through the explanation with the class. If students are not familiar with it, explain where they can find pronunciation information in their dictionaries.

1 Recording word stress

Answers

'Asian	'British
European	'Spanish
A'merican	'Mexican
Chi'nese	Japa'nese
Bra'zilian	Pe'ruvian

2 Consonant sounds

Answers

(Matching exercise)

1. d. 2. g. 3. h. 4. b. 5. c. 6. a. 7. f. 8. e.

1. /ʃ/ 2. /j/ 3. /dʒ/ 4. /tʃ/ 5. /ʒ/ 6. /θ/
7. /ð/ 8. /ŋ/

1. think 2. shot 3. crash 4. change 5. Asia
6. refugee 7. ring me later 8. I can imagine
9. dustpan and brush 10. the other day

3 Difficult sounds: /s/ and /ʃ/

Model and practise the sounds. Ask students if they can hear the difference. Then model the expressions. Get students to work in pairs saying the expressions to each other.

5 Buying things

Unit overview

General topic
Buying things, doing things around the house, clothing.

Conversation
Lisa tells Charlotte about some shoes she's just bought.

Reading
A woman complains about how her husband can't look after himself.

Listening
Three conversations that take place in shops.

Language input
- Clothing vocabulary: *top, bracelet, trainers.*
- Reference words: *I really like that shirt, I really like those jeans.*
- Prepositional phrases of location: *next to the cinema, just round the corner from the church.*
- Expressions describing household jobs: *do the washing, tidy up, lay the table.*
- Expressions with *not + enough: I don't have enough money, I'm not old enough.*
- Negative questions: *Don't you think it's a bit too big?*
- Expressions to talk about people's clothing and appearance: *It really suits her, She looks a bit too scruffy.*

Language strip

You can use the language strip as a way to lead in to the unit. Ask students to quickly look through the strip and find any expressions they have actually heard or seen before and any they think they could use themselves in the future. Explain that in this unit they will practise ways of talking about shopping, household tasks and clothing. Encourage students to choose a couple of expressions in the strip that look interesting and to find out more about them.

You might need to explain some of the following expressions:

- A *top* often refers to clothing worn on the upper part of the body like a sweatshirt, shirt or blouse. For example: *Do you think I should wear the white top with these black shorts?*
- If something is *reduced*, the price has been lowered. For example: *Everything on this shelf is reduced.*
- If you *lay the table,* you arrange the plates and cutlery on the table, ready for a meal.
- If you *do the hoovering*, you clean the carpet with a vacuum cleaner. For example: *You do the hoovering. I'll clean the windows.*
- If something *suits you*, you look good in it. For example: *Those glasses really suit you.*
- If you say something *looks ridiculous,* you think it looks silly. We often use it about the clothes someone is wearing. For example: *You can't go to work in orange trousers. They look ridiculous on you. Wear the black ones instead.*
- If someone or something *looks scruffy*, their appearance is untidy. For example: *Those shoes look a bit scruffy.*
- If someone or something *looks smart*, their appearance is tidy and quite formal. For example: *You look smart in that new suit.*

Remind students to record the expressions they like in their notebooks and to take note when they see similar expressions throughout the unit.

Use the language strip later on in this unit for a small group task. Here are some possibilities:

- Students find those expressions connected with clothing (e.g. *It's too tight*), those connected with household tasks (e.g. *Could you lay the table?*) and those connected with money (e.g. *It was £20 – reduced from 50*).
- Students discuss what *it* or *that* might refer to in several of the expressions (e.g. *It's directly opposite the bank*).
- Students choose five expressions from the list. They then create five variations by changing just one word in each. For example: *I hate doing the washing, I don't have enough money.* They can then talk about these with a partner. You should go around and advise on the appropriateness of these if necessary.

Lead in

You could lead in to this unit by bringing in lots of magazine pictures of people and ask students in groups simply to react to what they see. You can go around the class to find out what students know already and, more importantly, when they are having difficulties. You could repeat this activity at the end of the unit to see how students have improved.

Conversation

1 Using vocabulary: clothes and accessories

This is a basic vocabulary building exercise. Ask students to look at the picture on page 36 and label the items. You may want to extend the exercise by letting students ask about the names of other items of clothing. If you limit it to what people in the class are wearing that day, it can serve as a preparation for **2 Practice**. Using the picture, you could also work on descriptors (e.g. ***dark*** *sunglasses,* ***silver*** *bracelet*). This will help with the next task.

Answers

The woman is wearing a watch, a red bracelet and necklace, a dark green skirt and a green top. She is also wearing brown boots. The man is wearing a green baseball cap, sunglasses, a white T-shirt, a jacket, blue jeans and trainers.

2 Practice

Model the two examples for students first and get them to work in pairs. Go around the class and help with new vocabulary if necessary. You can then write these expressions on the board. A variation on the example questions is *Which one's Ana? (She's the one with the brown top.)* If you just want to practise clothing vocabulary, you could ask pairs of students to test each other with questions like *Can you remember what Nicole's wearing?* (You could even ask if anyone remembers what you were wearing yesterday!)

Talk about **Real English: guy / woman**. If you are teaching in the UK, you could mention that students might hear the word *bloke* used to refer to a man and *pet* to refer to a woman.

3 Talking about things you've bought

Explain the situation of the conversation and ask students to just listen for the answers to the two questions. Play the recording, making sure that students cover the text. Get them to discuss the answers in pairs. Remind them to keep the text covered as they do this. You might want to briefly ask them if they think £29.99 is a good price for a pair of shoes.

Answers

Lisa bought a pair of shoes that really suit her. The best thing about them is that they were reduced from £65 to £29.99.

Point out that we often omit the currency (e.g. pounds) when we talk about how much something costs and we are in the same country. Write some prices on the board and get students to practise saying them. For example:
They were 12.99.
It's 6.49 reduced from 6.99.

Play the recording again and ask students to try to fill in each of the gaps as they listen. They should then compare their answers with a partner. Play the recording a third time, but this time pause after each gap. Elicit the missing words and maybe write the complete expression on the board. Model the pronunciation and get students to practise saying it. Play the recording through one more time with students following the completed script.

Answers

1. Are they new? 2. suit you 3. get them
4. reduced from 5. do you know 6. on the left

Ask students to read the conversation in pairs using the tapescript on page 151. Remind them to try and follow the stress and phrasing as indicated. Then ask them to underline any expressions they find useful, particularly those they think they might use. Encourage them to transfer these into their notebooks. You might want to point out the following:
They really suit you.
They've got a sale on at the moment.

Students might ask you about the following expressions:

- *To begin with* is an alternative way of saying *at first.*
- *I can imagine* is an expression used when you understand how someone feels about a situation they have just told you about. *For example:*
  A: *We were two hours late. The food was terrible. The attendants were rude. It was the worst flight of my life.*
  B: *I can imagine.*
- *Brilliant* is a common way in British English of saying something was very good. For example:
  A: *How was the film?*
  B: *Brilliant!*
- If you *just couldn't resist* something, you couldn't stop yourself having or buying it. For example: *I know I'm on a diet, but they have really good cakes there. I just couldn't resist having one.*

Ask follow-up questions for further practice. For example:
Do you think my shirt suits me?
Do you know anywhere near here with a sale on?
Have you ever seen something you just couldn't resist?

4 Using grammar: reference words

Ask students to remember the first thing Charlotte said in the conversation (*Oh, I like those shoes*). Ask why she said *those* and not *these*? (If she had said *these*, she would have been referring to the shoes she was wearing.) Go over the instructions and ask students to cross out the wrong word. Model how the first item is said, focusing on the intonation and the contraction /ˈdɪdjə/. Then go through the answers by asking individual students to say the correct sentences and get them to practise the pronunciation. You might also mention that we sometimes use *a pair of* with the plural nouns here. For example:
I bought a nice pair of earrings at the market the other day.

Answers

2. that, it 3. that, it 4. those, them 5. those, them
6. that, it 7. that, it 8. those, them

5 Using grammar: prepositional expressions

Ask students if they can remember where the shop in **3 Talking about things you've bought** was located. Students might say *Hockley* or *Castle Street*, to which you could respond *Whereabouts exactly?* If no-one remembers, ask students to find the answer in the text (*It's halfway down Castle Street/the hill on the left*). Explain to them that in this activity they will practise other phrases to describe location. Get individuals or pairs of students to work on the matching task. After checking the answers, practise the pronunciation of these expressions. You may need to explain that *just* emphasises how close something is in *it's just round the corner* and *right* emphasises the exact position in *it's right next door to it*.

As a follow-up, ask students to write about the location of three places they know (they don't have to be shops; they could be other places like a bar, a park etc.) beginning *There's a great* … . They can then talk about what they wrote with a partner. You could also introduce expressions like *there's a nice little bar/park/bookshop*.

Answers

1. F (shoe shop) 2. A (clothes shop)
3. B (sports shop) 4. D (bookshop)
5. E (camping shop) 6. C (CD and record shop)

Refer students to G10 of the **Grammar commentary** on page 166, which they can read either in class or as homework.

6 Practice

Do a couple of example conversations with students first before they do the task on their own. You could also write some expressions on the board to help. For example:
I don't remember. I got them ages ago.
I don't know. It was a present from my sister.

You might need to explain that *the high street* is usually the main shopping street in a town and is usually preceded by *the*. You can also say *in the high street*, especially when you are focusing on the area rather than the name of the street. If students ask, Leith is part of Edinburgh.

7 Reading

1 Speaking

Go through questions **1–6** explaining any vocabulary if necessary. You might need to explain that if you *shop around*, you like to compare prices in different places before you decide to buy something. Also explain that if you *keep an eye open for* something, you pay particular attention in case you see it. For example:
A: *Do you know anyone who wants to sell their car?*
B: *Not really. But I always read the ads. I'll keep an eye open for any, if you like.*

2 While you read (Good mothers – real men)

Before asking students to discuss these questions in pairs or small groups, you might want to get them to ask you these questions first so you can provide them with a model.

Before students read the article, point out the title and ask what they think a *good mother* or a *real man* is. You don't need to spend too much time on this as students can talk about this further in **5 Speaking**. Explain that the article is about shopping and housework. Ask what they think the article is going to say about good mothers and real men in relation to these things. You could also play the recording, using it as a listening task first, and then get students to read the article.

When students have finished, ask them to share their reactions in pairs. Write some expressions on the board to help. For example:
He/She's just like my … .
He/She reminds me of … .
I think I'll be like that.
I'm exactly like that.

3 Comprehension

In this activity students try to remember particular details from the article. They are not only working on comprehension, but they are also focusing on useful expressions. Tell them not to worry if they can't remember everything. They can then re-read the article to find what they missed. You may need to explain that if you *make fun of someone*, you make jokes about them, sometimes in an unkind way.

Answers

Possible answers:

1. Her son's friends said he was a girl and he would never be <u>a real man</u>.
2. She sometimes has to go away on <u>business</u>.
3. She had an appointment at the <u>hospital</u>.
4. Her son's friends <u>made fun</u> of him one day when they found out he was making cakes.
5. Her husband forgot to buy <u>rice</u>. They normally eat rice every day. It was on the shopping list.
6. The cheese was reduced because the next day was its <u>sell-by date</u>.
7. Her husband bought six tins of pineapple because it was on <u>special offer</u>.
8. He is <u>thirty-two</u> years old.
9. The shopping took him <u>two hours</u> more than it normally takes her.
10. He doesn't know how the <u>washing machine</u> works.

Finish up by reading the article aloud or playing the recording while students follow the text. As they do so, ask them to underline any expressions they find interesting or they want to ask about. You may need to explain some of these expressions:

- If you *give someone a hand,* you help them. For example: *Can you give me a hand?*
- If you *get someone to do something*, you ask or persuade them to do it. For example: *I'll get my sister to come over and fix your computer.*

4 Word check

This activity helps reinforce some of the language from the article. Students can work individually or in pairs completing the sentences.

Answers

1. do 2. appointment 3. give 4. takes
5. shopping 6. tins 7. feel 8. company
9. keep 10. after

Here are some additional questions to ask if you want to give students further practice with the language:

Who does most of the housework in your house?
How long does it normally take you to do the shopping?
Do you usually write a shopping list?
What other food is sold in tins? (beans, tuna)
How would you describe someone's house if they didn't keep it clean? (messy, untidy)

5 Speaking

Before doing the discussion questions, you might want to go through **Real English: do the shopping** and do the sentence sharing activity so students can then use some of these expressions. You might need to explain that in **1,** if you *get on with someone*, you like them and have a good relationship with them.

6 Using vocabulary: verbs around the house

Explain the task and do the first item as an example. Students can then work individually or in pairs. Go through the answers and discuss any variations.

Answers

1. go to the shops / do the shopping / unpack the bags / put the things away
2. lay the table / have dinner / clear the table / wash up
3. invite some friends round / have a party / make a mess / tidy up
4. do the shopping / peel the vegetables / cut them up / cook dinner / clean up the kitchen
5. sort out the dirty clothes / put them in the washing machine / hang them up / iron them / put them away
6. put some water on to boil / make some tea / drop the cup on the floor / sweep up the bits / mop the floor

Model the miming activity with students before they work in pairs. Choose one of the groups of activities and act it out in the correct order. Encourage students to record any expressions they find useful in their notebooks. You could finish by asking them to find all the verbs here that use *up* (*wash up, tidy up, clean up, cut up, hang up, sweep up*) or all those that have irregular past forms (*put, did, went, laid, made, had, cut, hung, swept*).

7 Practice

Get students to complete the conversations individually and then check with a partner or by looking back at **6 Using vocabulary: verbs around the house.**

Answers

1. lay 2. peel 3. unpack 4. hang 5. boil
6. tidy up 7. put (these things) away
8. sort out, put

Model the pronunciation of the opening question and then get students to practise it before they practise the conversations **1–6** themselves. Teach some expressions for responding to these requests. For example:

Sure.

No problem.

OK.

For the second activity get students to wander around the classroom making their own requests. You might want to write the basic patterns on the board to help:

A: Can I do anything to help?

B: Yes … . Could you (just) / Could you (just) help me … ?

A: Sure. No problem.

Listening

1 Using vocabulary: problems with clothes

Focus students' attention on the pictures **A–F** on page 40. You could use this as an opportunity to revise some clothing vocabulary. Explain that there is a problem in each picture and ask them to find the appropriate phrase **1–6**. Even if students don't know *trendy* or *old-fashioned*, they will probably guess correctly. Go over the answers and check students' understanding of *trendy* by asking questions like *What kind of clothes are trendy now?* Also check they remember the use of *too* + adjective. Make sure they know that the expression *it doesn't fit me* is related to size and *it doesn't suit me* is related to style before they choose the appropriate follow-up expression.

Model and practise the pronunciation of the expressions. For further practice, you could ask students to test each other. One student covers the phrases and describes the problem in each picture while their partner listens and corrects if necessary. Tell students there may be more than one answer.

Answers

1. B/C 2. D 3. A/D/E 4. A/F 5. A/B/C/D/E/F 6. A/B/F

1., 2. and 3. can be followed by *It doesn't fit me.*

4., 5. and 6. can be followed by *It doesn't suit me.*

Before students talk about their own experiences, demonstrate by talking about yourself. For example: *I've got a wool jumper that my grandmother knitted for me ages ago. It's dark green and really warm. I used to wear it all the time, but then my husband said it was too boring and it didn't suit me, so I stopped wearing it.*

You might want to teach the phrase *I look good in green/blue/black*.

2 Using grammar: *not enough*

Read the first two examples and check students understand the meaning by asking:

*What's the problem in **1**? He needs more … ? (money)*

*How about in **2**? He needs a … ? (bigger size)*

Explain that *enough* is used before a noun (e.g. *enough money, enough room*) and after an adjective (e.g. *big enough, warm enough*). Students can then apply this guideline in the task.

Check that students know that if you *have experience*, you have worked in similar jobs before and that if you *are qualified*, you have passed the necessary exams. Here are some examples of further questions to ask as you go through the answers:

How old do you need to be to vote/drink alcohol/drive/leave school?

What other ways could you complete this sentence: 'I'd like to … but I'm not old enough'?

*What could the person do in **2**? (Add sugar.)*

*What could the person do in **3**? (Add more memory, get a new computer.)*

What could be an opposite of 'not qualified enough'? (too qualified, overqualified)

Answers

1. I'd like to vote in the next election, but I'm not old enough.
2. This doesn't taste right. It's not sweet enough.
3. This computer is terrible. It doesn't really have enough memory for me.
4. I didn't have enough time to finish all the questions in the exam.
5. I didn't get the job. They said I didn't have enough experience.
6. I didn't get the job. They said I wasn't qualified enough.

Refer students to G11 of the **Grammar commentary** on page 166, which they can read either in class or as homework.

3 Practice

Go around and help with vocabulary as students complete these sentence starters. As an alternative, you might want to ask them to explain their sentences in a small group. Get them to share some of their suggestions and write a few on the board. Encourage students to record a couple of their personalised examples in their notebooks.

4 While you listen

Explain the situation and ask students to just listen for the answers to the question. Play the recording and ask students to tell you the answers. Introduce the summarising task, explaining that they don't need to remember the exact words. You could also get students to work in pairs on this task. Play the recording again and let them add anything they missed before inviting them to share their answers.

Answers

Conversation 1 takes place in a camping shop.

Conversation 2 takes place in supermarket.

Conversation 3 takes place in a corner store or newsagent's.

Suggested summaries:

1. try another shop
2. not buy any and not wash his hair for a few days
3. take them back to the shop, give him coins

Play the recording again and ask students to follow the tapescript on page 151. Encourage them to underline any expressions they find useful or want to ask about. You may need to explain the following:

- If something is *just off this road*, it's on a side street.
- *The next size down* is the next smallest size. The opposite is *the next size up*.
- If you try to pay for something and the assistant asks if you *have anything smaller*, they want to know if you can pay with a smaller denomination note.
- In the UK we commonly refer to a bank's automatic cash machine as a *cash point*.
- Students might also ask about the way the person counts the change in Conversation 3. Explain that starting from the total, £1.10, the assistant gave the customer 90p and said *that's two*, meaning *that makes two pounds;* then gave another pound and said *three* etc.

You might also want to point out the following shopping expressions:

Have you got something like this, but in a smaller size?

They don't sell it in bottles.

Is that it then?

I need to cash some travellers' cheques.

5 Speaking

Read the questions to the class and explain any vocabulary if necessary. For **2** you may need to teach some expressions with *hair*. For example:

My hair's too dry.

I've got dandruff.

My hair's a bit greasy.

You can answer some of these questions yourself before students discuss their answers in pairs or small groups.

6 Using grammar: negative questions

This is an area of English that often causes problems for students. Here negative questions are practised in a meaningful context that helps students understand. Go through the examples and explanation and ask students to complete the conversations. Point out the expression *good value for money* and *good quality*. Ask them to tell you some things they think are *good value for money* or *good quality*. Explain that if we describe clothing as *baggy*, we mean it is very loose. For example: *baggy trousers/shorts/jumper/suit*. Model the conversations, letting students hear how *Don't you think* is said.

Answers

1. Don't you think it's a bit too bright?
2. Don't you think it's a bit too old-fashioned?
3. Don't you think it's a bit too expensive?
4. Don't you think it's a bit too big?
5. Don't you think it's a bit too trendy?

7 Using vocabulary: talking about clothes

Refer students to G12 of the **Grammar commentary** on page 166, which they can read either in class or as homework.

In this activity students are asked to translate expressions without a dictionary. You should explain the expressions so that the idea and the context are clear. Then students can think about what they would say in the same context to express the same idea in their own language. This way they will probably end up with a more appropriate equivalent. Stress that whenever they translate things in their notebooks, they should translate complete expressions and not just individual words.

One way to approach the first part of the task is to ask students to decide which expressions they think express a positive feeling (1., 2., 4., 5.) and which express a negative feeling (3., 6., 7., 8., 9., 10.). Then you can explain any expressions students don't understand. You might need to explain that if a piece of clothing or colour *goes with* another piece of clothing or colour, they look good together. For example: *White goes with everything!* Students can then practise talking about the people in the photos.

6 How are you?

Unit overview

General topic
Talking and asking about how people feel.

Conversation
Sarah tells Pete why she wasn't in class; Teresa tells Janet why she can't come to class.

Reading
James Phillips suffers from narcolepsy: he keeps falling asleep.

Listening
Five conversations about how people feel.

Language input

- Expressions to talk about being ill: *I've got an upset stomach, Have you taken anything for it?*
- Infinitives of purpose: *I'm just phoning to see what you are doing tonight.*
- Expressions to explain why you are tired: *I was up till three watching TV.*
- *Can't* and *couldn't* to explain why it is/was impossible to do something: *I can't read this. I haven't got my glasses, Sorry I couldn't come yesterday. My boss said I had to stay and work.*
- Expressions for greeting people: *How's it going? So what're you doing here?*
- Expressions for giving and responding to good news: *Guess what? We're getting married, Congratulations.*

Language strip

You can use the language strip as a way to lead in to the unit. Ask students to quickly look through the strip to see if they can predict the topic of the unit (talking and asking about how people feel, explaining health problems, sleep etc.). Encourage students to choose a couple of expressions in the strip that look interesting and to find out more about them.

You might need to explain some of the following expressions:

- If you say *you've been in bed all day*, you usually mean that you don't feel well and have been resting in bed.
- If *you've got a stomach bug*, you've got a (usually minor) bacterial or viral infection that causes an upset stomach. We can also use *bug* by itself in a more general sense. For example: *There's a bug going around at school.*
- If you say you were *up till* a particular time, it means you didn't get to sleep until that time. We can use *up* to mean *awake*. For example: *Are you up yet?*
- If you do something *in the middle of* something else, you do it while something else is going on. For example: *I started coughing in the middle of class, I can't help you at the moment, I'm in the middle of cooking dinner.*
- If you *oversleep*, you sleep longer than you planned to. For example: *You're late. Did you oversleep again?*
- If you have a *chronic illness*, you have an illness that goes on for the rest of your life or at least for a very long time. For example: *I've got chronic backache.*
- You might say *You're in a very good mood today* to someone who looks happy and you would like to know why.

Remind students to record any of the expressions they like in their notebooks and to take note when they see similar expressions throughout the unit.

Use the language strip later on in this unit for a small group task. Here are some possibilities:

- Students find those expressions connected with sleep (e.g. *I couldn't get to sleep last night*) and those connected with being sick (e.g. *I've got a stomach bug*).
- Students sort some of the expressions into two groups: those said by someone explaining how they feel (e.g. *I got woken up by the noise*) and those said by someone asking about or responding to how a friend feels (e.g. *You're in a very good mood today*).
- Students choose three or four expressions from the strip and – if necessary – change them so they are true about themselves. They can then talk about their choices with a partner.

Lead in

You could lead in by asking a few students about how they feel (e.g. *How are you? How's it going? How are you feeling?*). You could also talk about typical responses (e.g. *Not bad, OK, Fine, Good, Great*). You might get some answers like *Tired, I don't feel well,* to which you can follow up with questions like *What's wrong? Why?*. Write some of the answers you get on the board and reformulate if necessary. You can then explain to students that in the first few activities in the Coursebook they will practise ways of talking about when they don't feel well.

Conversation

1 Using vocabulary: *I'm not feeling very well*

Focus students' attention on the pictures on page 42 and explain the matching task. You could check the answers by pointing to a picture and asking individual students *How are you?* Get them to respond *I'm not feeling very well. I've got an upset stomach* etc. Talk about the time you had any of the problems before students talk to a partner about their own experiences.

> **Answers**
>
> 1. C 2. D 3. A 4. B

Point out the use of *a bit of a* when it is less serious and *a really (bad)* when it is more serious. Explain that unless we are talking to doctors, we tend to use *an upset stomach* rather than the more specific terms *vomiting* or *diarrhoea*.

You might want to use this opportunity to teach some other illness expressions. Let students ask what they want to know rather than giving them a comprehensive list. Give them some expressions to show how any words/expressions are used too. For example:
I've got a sore throat, I think I've got the flu.

2 Talking about being ill

Explain the situation of the conversation and ask students to just listen for the two problems. Play the recording, making sure students cover the text. Get them to discuss the answers in pairs. Remind them to keep the text covered as they do this.

> **Answers**
>
> Sarah has got a really bad cold. Teresa has got a really upset stomach.

Play the recording again and ask students to try to fill in each of the gaps as they listen. They should then compare their answers with a partner. Play the recording a third time, but this time pause after each gap. Elicit the missing words and maybe write the complete expression on the board. Model the pronunciation and ask students to practise saying it. Play the recording through one more time with students following the completed script.

> **Answers**
>
> 1. How are you 2. not very well 3. see anyone
> 4. a bit better 5. How's it going 6. that's awful
> 7. take it easy 8. got to go

Get students to read the conversations in pairs using the tapescript on page 151. Remind them to try and follow the stress and phrasing as indicated. Then ask them to underline any expressions they want to remember, particularly those they think they might use. Encourage them to transfer these into their notebooks. You might want to point out *That's really nice/kind of you* as a response to someone who has done or has offered to do something nice for you.

3 Questions and answers

Here students can focus on some typical expressions used in conversations about when people don't feel well. Explain the task and maybe do the first item together as a class. Students can then work individually on the rest before checking their answers with a partner. You may need to explain several of the expressions in this activity:

- If you say you've been *sick all night*, you usually mean you have been vomiting or have diarrhoea.
- *Painkillers* are drugs like *aspirin* or *paracetamol*.
- If you *just take it easy*, you relax and don't do anything that needs a lot of energy.
- *Herbs* refer to plants that are used as medicine (e.g. *camomile, eucalyptus*).
- *Pills* are medicine in the form of small tablets.

> **Answers**
>
> 1. a., d., f., i., l.
> 2. b., c., h., j.
> 3. e., g., k.

To help students with the conversation, write the basic patterns on the board:

A: *How are you?*
B: *Not very well, actually.*
A: *Oh no. What's the problem?*
B: *I've got …*
A: *Oh no. I'm sorry. Have you taken anything for it?/Have you been to see anyone about it?*
B: *Yes/No …*

Practise the pronunciation of these expressions with students before they have similar conversations based on some of the problems in the pictures on page 42.

Follow up by letting students talk about what they do when they feel ill. Here are some further questions you could feed in as necessary:

How do you try to keep healthy?
How often do you get sick?
How often do you take the day off work/class when you are sick?
Do you think herbs really work?
Have you ever tried acupuncture? Did it work?

4 Using grammar: infinitives of purpose

Before going through the explanation, ask students if they can remember why Pete phoned Sarah and why Teresa phoned Janet in **2 Talking about being ill**. (Students will probably answer with *because* but they might also use *to*.) Ask them to find what expression Pete used in **Conversation 1** that gives them the answer (*I'm just phoning to make sure you're OK*). Do the first re-ordering task as a class before asking students to work individually or in pairs on the rest.

There are a lot of different grammar patterns (tense, gerunds, indirect questions etc.) following the verbs in these expressions. Don't worry about going into the details. Tell students to concentrate on remembering the complete expressions. Students may have problems with the word order in **1**, **2**, **3** and **9**. As you go through the answers, ask them to tell you who they think the person is talking to and what that person might say next.

Answers

1. how you are
2. what you're doing tonight
3. where to meet tomorrow
4. for forgetting your birthday
5. about your English courses
6. sure you got home OK
7. still coming tonight
8. I'm going to be late
9. how much your flights to Chile are

Thinking of alternative endings for these explanations might be quite challenging. You might want to do the task together as a class, or the first few items at least. To make it easier, point out the basic patterns of some of the expressions (e.g. *apologise for + -ing, check you're still + -ing, let you know I'm going to be …*).

Pairs of students can then write and practise reading a similar conversation. Point out some of the other telephone expressions in the example: *Listen, I wonder if you can help me.*

Reading

1 Using vocabulary: feeling tired

Lead in by eliciting some reasons why someone might be tired. Listen to students' suggestions and maybe write a few on the board. Then explain that in this activity students will see some common ways of explaining why someone is tired. Encourage them to look for any that might express the reasons listed on the board. Do the first sentence as an example and then let students complete the rest on their own. They can then check their answers with a partner. You might ask a couple of students to read the answers to the class to check understanding.

Answers

1. day, lunch 2. couldn't, sleep 3. up, watching
4. up, reading 5. out, home 6. gym, did
7. week, late 8. get up, catch

You will probably need to explain the following expressions:

- If you can't do something *for some reason*, you don't know why you are not able to do it. For example: *For some reason, I can never remember my students' names.*
- If you say you *didn't even stop for lunch*, you mean you didn't take a lunch break. Here is another example: *It only took us five hours to get there because we didn't stop for lunch.*
- Explain that in English we can say *a busy morning/night/month/year* as well as *a busy day/week*.

For the practice part of the activity, students should cover sentences **1–8** and take it in turns asking each other. They can then look at the sentences again to check if they were right.

2 Before you read

These discussion questions give students the opportunity to personalise some of the expressions from **1 Using vocabulary: feeling tired** while also setting the scene for the reading task. Answer some of the questions yourself first to provide students with a model. Explain in **3** that if you *have a late night*, you go to bed late. You could also introduce the expression *I need (eight) hours of sleep*.

3 Reading (The sleeper)

Point out the title *The sleeper* and ask students to guess what the article might be about. Explain the first task and ask students read the introductory paragraph. Check that they understand what is wrong with James (*He's suffering from narcolepsy, which means he feels tired all the time. He keeps falling asleep all the time. You can't wake him up*) before asking students to list three possible problems narcolepsy could cause. This gives them a goal for the second reading task.

Let students read the rest of the article and compare with a partner to see how many of the problems were mentioned. You could also play the recording, using it as listening task first, and then get students to read the article. Finish up by reading the article aloud or playing the recording while students follow along. As they do so, ask them to underline any expressions connected with sleep – as well as any others – they find interesting or want to know about. You may want to make sure they notice the following:

He fell asleep

He often overslept in the mornings

He often has terrible nightmares

asleep at his desk

stay awake

You may need to explain some of these expressions:

- If you *have a great sense of humour*, you like to laugh and find things amusing; you aren't serious all the time.
- If you *give someone another chance*, you let them try to do something one more time, even though you were disappointed with their previous attempts.
- If two people *are a good match*, they get on well with each other.

Talk about **Real English: the loo**. You could also go over some alternatives, for example: *the men's/gent's, the women's/ladies'*. You might also teach students appropriate expressions for different contexts. For example:

Can I use your toilet?

Can I be excused?

4 Comprehension check

When students have finished marking their choices, ask them to explain the answers to each other rather than just checking to see if they agree. They can then re-read the article. Encourage them to find the expressions in the article that give the answers, for example in **1**: *He often got bad grades.*

Answers

1. F 2. T 3. T 4. F (He has a part-time job.)
5. F (He didn't even show up.) 6. T
7. F (He ate dessert.)

5 Speaking

Read the questions aloud to the class, explaining any difficult expressions. For example, we often use *live with someone* to mean *be in a relationship with someone*. Tell students about a personal experience in answer to **2** before they discuss on their own. For example:

Once I was coming home late on the train after a really busy day at work. I fell asleep and missed my stop. I woke up and realised what had happened. I got off at the next station but there were no more trains back. I had to sleep on a bench until the morning.

6 Using grammar: *can't / couldn't*

Introduce this activity by asking students to remember what James *can't* do (work full time, drive, have baths, stay awake etc.). Explain that *can't* is often used to show that something is not possible and let students read the three examples in the Coursebook. Check they understand the different meanings by asking for a couple of alternative examples for each one. For example:

1 *I can't drive. I never learnt.*
2 *We can't leave class until the bell goes.*
3 *I can't leave him alone. He's too sick.*

Then go through the examples with *couldn't*. Point out that the pattern in the second example *Sorry I couldn't … yesterday/the other day/last week etc.* is a common way of beginning an apology for something you were unable to do.

Ask students to do the matching task individually and then check their answersh with a partner. Model the pronunciation of the completed expressions and get students to practise along with you. Here are some examples of further questions to ask as you check the answers:

What are some other things to be 'scared of' or 'afraid of'? (the dark, flying)

What are other things to do with the body that we can lose? (I lost a leg/arm, I'm losing my hair.)

What are some other illnesses you can suffer from? (back pain, asthma, bronchitis)

What other things might you worry about so that you can't get to sleep?

What things were against the rules when you were at school? What happened when you broke the rules?

Are there places you know where it's against the law to smoke? Where can you smoke in public?

Answers

1. a. 2. f. 3. b. 4. d. 5. e. 6. c.

As a follow-up ask pairs of students to come up with alternative endings for some of the starters. For example:

I can't read this. It's in Arabic.

I can't speak very loudly. Someone might hear.

Refer students to G13 of the **Grammar commentary** on page 166, which they can read either in class or as homework.

7 Practice

This activity gives student the chance to personalise the language. Encourage them to record some of their examples in their notebooks. Remind them to follow up with an explanation. You may want to demonstrate a few examples yourself before they work on their own. For example:

I can't eat strawberries. They give me an upset stomach.

I really wanted to go to the Saturday market last week, but I couldn't. I had too much work to do.

Listening

1 Greeting people

Explain the task and read aloud the situations **a–e** first, explaining any expressions if necessary. (For example: If you *bump into someone*, you meet them by chance. It wasn't planned.) Then play the recording as students follow along in their Coursebook. Alternatively, get students to cover up the conversations **1–5** in the Coursebook while they listen for the first time, choosing the matching situations as they listen. They can then compare their answers with a partner. Play the recording a second time as they follow along in their Coursebooks.

Answers

1. e. 2. c. 3. a. 4. b. 5. d.

Ask students to underline any expressions they think are useful when greeting people. Make sure they notice the following:
Have you been waiting long?
I've only just got here myself.
Not too bad, thanks.
What're you doing here?
Did you have a nice weekend?
Do you mind if I join you?
Have a seat.
Did you sleep well?
So what've you been doing recently?

Talk about **Real English: What about you?** Tell students they might also hear *And you?* or even *You?* used as informal alternatives. Check that they can identify the question in each conversation that *What about you?* is referring to. Practise this further by asking individual students questions. For example:
A: How's it going?
B: Good. What about you?
A: Not too bad.

Practise the first conversation with a student before getting students to work on the conversations in pairs. This can give them ideas about how to extend the conversations.

2 While you listen

Explain the task and check that students understand that if you feel *annoyed*, you feel angry; and if you feel *awful*, you feel really bad. Before students listen, invite them to guess possible reasons why someone would have the feelings in **a–c**. Play the recording and then ask students to compare their answers with a partner.

Answers

Conversation 3 b.	(She got food poisoning on Friday night.)
Conversation 4 a.	(He was up until two and then was woken up at five by the people next door. He couldn't get back to sleep for ages.)
Conversation 5 c.	(She is pregnant. The baby is due in about six months.)

You can play the recording one more time as students follow the tapescript on page 152. Get them to underline any other expressions they want to remember or want to ask about. You may need to explain that if you are *a heavy sleeper*, you aren't easily woken up. Teach the opposite: *a light sleeper*. Ask if students know any other expressions with *heavy* (e.g. *heavy drinker, heavy smoker)*. Explain that if you are pregnant, you have several *scans* to check if the baby is OK. If someone asks a pregnant woman *Do you know what it is yet?* they are asking if she knows the baby's sex.

3 Word check

This activity focuses on several useful expressions from the listening task. Ask students to complete as many items as they can from memory first before they check their answers with a partner. Then they can listen to the recording again or check the tapescript.

Answers

1. feeling 2. sleep, actually 3. till, must
4. woken, heavy 5. busy 6. due

Get students to practise reading the conversations in pairs. Then ask them to test each other. One student reads the first part and the other – with their Coursebook closed – tries to remember the answer.

Use questions **1–4** to help personalise the language from this activity. Answer some of these questions yourself first – or as an alternative get students to ask you after they have finished talking in pairs.

4 Good news

Use the pictures as a warmer. Ask students to suggest what type of good news each picture shows (e.g. *they sold their house, they bought a new house*). Explain that in this activity they will practise some expressions for giving and replying to good news. Students can complete the task individually and then compare their answers with a partner.

Answers

1. f. 2. a. 3. d. 4. h. 5. e. 6. c. 7. b. 8. g.

Play the recording so students can check their answers. You could then play it again, pausing after each exchange so that students can repeat it, or just play the expressions in the box for students to repeat. Either way, make sure they get the intonation right for these expressions. Having practised the pronunciation, students can then test each other. Write the basic pattern of the conversation on the board to help students with the personalisation task at the end:

A: Hey, guess what? …

B: Oh really? Congratulations/That's great. …

Students can then wander around telling different people their good news. If they don't have good news, suggest they make something up.

Follow-up

Tell students to imagine they are at a party. They should circulate, chatting to each other, asking how they feel, what they've been doing recently etc. Give them a few minutes to look back through the activities in the unit and encourage them to use some of the expressions they find. To help, you could also elicit a list of feelings and write them on the board (e.g. *tired, awful, sick, excited, annoyed*). Tell students they should choose a different feeling each time they talk to someone, making up an explanation for why they feel that way.

7 School and studying

Unit overview

General topic
Studying at a university, classroom rules.

Conversation
Lee and Jane talk about what they do and their plans for the future.

Reading
Studying at a university in Britain is not like it was twenty years ago.

Listening
A student arrives late to class.

Language input
- Talking about plans for the future with *going to*: *I'm going to take a year off and go travelling a bit.*
- Common words and expressions connected with studying: *re-take an exam, hand in an essay, the summer term.*
- Asking for permission: *Is it OK if I close the window? Do you mind if I smoke?*
- Making requests: *Could you just move up a bit?*

Language strip

You can use the language strip as a way to lead in to the unit. Ask students to quickly look through the strip and find any expressions they have actually heard or seen before. Ask if they have seen any similar expressions in previous units (*Do you mind if I join you?* and *No, of course not. Have a seat* appear in **Unit 6** on page 46). Explain that in this unit they will learn expressions for talking about studying. Encourage students to choose a couple of expressions in the strip that look interesting and to find out more about them.

You might need to explain some of the following expressions:
- You use *Feel free* to show that it is OK for someone to do something. It is often used to answer someone asking for permission to do something. For example:
  A: Do you mind if I smoke?
  B: No. Feel free.
- A *mobile* is a mobile phone. For example: *You can call me on my mobile. I'll give you my number.*
- If you *get a grant*, you receive some money so you can do something. For example: *The university got a grant from the government to do some research.*
- If you say *my finals*, you are referring to your final exams. For example: *When do you finish your finals?*
- If you *take a period of time off*, you take a break from what you usually do (e.g. studying or working). For example: *I'm going to take the summer off and just be home with the kids.*
- If you *drop out of a course*, you stop attending before you have finished. For example: *I never got my degree. I dropped out in my second year.*
- If you *go on a demonstration*, you take part in a protest like a march. For example: *I didn't go on the demonstration. I overslept.*
- If you ask for a *loan*, you want to borrow some money from someone (your parents, friends or a bank). For example: *You need to take out a loan to study at university now.*
- The *deadline* refers to the date or time when something needs to be done. For example: *The deadline for the essay is 5:00 pm on Friday.*
- If something *has a good reputation*, it is well known for being good. We often use this to talk about universities. For example: *Bristol's got a good reputation. I don't want to go to … . It hasn't got a very good reputation.*

Remind students to record any of the expressions they like in their notebooks and to take note when they see similar expressions throughout the unit.

Use the language strip later on in this unit for a small group task. Here are some possibilities:
- Students find one expression that might be said by a teacher to a student (e.g. *Could you turn your mobile off, please?*) and one that might be said by a student to a teacher (e.g. *Could you play the tape again, please?*).
- Students choose a few expressions that are questions (e.g. *When's the deadline?*) and come up with a possible response (e.g. *Monday, I think*). Then they choose a few expressions that are responses (e.g. *I need to ask the bank for a loan*) and come up with possible prompts (e.g. *How are you going to pay the fees?*).
- Students find expressions that use *go* (e.g. *No, of course not. Go ahead*) and those that use *got* (*I've got my finals next term*).

Lead in

You can introduce the general topic of this unit by asking students some questions about school (rather than university). Of course, the kind of questions you ask depends on the make-up of your class. Here are some suggestions:
What age do children start school?
Did/Do you like school?

Did/Do you have a lot of homework?
What were/are your favourite subjects?
Did/Do you like your teachers?

Conversation

1 Vocabulary: your academic career

Read the stages aloud and then ask students to put them in order. Check the answers and discuss the typical ages for **1–4**. In the UK children start primary school at five and secondary school at eleven or twelve. You can leave school when you are sixteen but if you want to go to university, you stay until you are eighteen.

Answers

1. d. 2. b. 3. f. 4. a. 5. g. 6. c. 7. e.

Get students to talk to a partner about what they have done already. Write the following sentence starters on the board to help:
I started/went/did/left/graduated etc. … in (1986).
I'm going to start/do/leave etc. … (next year).
I want to do/go etc. … .
I hope I can do/go etc. …

If you have a multinational class, students will probably talk about how their school systems differ. In wrapping up, invite a few students to talk about any differences they learnt about.

Talk about **Real English: graduate**. Tell students about yourself (or some people you know) before asking them to think of their own sentences. You can either ask students to tell their sentences to a partner or ask for a few examples and write them on the board, reformulating if necessary.

You can use the picture of the graduation on page 48 to ask further questions. For example:
Are there any special celebrations when you leave school?
Do parents give presents?
What happens when you graduate from university?
Do you have ceremonies like this? Who usually comes?

2 Talking about university

Tell students to look at the photo of the two people on page 48. Explain that they are students. Ask the class to guess their ages and to describe how they are dressed. Invite them to guess what they might be studying. Give them the following pattern to help:
He/She looks (quite smart).
He/She's probably studying … .

This gives you an opportunity to revise some of the expressions from **Unit 5**.

Explain the first task and remind students to just listen for information about Jane. Play the recording, making sure that students cover the text. Get them to discuss their answers in pairs. Remind students to keep the text covered as they do this.

Answers

Jane is studying Business Management at the London Business School. She's in her third and final year. After she graduates, she's going to travel for a bit and then she wants to do a Master's in International Finance. She's interested in going to Leeds to do it.

Play the recording again and ask students to try to fill in each of the gaps as they listen. They should then compare their answers with a partner. Play the recording a third time, but this time pause after each gap. Elicit the missing words and maybe write the complete expression on the board. Model the pronunciation and get students to practise saying it. Play the recording through one more time with students following the completed script.

Answers

1. What year are you in? 2. my finals
3. take a year off 4. What in? 5. Have you applied
6. a very good reputation 7. go for an interview
8. what about you

Then ask students to underline any expressions they find useful, particularly those they think they might use. Encourage them to transfer these into their notebooks. Point out that *So what do you do?* is a common question between people who have just met. You might need to explain that in England a bachelor's degree is usually three years of study.

Get students to practise reading the conversation and to continue with what they think Lee would say. Tell the person playing Jane to use some of Lee's original questions. If you want, choose a couple of pairs of students to do the conversation again for the rest of the class. Play the rest of the recording and ask if anyone was right about Lee. Check that students have all the information. Then get them to read the tapescript on page 152 while you play the recording again.

Answers

Lee is doing a one-year art course at the moment. He wants to do art history at university and he has been offered a place at Goldsmith's College in London.

3 Using grammar: *going to*

Introduce this activity by asking students to tell you anything from **1 Vocabulary: your academic career** on page 48 that they plan to do in the future (e.g. graduate next year). Write a couple of examples on the board. Reformulate if necessary with *going to*. For example:
Olivier's going to graduate next year.

Ask if students remember what Jane's plans were. Ask them to find where in the text Jane explains her plans. Then go through the explanation of the use of *going to*.

Students may wonder when to use *going to* and when to use the present continuous for the future. Although there is some overlap, the present continuous tends to be used to talk about an arrangement that has already been decided on (e.g. *I'm meeting Bob for dinner later tonight*), whereas *going to* tends to be used to talk about something you intend or plan to do (e.g. *I'm going to take a few days off work*).

The questions in **a–f** are common uses of *going to*. Get students to work together if the task seems to be challenging. Play the recording so students can check their answers and then play it again, pausing after each one so that students can practise repeating. Make sure they are following the reduced pronunciation of *going to*.

Answers

a. (So what) are you going to study?
b. (So how) are you going to pay your college fees?
c. (Are you) going to go away in the summer?
d. (What are) you going to wear to the party tonight?
e. (So what) are you going to do when you finish?
f. (Which universities) are you going to apply to?

Get students to match the answers **1– 6.** Then in pairs they can practise asking and answering the questions. For further practice ask students to come up with two alternative answers for each question. For example:
A: *Are you going to go away in the summer?*
B: *No. I'm just going to stay here and take it easy/Yes. I'm going to America for a couple of weeks.*

Answers

a. 5. b. 3. c. 2. d. 6. e. 4. f. 1.

Explain the use of *might* for when we are not sure. Point out that *I'm/We're not (really) sure (yet), I haven't really decided yet, I don't really know yet* are often used in conjunction with *might*. You could also teach the pattern *I might … or I might …* . For example:
A: *What are you going to study?*
B: *I'm not sure. I might do History or I might do Politics. It depends what grades I get.*

Refer students to G14 of the **Grammar commentary** on page 166, which they can read either in class or as homework.

4 Practice

You can get students to work in small groups on this or alternatively, get them to wander around asking different people. Read the four additional questions to the class and practise the pronunciation. If you want to extend this into a role play based on the photos, you might want to ask students to write the dialogue first and then perform it to another group.

The photos on page 49 provide another opportunity to revise some of the expressions from **Unit 5** for describing how people are dressed (e.g. *He looks a bit scruffy*).

For further practice with *going to* get students into small groups to talk about their plans for the next few weeks or months, or the coming year.

Reading

1 Using vocabulary: studying at university

Write *lecture, exam, term, essay* and *course* on the board and elicit the connection between them – university. Get students to translate the words. Then explain the completion task and let students work by themselves. They can check their answers with a partner. You may want to pair up students with the same language for this. Explain any expressions students ask about. Encourage them to translate these complete expressions as well and to record them in their notebooks.

Answers

1. an exam 2. course 3. term 4. university
5. a lecture 6. an essay

Conversations **1–5** reinforce some of the expressions. After going through the answers, get students to practise reading them in pairs. You may need to explain that if you are *stressed-out*, you don't feel good because you are worrying about things. For further practice ask students to write six sentences that are true for them, using the words in the box. Give a few personal examples first to get them started. For example:
I failed my first English exam at university.
I'm going to do a part-time computer course next month.

Answers

1. go, asleep 2. got, fail 3. to, out, hard
4. end, long 5. deadline, handed

2 Speaking

The questions here give students the opportunity to practise some of the language from **1 Using vocabulary: studying at university**. Read the four questions aloud, explaining any expressions if necessary. When students have finished talking to each other, ask them to look at the questions again and memorise as many as they can. Tell them to close their Coursebooks and then ask you the questions.

3 Before you read

Use these questions to lead in to the topic of the reading task – how university education has changed in the UK. You can either check that students understand the difference between a *grant* and a *loan* now or wait until they have finished reading the article.

4 While you read (Students these days!)

Read the instructions and perhaps ask students to predict what changes they think they will read about. Point out the title *Students these days!* Explain that these days is a common expression people use when they are complaining that things are worse now than they used to be. For example:

Kids these days. They never do anything. They just stay at home watching TV and playing computer games.

Let students read the article and compare their answers with a partner. You might want to draw two columns on the board (*20 years ago* and *Now*) and elicit the answers from the class. You could also play the recording, using it as a listening task first, and then ask students to read the article.

Answers

Twenty years ago students didn't have to pay university fees. They were given a grant from the government. Now the course costs two or three thousand pounds and students get a loan. Before, most students didn't need to work while they were studying. Now most students have part-time jobs. Twenty years ago it was easier for students to choose what they really wanted to study. Now they have to think about what kind of subject will get them a good job. Twenty years ago it was easier to find work and students could take some time off before starting work. Now a lot people have to find a job straight away so they can start paying back the money they owe.

Finish up by reading the article aloud or playing the recording while students follow along in their Coursebooks.

5 Vocabulary focus

Ask students to work in pairs. Tell them to try to remember what was said without referring to the article. They can then re-read the article to check. Remind them to underline the complete expressions. Encourage them to record these in their notebooks.

Answers

I say concentrate on studying, … we just sat around and chatted to each other, … , went on demonstrations or went to parties.

He wants to drop out and apply to do American studies at a different university, but I say he shouldn't.

He says … he doesn't really have enough time to do the essays and projects he has to write.

I got a grant of over two thousand pounds …

He says he has to go to too many lectures, …
… , and I never had to pay any of it back at all.

The government gives you a loan, which you then have to pay back after you graduate. … , but he'll have to pay back the money he's borrowed.

6 Speaking

Read the first three questions out loud, explaining that in **3** students are being asked if they agree with Danny's or his father's thinking. Write some useful expressions on the board to help students discuss these questions. For example:

It's just the same in my country/here.
It's mostly the same, except we …
He's realistic/He's not being very realistic.
He wants what's best for his son.
I think Danny/his father has a good point.

Then ask students to look at the six choices. You may have to explain the following:

- If a course *leads to a good job*, you are more likely to get a good job if you do the course.
- If you do something *straight after* something else, you do it immediately you finish the first one. You can also use *go straight* somewhere to mean *go directly* somewhere without going somewhere else or doing something else first. For example: *go straight home, go straight to bed, go straight to work.*

Before getting students to discuss in pairs, go through the example conversations. Make sure you point out the highlighted patterns. Wrap up by asking one or two pairs of students to tell the class their choices.

7 Which degree?

Read through the list of courses explaining any if necessary. For example:

- *Fine art* involves painting, sculpture etc.
- *Media studies* involves the study of newspapers, TV radio etc.
- *IT* stands for *information technology*.
- *Pure mathematics* is concerned with the theory of mathematics rather than the practical applications of *applied mathematics*.

After students have marked their choices, model the three sentence starters and then get them to compare their choices in pairs or small groups. You might want to introduce the expression a *degree in (media studies)*. Here are some additional questions to ask:

What are the best degree courses for getting a high-paying job?

Is it difficult to get in to study these subjects?

What are some universities with good reputations for these courses?

Listening

1 Class rules

Read sentences **1–6** and then get students into small groups to discuss them. Check that students understand the expression *one … at a time*. Ask them to tell you, if that is the rule in your classroom, what they would have to do if they wanted to speak and someone else was already speaking (e.g. wait until that person finished).

To help students form the two rules for your class, point out the basic patterns:

If you … , you should/shouldn't …

You should always …

Ask groups of students to share their ideas and vote on the best rules.

Use the picture on page 52 to revise the use of *couldn't* (or *can't*, if students are young enough). Get them to tell each other about any of the things the person is doing that were against the rules when they were at school. For example:

We couldn't put our feet up on the table.

We couldn't smoke at school.

Get students to continue talking and asking about other rules.

2 While you listen

Explain the task and play the recording once. Ask students to compare their answers with a partner and then play the recording again. Play the recording a third time while students follow along with the tapescript on page 152.

Answers

Adam broke rules 1 and 2. He was late for school because his alarm clock didn't go off. He didn't turn his mobile off and someone rang him in the middle of class. He said he did his homework, but he didn't bring it to school.

3 Speaking

Use these questions so students can talk about some of their ideas. Explain *strict* if necessary. Ask students who or what, apart from a teacher, we can describe as *strict* (*parents, a law*).

4 Asking for permission

Here students practise a common way of asking for permission. You might want to elicit the ways they know already by asking *What would you say to me if you wanted to leave the room?* Write some of their suggestions on the board. For example:

Can I leave the room?

Could I leave the room?

May I leave the room?

If no-one suggests *Is it OK if … ?*, ask students to remember what Adam said and then to complete the question in the Coursebook. Explain that *Is it OK if … ?* is a common informal way of asking permission.

Ask students to do the matching task and then compare their answers with a partner. Play the recording so they can check their answers. Point out that *Well, actually, I'd rather you didn't* is used when the person wants to say that it isn't OK. Explain that we use *boiling* and *freezing* to describe something very hot and very cold. We can say both *it's boiling/freezing* and *I'm boiling/freezing*.

Answers

1. a. 2. d. 3. e. 4. b. 5. c.

5 Pronunciation: linking

Practise the linking of the phrase *Is it OK if I … ?* with the class and then get them to practise the conversations from **4 Asking for permission**.

Talk about **Real English: Do you mind if I … ?** Students often have problems answering this kind of question because *yes* would mean it's not OK and *no* would mean it is OK. Explain that *Do you mind if I … ?* means *Is it a problem if I … ?* To avoid confusion, we rarely answer with just *no*; we use *No, of course not, Go ahead, No problem, Feel free*. If it isn't OK, we don't usually use *yes* at all. We say things like *Well, actually, I'd rather you didn't*.

After students have practised the conversations with *Do you mind if I ... ?* ask them to write their own questions. They can then either work in pairs or wander around having conversations with different students. Refer students to G15 of the **Grammar commentary** on page 167, which they can read either in class or as homework.

6 Making requests

Ask students to look at the cartoons on page 53. Get them to explain what the problem is in each one (e.g. *the suitcase is too heavy, she doesn't understand, the music is too loud*). Then choose one of the pictures and elicit what the person might be saying. Write a couple of the students' suggestions on the board, including any with *could*. Explain that we often start requests with *Could you just ... ?*

Explain the matching task and then get students to compare their answers with a partner. As you go through the answers, point out that as well as meaning *a little*, *a bit* can soften a request to make it sound more polite. Make sure students notice how we use *Sorry, but ...* to say that we can't or don't want to do something. Follow up by asking students where they think the speakers are in each conversation.

Answers

1. c. 2. e. 3. a. 4. b. 5. d.

There are several useful expressions here, so encourage students to record those they want to remember in their notebooks. Point out the following:

I can hardly hear it

let a bit of fresh air in

There you go

Have you got enough space?

Ask students to practise the conversations in pairs before they have their own conversations based on the pictures.

Follow-up

Ask pairs of students to choose four or five expressions from the language strip on page 48. They should write a conversation containing those expressions. They should then role-play the conversation to another group or to the class as a whole.

8 Work and jobs

Unit overview

General topic
Talking about work and different kinds of job, applying for jobs.

Conversation
Nori and Sue explain what their jobs are like.

Reading
A man explains why he likes doing temping work.

Listening
Sue tells Vic about a disastrous job interview.

Language input

- Questions about people's work: *Do you get much holiday? What are the hours like?*
- Expressions with *get*: *I only get ten euros an hour, I've finally got a job.*
- Expressions with *have to* and *don't have to*: *I have to do a lot of paperwork, I don't have to work weekends.*
- Compound nouns: *taxi driver, web designer, fitness instructor.*
- Present perfect simple: *I've done lots of other jobs as well, Have you done this kind of work before?*
- Past time expressions: *the day before yesterday, a couple of years ago.*
- Expressions with *I'm good/terrible at/with … : I'm good at languages, I'm good with people, I'm terrible at maths.*
- Expressions with *want: My parents want me to get a job when I leave school.*

Language strip

You can use the language strip as a way to lead in to the unit. Explain to students that they will practise talking about jobs. Ask them if they remember the expression *So what do you do?* Then ask them to find three expressions from the language strip that could answer that question if they were changed to *I: (I work in the media, I'm a fitness instructor, I'm a real estate agent).* Encourage students to choose a couple of expressions in the strip that look interesting and to find out more about them.

You might need to explain some of the following expressions:

- If you are *good with people*, you like being with other people and are friendly. For example: *I'd like to be a teacher because I'm really good with people.*
- If someone *gets sacked*, they lose their job because they have done something wrong. For example: *I got sacked for falling asleep at my desk all the time.*
- If you describe something like an interview as a *disaster*, it didn't go well. For example: *My date last night was a disaster. I got there late. The restaurant was full. And we ended up fighting.*
- If you *send something off*, you send it by post. For example: *I'm sorry. I didn't send your birthday card off until today.*
- An *estate agent* is someone who helps sell and buy houses. They usually receive money (*a commission*) from the sale.
- If you get a certain amount of money an hour, you receive that amount for working each hour. You can also say *a week* or *a month*. If we talk about *a year*, we often use *make*. For example: *I make £30,000 a year.*

Remind students to record any of the expressions they like in their notebooks and to take note when they see similar expressions throughout the unit.

Use the language strip later on in this unit for a small group task. Here are some possibilities:

- Students find those expressions connected with applying for a job (e.g. *Could you send me an application form?*) and those connected with describing a job (*I have to wear a suit to work*).
- Students find expressions that are about something good (e.g. *I don't have to work tomorrow!*) and those about something not so good (e.g. *He got sacked!*).
- Students discuss what questions might prompt several of the expressions. For example:
  A: Where's Lee? I haven't seen him for ages.
  B: He got sacked!

Lead in

Elicit from the class things we often want to know about someone's job (e.g. pay, holidays, hours etc.). Write these topics on the board. Ask students to think about how they would actually ask someone about these things in English. Then introduce the first activity.

Conversation

1 Questions about work and jobs

Explain that in this activity students will see some common ways of asking someone about their job. As they complete the sentences, ask them if any of these expressions are similar to the ones they thought of in the **Lead in** activity.

Answers

1. studying 2. do 3. enjoy 4. weekends 5. get 6. travel 7. people 8. money 9. boss 10. hours

Explain the translation task and encourage students to record some of these questions in their notebooks along with the translation. You may need to explain that in **1** *or what?* is an informal way of saying *or do you do something else?* Make sure students notice the use of *like* in **8–10**. In a multinational class, ask students to work with someone who doesn't share the same language and discuss with them if any of these questions aren't appropriate in their culture. They could also tell each other about any other questions that aren't considered appropriate in their culture. Finish up by inviting a couple of students to report back on what they discussed and then explain that all these questions are acceptable in English. Point out that we usually ask *What's the pay like?* rather than *How much do you get?* You could then get pairs of students to think of possible answers to some or all of these questions. For example:

A: *What's your boss like?*

B: *Very nice. She's quite friendly and always chats with us.*

2 Talking about what you do

Focus students' attention on the photo on page 54. Ask what kind of job they think the person has. Ask them to explain their guesses. For example:

I think he's a businessman or something because he's wearing a tie.

Read the instructions for the listening task aloud. Play the recording, making sure students cover the text. Then get them to discuss their answers in pairs. Remind them to keep the text covered as they do this.

Answers

Jenny asks questions 1., 2., 3., 4., 5. and 6.

Play the recording again and ask students to try to fill in each of the gaps as they listen. They should then compare their answers with a partner. Play the recording a third time, but this time pause after each gap. Elicit the missing words and maybe write the complete expression on the board. Model the pronunciation and have the class practise saying it. Play the recording through one more time with students following the completed script.

Answers

1. a couple of years ago 2. civil servant 3. quite boring 4. a bit bored 5. a twelve-hour day 6. three weeks a year 7. spend a lot of time

You may need to explain some expressions:

- Someone who *does a lot of paperwork* writes letters and reports, fills out forms etc.
- Point out the expression *kill time*. Ask students what they would do to *kill time* if they were Nori (e.g. *read a book, stare out the window, play solitaire on the computer*).
- *Thank goodness* is another way of saying *and it is a good thing that this is the case*. Give students some more examples:

  A: *Do you have to commute to work?*

  B: *No, thank goodness. I live five minutes away.*

  A: *Did you find your watch?*

  B: *Yes, thank goodness. It's a really expensive one.*

Point out the expression *spend a lot of time + - ing*. Ask students to say something true about themselves using this pattern. Then get them to read the conversation in pairs, adding how they think the conversation will continue.

Play the second part of the conversation. Get pairs of students to compare their answers. Finish up by playing the recording again while they read the tapescript on page 153.

Answers

Jenny is an estate agent in Leeds (in the north-east of England). Her job is quite stressful and she doesn't get paid much. She gets on OK with the other people at work. She has been doing this job for a year and a half. She is not sure if this job is what she really wants to do.

3 Speaking

Ask students to discuss these questions in pairs or small groups. Write up some patterns on the board to help them in the discussion of the first question. For example:

...'s job is better because he/she ...

...'s job is stressful/boring, but at least he/she ...

You could then ask the class questions like this:

What are the most stressful jobs?

Do people get paid a lot if their jobs are stressful?

What are the least stressful jobs?

For the conversation activity, you may want to get pairs of students to spend a few minutes writing down notes and then practise having the conversation a couple of times.

4 Using vocabulary: expressions with *get*

If you haven't done so already, talk about collocation with your class. Explain that knowing what words typically go together (and which words don't) is very important. Ask students if they can remember some examples of words that go with *get* from previous units (e.g. *get married*). They can then complete the sentences individually and compare their answers with a partner.

Answers

1. a job 2. an interview 3. bored 4. to work
5. ten euros an hour 6. six weeks' holiday
7. a half-hour break 8. sacked

You can read the completed sentences again. Then students can underline the expressions with *get* and try to memorise them. Next, play the recording, pausing after each one, so students can hear which words are stressed.

Answers

1. I've finally got a job.
2. I've got an interview for it.
3. I get a bit bored with it sometimes.
4. How long does it take you to get to work?
5. I only get ten euros an hour.
6. I get six weeks' holiday a year.
7. I get a half-hour break at lunchtime.
8. I got sacked!

5 Speaking

These questions help reinforce some of the expressions from **4 Using vocabulary: expressions with get**. Ask students to discuss them in small groups or in pairs. When they have finished, invite a few students to report back on what they found out. Then ask them to look at the questions again and try to memorise as many as they can. Ask them to close their Coursebooks and ask you similar questions.

6 Using grammar: *have to*

Introduce this activity by asking students if they remember what kinds of things Nori does in his job (*a lot of paperwork*). Then ask if he likes doing this (*Not really. It's 'quite boring'.*) Next, ask them to find what expression he used in the conversation on page 54 (*I have to do a lot of paperwork*). Go through the explanation at the start of this activity and the two examples. Ask students to make two more statements about Nori using *has to* (*He has to work a twelve-hour day, He has to spend a lot of time commuting*) and then one with *doesn't have to* (*He doesn't have to work weekends*).

For further practice ask the class to think of two things they have to do as students and two things they don't have to do. For example:

I have to do homework every day.
I don't have to come to school at the weekend.

Check that students are getting the idea of choice (*don't have to*) and no choice (*have to*) by asking questions like:
Do you have a choice?
What would happen if you didn't … ?

Introduce the next task. Explain that *awful* means *very bad*. Ask what else we can describe as *awful* (e.g. *these clothes look awful, this food tastes awful*). Ask students to work on **1–5** and then **6–10** individually, and then compare their answers with a partner. Here are some additional questions you can ask:
In what kind of jobs do you have to start work at six/work long hours/wear a uniform etc.?
Why might someone have to do a lot of travelling?
What's good about not having to take work home with you?

Answers

1. start 2. work 3. wear 4. do 5. make
6. start 7. wear 8. go 9. work 10. take

Ask students to work with a partner, talking about which sentences are true for them or someone they know. You can also ask them to change any sentences so they are true for them (e.g. *It's great where I work because I don't have to wear a suit and tie in the office).*

Refer students to G17 of the **Grammar commentary** on page 167, which they can read either in class or as homework.

Reading

1 So what do you do for a living?

Point out the title and explain that *So what do you do for a living?* is another way of asking *So what's your job?* Explain to students that in this activity they will learn the names of several different jobs. Encourage them to record any they want to remember – along with a translation – in their notebooks.

Answers

1. driver 2. designer 3. guard 4. clerk 5. agent
6. instructor

After students have done the first task individually, put them in pairs to think of other kinds of *guard, instructor, driver* and *designer*. They can use the pictures if they want to or think of other examples.

Answers

Possible answers:
In the pictures: lifeguard, fashion designer, bus driver, skiing instructor

Other: prison guard, coast guard, shoe designer, interior designer, stage designer, train driver, lorry driver, driving instructor, flying instructor, karate instructor

To revise expressions with *have to/don't have to,* ask students to talk about what some or all of the people mentioned in this activity have to or don't have to do (e.g. *A taxi driver has to work long hours, A web designer usually doesn't have to wear a suit and tie*).

2 Pronunciation: compound nouns

Go through the explanation and model the three examples. Ask students to mark the stress in the compound nouns in **1 So what do you do for a living?** and then practise saying the sentences. Get students to work in pairs. For example:

A: *So what do you do for a living?*

B: *I'm a taxi driver? What about you?*

A: *I'm a web designer.*

3 While you read (Work or life?)

This article includes a lot of useful language connected to work and raises some interesting questions for discussion. Explain that the article is about someone who does *temping*. If students don't know what *temping* is, explain that they will find out from the article. Point out the title *Work or life?* Ask them what they think it means (*What is more important: your work or your life?*).

After students have read the article, check that they know what *temping* is and how they think the author would answer the question in the title. You could also play the recording, using it as a listening task first, and then get students to read the article.

Answers

Possible answers

1. Temping work is temporary work for different companies. You often do different jobs and it can be for a short time (one day) or several months. A temping agency finds the work for you and pays you. You do temping work if a company has extra work, or to cover for someone who is off sick, having a baby or holiday.

2. He does temping work because it's varied – he doesn't have to do the same thing every day and see the same people; it's flexible – he doesn't have to work if he doesn't want to; he can take more holidays; he doesn't want to be like his father and become a workaholic.

4 Word check

The focus here is on several useful expressions from the article. Ask students to complete as many as they can from memory and compare their answers with a partner. They can then re-read the article to check if they were right. Here are some additional questions to ask as you go though the answers:
What often happens when you get promoted? (You get more money, a bigger office etc.)

What would happen to someone who was unreliable at work? (They might get a warning/get the sack.)

Do you usually get paid if you take a day off sick? (If you're doing temp work, you don't, but most other jobs have to pay you.)

What would you do if you were getting a bit fed up with your job? (You might look for another one.)

What are some other jobs that you could describe as 'disgusting'?

Answers

1. hours 2. promoted 3. reliable 4. off 5. over
6. office 7. fed 8. disgusting

Finish up by reading the article aloud as students follow in their Coursebooks. Ask them to underline other expressions they find interesting or would like to ask about. You might want to ask them to find all the expressions in the article that use get (e.g. *get a permanent job, got home after nine o'clock at night*).

5 Using grammar: present perfect simple

This tense has several different uses and is often a difficult tense for students to feel comfortable with. Here the focus is on one common use of the present perfect simple: as a way to talk about experience in the past. Before reading the explanation, ask students if they can remember the different jobs the writer of the article on page 56 mentioned (*security guard, barman, washing cars, working in a hotel, working in an abattoir, working in a chocolate factory*). Get them to find the expressions in the text that mention the jobs. Ask if they notice how the tenses of the verbs are formed. They might not come up with the names of the tenses, but they should at least see that some of them use the auxiliary *have*.

Then read the explanation of the present perfect as a class. Explain that the present perfect is used when we want to talk about our experience in the past. The experience itself is what is important. When we want to give details such as times and places, we usually do so with the past simple. Check that students know how to form the present perfect by asking them to complete the following:

I … done many jobs.

… you done any other jobs?

Where … you worked before?

I … never done web design before, but my brother … .

Next, ask students to find the past participle forms of the verbs in the box. Check that they know that the regular way to form a past participle is by adding *-ed* (or *-ied* if the verb ends in *-y*).

Answers

been done found gone heard played
seen travelled tried visited

Talk about **Real English: I've been (to) and He's gone (to).** Go through the explanation and then write some examples on the board for students to complete with either *gone* or *been*. For example:

I'm afraid she's … home. She feels sick.

Have you … here before?

Where have you … ? I've been waiting for ages.

They've … camping for the weekend. They'll be back on Monday.

After students have completed the conversations and compared their answers with a partner, check the answers as a class. Then ask them to practise reading the conversations in pairs. For extra practice get pairs of students to change some of the questions a bit and ask each other. For example:

We're going to a concert tonight. Would you like to come with us?

Have you travelled round Europe much?

Answers

1. done 2. seen 3. heard, found 4. visited, been
5. tried 6. played, played 7. travelled, been

Refer students to G18 of the **Grammar commentary** on page 167, which they can read either in class or as homework.

6 Practice

One way to do this activity is to ask students to work on the reordering task and then choose individual students to ask you the questions. In your answers you can demonstrate how we switch to the past simple when we want to give details. For example:

S: *Have you travelled much?*

T: *Yes, I have actually. I've been to lots of countries in Asia and Europe and last summer I spent a month travelling around Africa.*

Then students can ask each other the questions.

Answers

1. Have you travelled much?
2. Have you tried much foreign food?
3. Have you seen any good films recently?
4. Have you bought any good CDs recently?
5. Have you had many jobs before?
6. Have you studied this grammar before?

Ask students to write a few more questions using the present perfect. Go round the class and help where necessary. Then students cab either ask each other in pairs or wander around, asking their questions to several of their classmates.

Listening

1 Looking for and getting a job

You could introduce this section by asking students to tell you the different ways people find out about jobs (e.g. from newspaper advertisements, on the internet, by writing directly to a company etc.). You can then work on some basic verb + noun phrases by asking students to tell you the different stages for getting a job. For example:

see an advertisement

call the company

ask for an application form

send in your CV

write a letter

get an interview

get the job

receive a letter

start work etc.

Write the phrases on the board and reformulate if necessary. Then you can tell students they will now see some more expressions on the topic of getting a job in conversations **1–8**.

Answers

1. looking for 2. interested in 3. advertised 4. fill in 5. applied for 6. Good luck 7. offer 8. go

After students have completed the conversations, go through the answers explaining any difficult vocabulary and asking follow-up questions. For example:
What would you give someone if they asked for your details? (your name, address, telephone number)

What do you usually do when you send off a form? (You take it to the post office and put it in the post box.)

What kind of clothes do you wear to an interview? (a suit and tie, smart clothes)

What would you do in **7** *if you weren't interested? (turn the job down)*
How would you celebrate if you were offered a great job?

Model the example conversation first before students practise in pairs. Then ask a few pairs to read one or two of the conversations for the whole class.

For the last task, you could get students to close their Coursebooks and listen to you say each of the gapped sentences. With a partner they can discuss what word is missing before opening their Coursebooks to check their answers in the conversations **1–8**.

Answers

a. give b. send off c. got d. start e. got

2 Before you listen

Read the situation of the conversation. Explain *disaster* if necessary. Ask students to tell you other things about which someone might say *It was a disaster* (e.g. *a date, a presentation*). Check that students know about *accountancy* by asking a few questions. For example:
What do we call a person who works in an accountancy company? (an accountant)
To become an accountant, what kind of subjects do you study? (maths, economics, business, law)

Would you like to become an accountant? Why/why not?

3 Listening

Ask students to think about what went wrong on their own before comparing their ideas with a partner. Then invite them to share their suggestions. This gives you a chance to work on some vocabulary. For example:
She turned up late.

She insulted the boss.

Her mobile phone went off.

Ask students to listen for what went wrong in Sue's interview and play the recording. Get them to share what they heard with a partner.

Answers

Sue said she had experience working in an accountancy company when she hadn't really. They asked her lots of difficult questions that she couldn't answer.

4 Comprehension check

Read the statements aloud for students. Then play the recording. Ask them to compare their answers with a partner and form correct statements. Play the recording again and then invite students to tell you their answers. For example:
Sue missed class yesterday because she had to fill in an application form before the deadline.

Answers

1. False (She had to fill in an application form before the deadline.)
2. True
3. False (She's studying biology.)
4. True
5. True
6. False (She made the tea and posted letters.)

You can play the recording again while students follow the tapescript on page 153. Ask them to underline any expressions they find interesting or want to ask about. You might need to explain that *you live and learn* means *we learn by experience and we shouldn't repeat the mistakes we have made.*

5 Speaking

Introduce this activity by giving your own answer to question 1. Teach the phrase *When I was a kid, I always wanted to be a …/work in …* . Explain *qualifications* if necessary. Ask follow-up questions. For example:
What qualifications do you need to be an accountant/a police officer/a teacher?

Finish up by asking a few students to tell you what they talked about.

6 Using vocabulary: *good at … / good with …*

Ask students if they remember why Sue applied to be an accountant even though she is studying biology (*She was quite good at maths*). Write the pattern *I'm quite good/not very good/terrible at …* on the board. Explain that we can follow this type of phrase with a noun (e.g. *maths*) or with a *-ing* form (e.g. *drawing*). Ask students to complete the sentences **1–10** and then compare their answers with a partner.

Answers

1. maths 2. languages 3. English 4. cooking
5. sports 6. fixing 7. listening 8. computers
9. people 10. my hands

Ask students if they noticed **9** and **10** used *good with* + noun. We use *good with* when we refer to the things or people we work with. Give students some more examples:
I'm good with children.
I'm good with a pen, but terrible with a brush.

Demonstrate the final task by giving a couple of examples yourself. You could also get students to talk about any other things that they are *good at* or *terrible at*.

7 Career or job?

Read the explanation of the difference between these two words and then maybe ask students to think of a career that would suit Sue (*She's studying biology, so maybe a career working in a zoo would be good*). Explain the task and ask students to work individually or in pairs sorting the words. As you go through the answers, check students' understanding by asking questions. For example:
What does a (vet) have to do?
What do you have to be good at to be a (lawyer)?
What kind of jobs are there in (the media)?
Are there many well-paid jobs in (IT)?

Answers

Careers: marketing, business, IT, the media, tourism

Jobs: teacher, doctor, accountant, vet, civil servant, fitness instructor, lawyer

Point out a couple of useful expressions in the example before asking students to discuss what they would be good at:
I'd quite like to be a … because I …
I'd quite like to work in … because I …

You could also include a couple of variations. For example:
I could never be a …/work in … because I …
I don't think I'd like to be a …/work in … because I …

8 Using grammar: *they want me to*

An alternative way of introducing this expression is to write *He/She wants us to …* on the board and then ask students to complete the phrase with something they know you want them to do. Write their suggestion on the board. For example:
She wants us to write down complete expressions in our notebooks.

Get students to work in pairs to think of more examples. Then go through the explanation in the Coursebook and get them to complete the sentences. Check their answers by asking them to say the complete sentence.

Answers

1. wants us to get married
2. want me to get a job
3. wants me to finish
4. wants my dad to retire
5. want me to have a party
6. want my boyfriend to take me out
7. wants people to spend

Here are some extra questions to ask as you go through the answers:
What age do people usually leave school?
When do people usually retire?
Why do you think some parents want their children to get a job after leaving school instead of going to university?
Why don't some parents let their children have parties?
What kind of place would you take a girlfriend/boyfriend out to?
Why do you think the government wants people to spend more money? What is the opposite of this? (The government wants people to spend less money.)

Point out some useful phrases. For example:
I can't do it by then.
(I) can/can't afford it.
(I) can/can't afford to.
(I'm) not ready yet.

Follow-up

Get students to role-play an interview. Put them in pairs and ask them to agree on a particular job. You could ask them to choose one that was mentioned in this unit. Explain that one person should be the person applying for the job and the other the interviewer. Give them a few minutes to think of questions to ask each other. For example:
Have you done this kind of work before?
Do I have to wear a uniform?

Encourage them to look back through the unit for useful language to use. They can either write the conversation and then act it out, or just use notes to act it out.

Review: Units 5-8

Most of these exercises should be done in pairs or small groups.

1 Act or draw

Get students to read through the list individually first. Then ask them in turns to draw or act out the five words or expressions they have chosen. Next, they should ask their partner about any of the words or expressions they are not sure of.

2 Tenses

Answers

1. I've had it 2. I can't 3. I couldn't 4. I might do 5. I'm going to 6. been 7. I had, I didn't really like it 8. I've never been here before, we only arrived here

3 Grammar

Answers

1. Could you 2. Is it OK 3. Do you mind 4. Do you want 5. enough 6. I don't have to 7. too 8. I have to

4 Questions and answers

Answers

1. e. 2. d. 3. c. 4. b. 5. a. 6. h. 7. j. 8. i. 9. f. 10. g.

5 What can you remember?

When students have finished working in groups of four, invite a few students to tell you what they remember.

6 Verb collocations

Answers

1. arrange 2. enquire 3. look after 4. keep 5. suffer from 6. drop out of 7. go on 8. apply 9. do 10. find out

Examples of other collocations:

1. (arrange) the chairs in a room
2. (enquire) about a job
3. (look after) my bag for me
4. (keep) going straight
5. (suffer from) migraines
6. (drop out of) school
7. (go on) a tour
8. (apply) for a visa
9. (do) a computer course
10. (find out) where it is

7 Look back and check

Ask students to choose one of the activities. You could then get them to do the other one on another day.

8 Expressions

Answers

1. kind 2. telling 3. resist 4. sorry 5. imagine 6. see 7. suits 8. better 9. help 10. interesting

9 Vocabulary quiz

Answers

1. Possible answers: A doctor, a hairdresser.
2. Around your wrist.
3. You shouldn't buy or eat it.
4. Trainers.
5. Before dinner.
6. The wrong colour.
7. You have to go to the toilet a lot.
8. Yes.
9. Possible answers: Forgetting someone's birthday, being late.
10. If you have a cold or have been speaking too much.
11. From university (but from both in the US).
12. You are late handing it in. The teacher might not accept or mark it.
13. You failed the first time you took it.
14. Possible answers: Always coming in late for work, stealing money from work.
15. After university.
    Possible answers: In journalism, education, marketing.
16. Making things.

Pronunciation

1 Word stress

Go through the explanation with the class and perhaps ask them to find the stress pattern in the dictionary of one or two words you write up on the board.

Answers

Pattern 1: upset, career, enquire, arrange
Pattern 2: bracelet, lecture, details, necklace
Pattern 3: library, opposite, sensible, restaurant
Pattern 4: directly, revision, imagine, appointment

Answers

Unstressed sounds

/ə/: **ca**reer, **a**rrange, res**tau**rant, op**pos**ite, appoint**ment**, sen**si**ble **re**vision

/ɪ/: **en**quire, brace**let**, neck**lace**, oppo**site**, ima**gine**

Ask students to check their answers against the recording.

2 Words with two stresses

Answers

1, 2 pattern: graduate, apologise, deadline, lifeguard, uniform, bus stop,

2, 1 pattern: reputation, drop out, go away, demonstration, sort out

3 Consonant sounds: /b/, /d/, /dʒ/ and /g/

Model and practise the sounds. Ask students if they can hear the difference. Then model the expressions. Ask students to work in pairs saying the expressions to each other.

Answers

Britney, Brian, Debbie, Dan, Jane, Jack, Gail, Graham

4 Difficult sounds: consonant clusters

If students have difficulty with any of these, get them to lengthen the sound of the first consonant.

9 Eating out

Unit overview

General topic
Eating in restaurants.

Conversation
Mel and Kenny discuss where to eat.

Reading
Enrico tells a friend about how a meal at a restaurant turned into a disaster.

Listening
Kenny and Mel order a meal in a restaurant.

Language input

- Expressions for describing restaurants: *The portions were really big, The service was really slow.*
- Expressions for saying no to food and drink: *No thanks. I mustn't. I'm on a diet.*
- Expressions with *some* and *any*: *Have you got anywhere in mind? Does anyone want to go for a coffee after class?*
- Irregular past simple verbs: *I spilled coffee down my shirt, I drank too much.*
- Restaurant vocabulary: *Could we see the menu please? Let's leave them a big tip.*
- Stress in comparisons: *Sorry, but I ordered RED wine, not ROSË.*

Language strip

You can use the language strip as a way to lead in to the unit. Ask students to quickly look through the strip and find any expressions they have actually heard or seen before, any that they think they could use in the future and any that look unusual. Explain that in this unit they will learn expressions for talking about going out to eat. Encourage students to choose a couple of expressions in the strip that look interesting and to find out more about them.

You might need to explain some of the following expressions:

- If you *mix something up*, you make a mistake because you have confused two or more things. For example: *Bill and Ben look so much alike. I'm always mixing them up.*
- We often refer to a dish on a menu by using *the*. If there is only one lamb, pork, fish etc. dish on the menu, we can say *I'll have the lamb/pork/fish* etc.
- If you say someone *eats like a pig*, you think that they eat a lot and eat in a very messy and unpleasant way. We can also say *I made a pig of myself* to mean that you think you ate too much. For example: *They've got great desserts, so I always make a pig of myself.*
- If someone *overcharges* you, they ask you to pay more than you should. The opposite is *undercharge*. For example: *Look, they've undercharged us. Should we tell them?*
- If you ask someone if they *have anything* or *anywhere in mind*, you are inviting them to tell you what they want to do or where they want to go. For example:
  A: Let's do something this weekend.
  B: OK. What do you have in mind?
  A: How about trying that new German restaurant?
- We can refer to a particular French, Thai, Greek etc. restaurant as *that French/Thai/Greek* etc. *place*.
- If you say *the portions are huge*, you think the amount of food served is very big. For example: *I spent a week in New York last month. The food was great, and they always give you huge portions.*
- If someone offers you an alcoholic drink, you can say *No, thanks. I'm driving* to explain why you don't want one.

Remind students to record any of the expressions they like in their notebooks and to take note when they see similar expressions throughout the unit.

Use the language strip later on in this unit for a small group task. Here are some possibilities:

- Students find those expressions that may be said by a customer to a waiter (e.g. *A table for three, please*) and those said by one customer to another (e.g. *Should we leave a tip?*).
- Students find those expressions that are about something negative (e.g. *I spilled wine all over her dress).*
- Students find an example of the present perfect (e.g. *He's mixed up our order),* the present simple (e.g. *I'm afraid we don't have any left),* the past simple (*Sorry, but I ordered baked potatoes, not fried*) and the present continuous (*No, thanks. I'm driving*).

Lead in

Point out the title of the unit: *Eating out*. Ask students what they think it means (*having a meal in a restaurant, café etc.*). Ask what the opposite is (*eating in*). Then follow up with some questions on this topic: For example:
Do you like eating out?
How often do you go out for a meal?
How often do have lunch out?

Do you ever go out for breakfast? Where do you go? What do you eat?
What are some positive things about eating out? What are some negative things?

Conversation

1 Using vocabulary: eating out

Introduce this activity by asking students to suggest what makes a restaurant good or not good. You may elicit things like *the price, the atmosphere, the taste of the food* etc. Reformulate any suggestions if necessary and then explain to students that in this activity they will see some examples of how to describe what a restaurant was like. Students can work individually on the matching task and then check their answers with a partner. Here are some questions you can ask about the language as you go through the answers:
What are some foods that are spicy? How about too spicy?
What are some foods that are delicious?
What could be wrong with food you describe as horrible? (e.g. no taste, burnt, too greasy)
Why might a restaurant be really empty? (e.g. because of the time of day, because it's not popular)
How long do you think you would need to wait before you could say 'the service was slow'?

Answers
1. c. 2. e. 3. a. 4. h. 5. b. 6. d. 7. f. 8. g.

2 Practice

Go through the list of restaurants, explaining what they are if necessary. Ask students to tell you what kind of food you would find in each place. For example:
You can get chicken tikka in an Indian restaurant.

You may need to explain that a *tapas bar* is a Spanish-style restaurant that serves snacks to accompany drinks.

Before students talk to their partner, model an example by telling them about one or two of the places that you have been to. You might want to finish up by asking students if they know any good examples of these restaurants in the place where they are studying.

3 Restaurants

Explain the situation and ask students to look at the conversation by themselves before discussing with a partner. They should be able to guess the topic fairly easily. You could also ask if anyone wants to guess what some of the complete expressions are (e.g. *Are you hungry?*). Play the recording once all the way through while students listen. Ask a few comprehension questions. For example:
Is Kenny very hungry? (Just a little.)
Do you think he's tried Thai food before? (No. 'I'll try anything once.')
Does he like spicy food? (No.)

Play the recording again and get students to follow the tapescript on page 154. Point out and explain some of the useful expressions in the conversation if necessary:
Have you got anywhere in mind?
just round the corner
There's a really nice (Thai) place
I'm sure you'll like it
I'll try anything once.

Explain that we say *I don't mind. It's up to you* when we want the other person to decide.

Put students in pairs and ask them to practise reading both roles using the tapescript on page 154, focusing on the stress and phrasing. Then explain the next task and allow them enough time to memorise the conversation. Point out that this exercise will help their fluency. Remind them to use the notes on page 64 to help them remember. You might want to get them to practise the conversation a second time with a different partner.

4 Speaking

Go through the three different kinds of place, explaining that *a top-class restaurant* is somewhere with really good food, great chefs, a great atmosphere, but probably very expensive; and that *somewhere really different* might be a place that is unusual, unique or not well-known. If possible, give examples that you know from your home town or from some other place that you have visited or know well. Point out that for restaurants we often use *do* to mean *cook and serve (food)*. We sometimes use it about people too. For example:
My mum does a great Sunday dinner. I'll invite you over one weekend.

5 Saying no to food and drink

Introduce this activity by eliciting some reasons why a person might say no to some food or drink. For example:
I've had enough.
I don't like it.
I don't/can't eat that kind of food.

Then explain that when we refuse food or drink, we usually give a reason. (However, if we don't like something but we want to be polite, we usually pretend there is another reason.) Ask students to complete the conversations and then compare their answers with a partner.

Answers

1. I'm driving
2. I don't drink
3. I'm on a diet
4. I won't be able to sleep
5. I don't really like anything spicy
6. I'm full, I couldn't eat
7. I don't really like anything sweet
8. I've actually just had one

As you go through the answers ask questions to focus on some of the language. For example:
What does 'I don't drink' mean? (It means the person doesn't drink alcohol.)

What similar expressions do we use to refuse a cigarette? (No thanks, I don't smoke.)

What kinds of food should you avoid if you're on a diet?

What kind of coffee could you have if you're worried about being able to sleep? (decaffeinated)

How many cups of tea do you drink a day? How about cups of coffee?

Ask students to go back and underline the complete expressions for saying no (e.g. *No thanks. I've had enough. I'm full*). Encourage them to record any they want to remember – along with a translation – in their notebooks. Finish up by getting pairs of students to practise reading the conversations. Then ask one person to read the question while their partner, with their Coursebook closed, tries to remember the answer.

You could also teach some expressions giving other reasons for refusing food. For example:
Actually, I can't eat nuts. I'm allergic to them.

Actually, I don't eat meat. I'm a vegetarian.

Actually, I don't usually drink coffee in the evening. It keeps me awake.

6 Practice

Make sure students know what the food and drink in the pictures is (*ice cream, beer, chocolate cake, coffee, cheese and crackers, chillies*). Model an example with a student first before students work in pairs. As a follow-up, ask them to do the task again, but this time they should accept the food/drink. Teach some appropriate expressions. For example:
Thanks, I'd love some/one/a piece.

OK. Just one more.

7 Using grammar: *some / any*

In this activity, students practise using expressions with *some* and *any*. You could lead in by asking them to find all the examples of *any/anything* and *some/something* in **5 Saying no to food and drink**. Then elicit other words or expressions that start with *any* or *some* (*some/anywhere, some/anyone, some/anybody*). Explain to students that in this task they will see several common expressions using *any* and *some*.

Get students to work individually on the completion task and compare their answers with a partner. Then play the recording so they can check their answers.

Answers

1. something to eat, anywhere in mind
2. do something, anything in mind
3. sometime next week
4. any time after five
5. anyone want
6. Someone has taken
7. any more, have some more
8. not any more

Model the first conversation with a student as an example before asking students to practise the conversations in pairs. For example:

T: *Do you want to go and get something to eat?*

S: *Yes, great. Have you got anywhere in mind?*

T: *Well, there's a great sandwich place just over the road.*

S: *I don't know. I always have sandwiches for lunch. I'm a bit fed up with them.*

T: *OK, then. How about that new Mexican place in the High Street? It's cheap but really good.*

S: *That sounds good. I'll meet you downstairs in a minute. I just need to finish writing this letter.*

Refer students to G19 of the **Grammar commentary** on page 167, which they can read either in class or as homework.

Reading

1 Deciding where to eat

Here is one way to make sure students understand the vocabulary in the box. Ask a student to remember one of the restaurants they talked about in **2 Practice** on page 64, and that they really liked. Ask why they liked it. You might get reasons like *the food was really fresh, it was quite cheap, the people were very friendly* etc. Then focus students' attention on the words and expressions in the box. Use the reasons the student gave you to help explain the vocabulary by asking:
If Maria said the food was really fresh, she was talking about the … ? (quality of the food)

She said the people were very friendly, so she was talking about the … ? (service)

Ask students to rank the five criteria and then compare their suggestions with a partner. If you want to extend the practice, you could put students in groups of four or five to discuss further.

Get pairs of students to make a list of problems you could have when you go to a restaurant. Then ask them to tell you what they came up with. Write the problems on the board, reformulating them into appropriate expressions. You might want to start off with what's shown in the picture (e.g. *I spilt my wine, we waited for a long time to get in, there wasn't much room to sit, the food was disgusting*).

2 While you read (I wouldn't recommend it!)

Explain the situation and ask students read the e-mail to find out which of the problems listed on the board from **1 Deciding where to eat** actually happened. Get students to compare their answers in pairs.

Answers

There was a huge queue. They had to wait for ages to get a table. The service was slow. The waiter mixed up their order. The food was terrible. They overcharged them on the bill. It was quite expensive. The writer spilt coke all over Martina's dress.

3 Comprehension check

Students can work on this individually before checking their answers with a partner. Remind them to see how much they can remember without looking back at the e-mail. They should try to correct the false statements. They can then re-read the e-mail.

Answers

1. True
2. True
3. False (The waiter mixed up the order and then overcharged them.)
4. False (The fish was cold and the pizza didn't taste of anything.)
5. True
6. True

Finish up by reading the e-mail aloud or playing the recording while students follow along in the Coursebooks. You may want to take this opportunity to point out some typical e-mail styles, for exmple, using a noun or noun phrase for the subject (*Disaster!*), and common correspondence expressions, for exmple, *I just thought I'd send you a quick e-mail, Anyway, I hope you're well, See you soon, All the best.*

Talk about **Real English: spilt or spilled.** Tell students about a personal experience before inviting them to tell the class or a partner about their own experience. For example:
I used to wear beige trousers all the time, but I don't any more. I always spilt coffee on them.

4 Speaking

Read the three statements aloud, explaining any vocabulary if necessary. You may want to write a few expressions on the board to help students with the discussion. For example:
It's my money!
I don't like to cause trouble/make a fuss.

Note that in this activity students are seeing some examples of *would* to talk about hypothetical situations. However, you probably don't want to go into a full explanation at this stage.

Ask students to tell each other about their worst restaurant experience in pairs or small groups. You could then invite a couple of students to retell their story to the whole class. You might want to teach some expressions for sending something back. For example:
Excuse me, but I ordered the chicken.
I'm sorry, but this fish is cold.

5 Word check

This activity focuses on several useful expressions from the e-mail. As an alternative, tell students to close their Coursebooks. Read each gapped sentence aloud while students discuss what word is missing with a partner. They can then open their Coursebooks and check the e-mail to see if they were right. Here are some questions to ask as you go through the answers:
Where else is it common to see queues? (at a bus stop, outside a cinema, at ticket counters, in post offices)
Apart from 'orders', what else can we 'mix up'? (names, faces, words)
What do they charge for a cup coffee in … ?
What do you usually order with your meal?
Why else might you 'get something on the house'? (you're a regular customer, you're a friend of the waiter/manager)
What would we say in ***7*** *if we included the wine in the total? ('… and that was with the wine' or '… and that included the wine')*
What would you expect the waiter to say if they split wine all over you? (I'm terribly sorry. Let me get a cloth.)

Answers

1. disaster 2. queue 3. mixed 4. charge
5. order 6. apologised 7. cost 8. spilt/spilled

6 Using grammar: irregular past simple verbs

Students worked on one set of irregular past forms in **Unit 1**. This activity focuses on several more. Encourage students to record examples of the collocations from **1–8** for those forms they want to try to remember.

Answers

broke drank ate fell felt sent spilt/spilled tore

As you go through the collocations, ask further questions whenever appropriate. For example:
Why might you say 'I drank too much'?
What did the person do after they spilt water on the floor? (They mopped it up.)
What made the person feel dizzy? (They stood up too quickly. They were on a roundabout.)
What could the person be talking about if they said 'I tore it into little pieces'? (a letter, a receipt)
If you ate something that was off, what might happen? (You might get an upset stomach.)
Who do people usually break up with? (their boyfriend/girlfriend)
*Why do you think the person in **8** broke up with her? (They had an argument. She found someone else.)*

Answers

1. drank 2. spilt 3. felt 4. tore 5. sent 6. ate 7. fell 8. broke

7 Practice

Give students a model by telling them first about one of the occasions when you did something in **1–5**. Encourage them to ask you follow-up questions. Then ask them if they can remember any good expressions you used to tell the story. For example:
One time a few years ago …
I felt really full/embarrassed/bad.
I'll never forget it.

Write these on the board to help students when they tell their own story. When they have prepared their story, ask them to tell it to their partner. Then ask them to tell the same story to a different person. Explain that this will help them improve their telling of the story. You can finish up by choosing a couple of students to tell their story to the whole class.

Listening

1 Restaurant vocabulary

Ask students to look at the photos and compare their answers in pairs. Encourage them to share any other restaurant words they came up with. Talk about the difference between a *chef* and a *cook*. A *chef* works in a restaurant and is usually more respected than a *cook*. They usually have more training than a *cook*. A *cook* usually prepares food in places like a school or hospital.

Answers

First photo: a bill and a tip
Second photo: a chef
Third photo: a customer holding a menu/wine list, ordering a meal/wine; a waiter pouring a glass of water

Explain to students that they will see examples of how some of these words and others are used in conversations **1–6**. Ask them to complete the conversations and then compare their answers with a partner. Explain that if you *try to catch someone's eye*, you try to get their attention, for example by looking at them.

Answers

1. book 2. wine list 3. menu 4. order 5. bill, waiter 6. tip, service

You may want to teach some other related collocations and expressions. For example:
book a room for the night
book a flight
order a bottle of champagne
pay the bill
pick up the bill
the service was terrible
leave a generous tip

Finish up by asking students to read the conversations in pairs.

2 Speaking

Read through the questions with the class and then have them discuss in pairs or small groups. You could then turn this into a class discussion on the question of tips, especially if students are studying overseas and are unsure of the correct etiquette. Ask them if they have been to places where they tip all the time, or never tip; how they feel about tipping; if they have ever worked somewhere where they got big tips all the time.

3 Before you listen

Explain the first task and then get students to say the questions so you can work on pronunciation. Explain that *lychees* are fruit. Ask students to work in pairs on the ordering task.

Answers

Possible answers:
Waiter to customer: b., d.
Customer to waiter: e., f.
Customer to customer: a., c.

Order: d., a., c., b., f., e.

4 While you listen

Explain the situation of the conversation and ask students to listen if their answers in **3 Before you listen** were correct. Play the recording and get them to discuss their answers in pairs. Play the recording again so they can check. You can also play it one more time while students follow the tapescript on page 154. Make sure they understand *still* and *sparkling water*.

Answers

1. Have you booked? (No, I'm afraid we haven't.) Waiter to customer.
2. Can you recommend anything? (It's all nice really, but when I've been before we've usually just ordered one of the set menus here.) Customer to customer.
3. Do you know what lychees are? (Oh, they're a kind of fruit. They're really nice and sweet.) Customer to customer.
4. Are you happy having wine? (Yes. Red or white?) Customer to customer.
5. Are you ready to order? (Yes, we'd like the set menu D, please) Waiter to customer.
6. Could we have some water as well, please? (Still or sparkling?) Customer to waiter.

5 Speaking

Explain that a *set menu* usually has the choices already made for you, although sometimes you can choose between one or two options. Write some expressions on the board to help with question **5**. For example:
I can't eat … because I'm allergic to it/them.
I can't eat … because it isn't kosher/halal.
I can't eat … because it gives me an upset stomach.

6 I'm afraid that's off

Point out the title. Explain that if a dish *is off* in a restaurant, it means that it is no longer available because they have run out. We also say food *has gone off* or *is off* when it is old and can't be eaten. For example:
Smell this meat. I think it's gone off.

Ask students to put the conversations in the right order an then go through the answers. Then get students to practise reading the conversations in pairs. You may need to explain the following:

- *Paella* is a Spanish rice dish made with seafood.
- A *tart* is a dessert made of pastry, like a pie, but without a top.

Answers

Conversation 1: c., b., d., a.
Conversation 2: b., a., d., c.
Conversation 3: a., d., c., b.

Go through the menu, explaining any items if necessary. For example:

- *Dumplings* are made from flour and water and then boiled or fried.
- *Mussels* are small shellfish.
- *Sorbet* is like ice cream, but it is made from fruit juice.

7 Sorry, but I didn't order this

You may want to write the basic pattern on the board to help students with their conversation:
A: Could I/we have the … ?
B: I'm afraid …
A: Oh, right. In that case I'll …

This activity focuses on a common function of stress or emphasis: comparison. It also introduces some more common collocations for food. Ask students to record those they want to remember in their notebooks. Explain the first task and get students to complete the sentences, explaining any vocabulary first.

Answers

1. not rosé 2. not well done 3. not still
4. not boiled 5. not brown 6. not tomato salad
7. not scrambled 8. not carrots 9. not ice cream

Now go over the explanation of the stress pattern. Demonstrate the example a couple of times. Ask pairs of students to mark the stress in sentences **1–8** and then play the recording so students can check which words are stressed. Play the recording one more time, pausing after each sentence so students can repeat, following the same stress pattern.

Answers

1. Sorry, but I ordered RED wine, not ROSÉ.
2. Sorry, but I wanted my steak RARE, not WELL DONE.
3. Sorry, but I ordered SPARKling water, not STILL.
4. Sorry, but I ordered MASHED potatoes, not BOILED.
5. Sorry, but I ordered WHITE bread, not BROWN.
6. Sorry, but I ordered GREEN salad, not toMAto salad.
7. Sorry, but I ordered FRIED eggs, not SCRAMbled.
8. Sorry, but I ordered GREEN BEANS, not CArrots.
9. Sorry, but I ordered the apple pie with CREAM, not ICE cream.

Finish up by asking students to complete the collocation task. You may need to explain the following:

- *Stale bread* is bread that is too old.
- A *side salad* is a salad that accompanies your main meal.
- *The house wine* is usually the cheapest wine a restaurant serves.

8 Speaking

Use these questions to practise some of the collocations from **7 Sorry, but I didn't order this**. Teach some expressions to help students in the discussion. For example:
I like my eggs scrambled/my steak well-done etc.
I like red wine with … and white wine with …

Finish up by getting students to ask you the questions.

Follow-up

Ask students in threes to write their own conversation like the one between Kenny and Mel. Get them to look back through the unit and find language they would like to use. They can then act the conversation out for the class.

If you would like your students to do a writing task, ask them to write an e-mail to a friend describing a great restaurant they went to. They can describe one they have actually been to or make one up.

10 Family

Unit overview

General topic
Talking about your family.

Conversation
Stella tells Mary about her much older sister.

Reading
Jerry talks about getting married eight times.

Listening
Beth and Salma talk about how they both know Mark.

Language input
- Questions about families: *Have you got any brothers or sisters? Are you married?*
- Comparatives: *Mary's a bit taller than me, I'm more relaxed.*
- Expressions with *we both* and *we all: We both love swimming, We're all from the same town.*
- Expressions explaining how we know someone: *She's a friend from university.*
- Expressions with *die: She died in her sleep, She died of a heart attack.*
- Internet vocabulary: *use the internet, download music.*

Language strip

You can use the language strip as a way to lead in to the unit. Ask students to quickly look through the strip and find any expressions they could use about someone they know. Explain that in this unit they will learn ways of talking about families. Encourage students to choose a couple of expressions in the strip that look interesting and to find out more about them. You might need to explain some of the following expressions:

- *Identical twins* are twins that look exactly the same. They are always the same sex.
- If someone is *open*, they tell you how they feel, what they want etc. They don't try to hide their emotions. For example: *My parents are both very open with me. They're always telling me their problems.*
- If you *have a lot in common with someone*, you have similar personalities and share the same interests as them. For example: *I don't know why she married him. They've got nothing in common.*
- If you *get engaged to someone*, you have promised that you will marry them. If you decide later not to get married, you *break off the engagement*. For example: *He's really upset. She broke off the engagement last week.*
- An *old people's home* is a residence where old people can go and live and where there is staff to look after them.
- If you say someone *passed away*, you are saying they died. However, you are using this expression to avoid using the word *die*, which might be too direct. For example: *I'm afraid I've got some sad news. Jill's dad passed away last night, so she won't be here for the rest of the week.*
- We say *I'm sorry to hear that* when someone has told us some sad news. For example:
  A: We've decided to get divorced.
  B: Oh no. I'm really sorry to hear that.

Remind students to record any of the expressions they like in their notebooks and to take note when they see similar expressions throughout the unit.

Use the language strip later on in this unit for a small group task. Here are some possibilities:

- Students discuss who *she, he, her* and *they* probably refer to in several of the expressions. For example, *They* in *They got divorced when I was a kid* probably refers to the person's parents.
- Students choose expressions that are questions (e.g. *How do you get on with her?*) and come up with a possible response (e.g. *Quite well, actually*). Then they choose expressions that are responses (e.g. *He's much fitter than I am*) and come up with possible prompts (e.g. *What's your brother like?*).
- Students find expressions in the language strip that use *get* (e.g. *My sister has just got engaged)*. Then later on, you can write all the *get* expressions on the board but with *get* gapped out. Ask students which word is missing from all the expressions.

Lead in

One way to lead in is to ask students what kinds of things we often want to know about each other's families. Write down their ideas on the board. List the things we want to know rather than the actual questions. For example: the size of the family, who is in the family, who is still alive, if they like each other, what the members of the family do etc. Then explain to students that they are going to see typical ways of asking someone about these topics, and do **1 Questions we ask about families**.

Conversation

1 Questions we ask about families

In this activity students practise the fairly fixed expressions we use when asking about someone's family. Ask them to do the first task individually and then check their answers with a partner. If they are having trouble, remind them that the first word in the question has a capital letter. Play the recording so they can check their answers. Then play the recording again, pausing after each question so that they can say it, following the same pronunciation.

Answers

1. Have you got any brothers or sisters?
2. How old are they?
3. What do your parents do?
4. Are you married?
5. Have you got any kids?
6. What are they like?
7. Do you get on with them?
8. Are your grandparents still alive?
9. Have you got a girlfriend/boyfriend?

Get students to ask you these questions so you can provide them with an example of how to answer. You will need to explain that often questions can be grouped together. For example:
Have you got any brothers or sisters? How old are they? What are they like? Do you get on with them?

You should also explain which follow-up questions aren't really appropriate. For example, you wouldn't ask a person with young children:
Have you got any kids? Do you get on with them?

When students have asked each other the questions, ask them to record those they want to remember, along with a translation. You might want to take this opportunity to discuss if any of these questions are inappropriate – or in what situations they could be inappropriate – in the students' own countries.

2 Talking about your family

Read the instructions for the task and then play the recording. You may want students just to listen for which questions from **1 Questions we ask about families** were used first, and then play it again so they can listen for the information about Stella's sister. Get students to compare what they heard with a partner. Then play the recording again, if necessary, so they can check they got everything. You may need to explain that if we are talking about brothers or sisters, or couples, where there is a big difference in age, we often use the expression *a big age gap*. Also, if someone *treats you like a baby*, they don't behave towards you as an equal. They act as if you were a child.

Answers

Stella's sister lives in Pinedo. She works in Central Hospital. She is 35 years old (15 years older than Stella). They get on well. She's quite similar to Stella, but a bit more organised. She is funny, easy to talk to and doesn't treat Stella like a baby. She has been married for 12 years. She's expecting her first baby in November.

Explain the second task. To make the task easier for students, remind them which questions in **1 Questions we ask about families** were used. Make sure they understand they should continue the conversation about their own family. Then get them to swap roles and repeat the role play.

For the listening task, play the recording and ask students to try to fill in each of the gaps as they listen. They should then compare their answers with a partner. Play the recording again, but this time pause after each gap. Elicit the missing words and maybe write the complete expression on the board. Model the pronunciation and get students to practise saying it. Play the recording through one more time with students following the completed script.

Answers

1. twin sister 2. taller than 3. what's she like
4. quieter than 5. more relaxed 6. quite close

Play the whole conversation one more time while students follow the tapescript on page 154. Ask them to underline any expressions they find interesting or want to ask about. You may need to explain the following:

- If you *are used to something*, it happens often, so you don't feel uncomfortable. For example:
  A: *Doesn't his snoring annoy you?*
  B: *Not really. I'm used to it.*
- If you say *we're close*, it means you get on really well and like each other very much. For example: *I haven't spoken to my brother for ages. We're not that close really.*

You could also teach the expressions *a close friend*. Ask students to tell you who they are close to in their family or about a close friend.

3 Speaking

Go through the questions, making sure students know what *identical twins* are. Write some expressions on the board to help with the discussion. For example:
They don't look alike at all.
I'm always mixing them up.
A good/bad thing about being a twin is that …

You may need to explain that in English you can be an uncle by marriage too. For example, if Stella had a baby,

Stella's sister would be its aunt and her sister's husband would be its uncle. Ask students if this is similar in their language, or if there are different terms.

For extra practice ask students to describe the twins in the photograph on page 70. Teach some appropriate vocabulary. For example:
How do you know who the older twin is?
Do you think that each twin knows how the other is feeling?

4 Using grammar: comparatives

Ask students if they can remember the differences between Mary and Alison. Tell them to find the expressions in the conversation that give us the information. (*Alison's a bit taller than me, her hair is darker, she's a lot quieter than me, she's a more serious person than I am, I'm more relaxed*). Then write the following on the board:
Stella is a lot … than her sister. (young)
Her sister is a bit … than she is. (organised)

Ask students to complete the sentences using the adjectives in brackets. Then ask if they can explain why *young* becomes *younger* and *organised* becomes *more organised*. Listen to their suggestions and then ask them to read the explanation in the box. Answer any questions they may have and then get them to work individually on the completion task and apply the 'rule'. Make sure they get the spelling right in **6, 7** and **8**. You may want to remind them about the spelling rule of doubling a single final consonant of a word when the last syllable contains a single vowel and is stressed: (*fit–fitter, big–bigger*; but *cool–cooler, rough–rougher*).

Answers

1. more relaxed 2. easier, more open
3. older, more serious 4. younger, older
5. quieter / more quiet 6. fitter 7. nicer 8. lazier

Focus attention on some of the expressions in this activity by asking questions as you go through the answers. For example:
*In **1**, what do you think the mum doesn't let the person do? (go out at night, stay the night at a friend's house)*
*Who would the person in **2** talk to if they had problems? (their mum)*
What else can you do to be fit? (work out in a gym, swim)
Why would you describe someone as horrible? (they're rude, they're not friendly, they make fun of people)

Talk about **Real English: a bit / a lot / much older.** Ask students to tell you one or two personalised sentences using these modifiers. For example:
I'm a lot quieter than Georgi in class but I'm much more hard-working.

Encourage students to use modifiers when appropriate as they talk to their partners about which of the sentences **1–8** are true for them.

5 Using grammar: *better / worse*

Explain that just as some common verbs have irregular forms, so a few common adjectives have irregular comparative forms. Here students focus on the two most important: *good* and *bad*. Ask students to complete the sentences with either *better* or *worse* and then discuss their answers with a partner.

To extend the discussion get them to write two or more extra sentences of their own. Point out that it is much more common to say *more good-looking* than *better-looking*. We can sometimes say *not bad-looking*, though. Refer students to G20 of the **Grammar commentary** on page 168, which they can read either in class or as homework.

Reading

1 Using vocabulary: *a lot in common*

Before reading the explanation in the Coursebook, tell students about a person you have a lot in common with. Try to use expressions with *we both* … . Then read the explanation with the class. Ask students to tell you any details they remember from what you told them about your friend. This can give them ideas for the sentence completion task. As they work on this, go around and help with vocabulary if necessary. You may want to get students to talk to more than one person or work in small groups.

2 Further practice

There are lots of questions students could ask in this activity. However, you might want to elicit a few model questions and write them on the board. For example:
What kind of music do you like?
Do you like sports? What kind?
What were you good at in school?

Also, teach some expressions students can use when they find they have something in common. For example:
Me too.
So do I.

Give students a set time to talk with their partner before getting them to change and talk with another person. Finish up by inviting students to report back, using expressions with *all*. For example:
José, Martin and I all like (football).
All five of us (were born in 1989).

3 Before you read

Ask students if they have heard of Elizabeth Taylor, what she does, where she is from, why she is famous. Ask if they have ever seen any of her films, or seen her on television. If students don't know much about her, you can tell them a little more after they have read the introduction. Elizabeth Taylor starred in the film *National Velvet* when she was still a child. She married the Welsh actor Richard Burton twice. Her other famous films include *Cleopatra* and *Who's afraid of Virginia Woolf?*

Ask students to read the short text and to tell you what Jerry and Elizabeth have in common. You may need to explain the following expressions:

- If something is an *extreme example*, it is an unusual one.
- If something is *a growing trend*, it is something that is becoming more common.

Answers

Both Jerry and Elizabeth have the same surname (Taylor). They are both in their seventies. They were both born in England. They both moved to America. They have both been married eight times.

4 Speaking

Be sensitive to the fact that the topic of divorce might make some students uncomfortable. Read the questions aloud to the class and write some sentence starters on the board to help. For example:

My … 's been married (three) times.

Unfortunately, her first husband/his first wife …

I think it's better to get divorced because …

I think it's better to stay married because …

5 Reading (Eighth time lucky!)

Point out the title *Eighth time lucky!* and ask what it refers to (*Jerry has got married for the eighth time*). Then focus students' attention on the photograph. Ask students if they can guess what Jerry's main interest is (*Elvis Presley*). Then ask them to tell you what they know about Elvis: have they ever heard his music before; do they like it; can they name any of his hits etc.

Now ask students to read the article and find out why Jerry's seven previous marriages failed.

6 After you read

You could get students to complete sentences **1–7** in pairs. Remind them not to look back at the article. They can check their answers by re-reading. Here are some questions to ask as you go through the answers:

What would you do if someone didn't want you around the house? (find a job, go for long walks)

How might you find out if someone is having an affair? (a friend might tell you, you might find a love letter)

What are some other ways to complete the phrase 'died of … '? (cancer, a drug overdose, natural causes)

If you're a tidy person, what do you do? (put things away, clean things up, pick things up off the floor)

Alternatively, you could do this as a listening task first. Play the recording while students listen with the text covered, and then get them to read the article.

Answers

1. around, born 2. found, affair 3. a heart attack
4. left, for 5. disappeared 6. crazy 7. crazy

Finish up by reading the article aloud or playing the recording while students follow along. As they do so, ask them to underline any expressions they find interesting or want to ask about. You may want to point out the following expressions:

bad habits

she joined me at my table

we fell in love

in those days

I'm a big fan

You may need to explain some of these expressions if students ask:

- You say someone is *the love of your life* when you are really in love with them and think you have found the person you want to live the rest of your life with.
- If you are a *difficult person to live with*, people don't find it easy to live in the same house as you because you have annoying habits or have an unpleasant personality.
- If you have *high standards*, you like the quality of things to be very good.

7 Speaking

Explain the expression *Whose fault was it?* and teach a couple of related responses:

It was his/her fault.

He/She was to blame.

Read through the statements, explaining any vocabulary if necessary. Explain that if you *feel sorry for someone*, you feel sympathy for them, but that if you think someone is *a bit sad*, you think what they do or think is a bit silly. After students choose their answers, ask them to share their ideas in pairs or small groups.

8 Using vocabulary: collocations

In this activity, students see several typical collocations and one that doesn't work. Remind students that knowing when something doesn't collocate is also important. When they have finished, ask them to work in pairs and think of an appropriate verb for each of the expressions they crossed out.

Answers

1. (I had) a baby this year.
2. (I was brought up) by my grandparents.
3. (I left my) country.
4. (She had) a baby.
5. (I stayed) in a hotel for the weekend.
6. (I was) crazy.

Demonstrate the personalisation task by telling students about yourself. For example:
I was born in … but I grew up in … . I went to university in … . When I graduated, I moved to … . In … I got married and moved back to … . etc.

Encourage students to ask you questions. Then get them to talk about themselves in pairs. Then ask students to do the second completion task and revise any vocabulary if necessary.

Answers

a. move b. change c. buy d. leave e. get

Before students talk in pairs about what they have done and what they plan to do, make sure they remember the irregular forms of *buy*, *leave* and *get* *(bought, left, got)*. Then write up some example patterns on the board:
I … last year/in 1997/a few months ago.
I'm going to … this year/next week.
I want to … in a few years time/when I'm 30.

Listening

1 Using vocabulary: *How do you know her?*

In this section, students practise ways of talking about where they met their friends and asking other people about the same thing. You can introduce the first activity by briefly telling students about one of your friends. Tell them all sorts of things, making sure you include information about where you first got to know them. When you have finished, ask if anyone can remember how you met your friend. Point out the question *How do you know her?* and explain to students that in this activity they will learn different ways of explaining how they met their friends. You may need to explain that if you *used to do something*, you don't do it any more.

Answers

1. university 2. the tennis club 3. work 4. school 5. my old job 6. Germany 7. church

Get pairs of students to ask each other about five of their friends. Encourage them to ask follow-up questions. For example:
What's she like?
Is she older than you?
Do you have much in common?

As an alternative, ask students to choose five people from anywhere in the Coursebook and make up a story about how they know each of them.

2 While you listen

Explain the situation and ask students to listen for the answers to the question. Get them to compare their answers and then play the recording again.

Answers

Salma knows Mark from the old school she went to.
Beth met Mark in an internet chat room.

3 Comprehension check

Read the questions to the class. Explain that if you are *going out with someone*, they are your boyfriend/girlfriend. Make sure students remember the expressions *What do you do for a living?* and *get on well with*. After they have discussed their answers, play the recording again.

Answers

1. Beth and Mark haven't been going out very long. They have only been out three or four times.
2. Mark is a policeman.
3. Beth's parents haven't met Mark yet.
4. She died in her sleep, probably of a heart attack
5. Beth got on really well with her. They were really close.

Follow up by playing the recording a final time while students read the tapescript on page 155. Ask them to underline any expressions they think are interesting or that they want to ask about. You may need to explain the following:

- If you *lose touch with someone*, you no longer see them or write to them.
- We say *You're joking* when someone says something that's surprising to us.
- If you're *anti* something, you don't like it or are opposed to it. For example: *I'm anti death penalty.*

4 Speaking

These questions let students talk about some of the things mentioned in the conversation. Teach a few useful expressions for the last part of the task. For example:

They're a bit prejudiced/old-fashioned.

They're not very open-minded.

Actually, they wouldn't care.

5 Keyword: *die*

Ask students if they remember how Beth's grandmother died and what she was doing at the time (*she probably died of a heart attack while she was sleeping*). Explain that we say *die of* with the cause of death, for example, a disease, and *die in* with the circumstances, for example, what was happening at the time. Then get students to complete the expressions.

Answers

1: c., e., f., h., i.
2: a., b., d., g., j.

Finish up by asking students about some famous people who are dead. Here are a few examples if you need them:

The singer Sonny Bono died in a skiing accident.

The singer Buddy Holly died in a plane crash.

Princess Diana died in a car crash.

Freddie Mercury of the rock group Queen died of AIDS.

Talk about **Real English: He passed away last year.** Ask students if they have different or 'nicer' expressions to say someone has died in their own language.

6 Using vocabulary: the internet

Lead in to this activity by brainstorming a list of things connected with the internet. For example: *e-mail, websites, instant messaging, chat rooms, news groups, free software, e-commerce, e-learning.* You can explain any vocabulary if necessary. Then explain to students that they are going to see some of these words used in context. Ask them to read questions **1–10** and ask you about anything they don't understand. Then get pairs of students to ask each other. Finish up by asking them to memorise as many questions as they can, close their Coursebooks and ask you some of the questions they have learnt.

Follow-up

You could develop this into a class discussion by asking further questions. For example:

Are there any bad things about the internet?

Do you think governments should control what people look at on the internet?

How about schools? Would you ever study English over the internet?

To work on comparisons, ask students to think of five things comparing life before the internet with now. Ask them if life is better now or worse, or if things are easier or harder.

11 Getting around

Unit overview

General topic
Asking for and giving directions, talking about transportation.

Conversation
A tourist asks how to get to The Gagosian art gallery.

Reading
A writer explains why she prefers cycling and taking public transport to driving.

Listening
Four conversations involving tourists.

Language input

- Expressions for asking for and giving directions: *I'm looking for a gallery called The Gagosian, It's down there somewhere.*
- Indirect questions: *Do you know if there's a post office near here? Do you know how old he is?*
- Expressions explaining how long it takes to get to work: *It takes me about forty minutes, I have to change trains twice.*
- Comparatives to explain decisions: *No, I'll just phone him. It'll be quicker.*
- Expressions with *right* and *wrong: Is this the right platform for Opera? I got off at the wrong stop.*

Language strip

You can use the language strip as a way to lead in to the unit. Ask students to quickly look through the strip and find any expressions they have actually heard or seen before. Explain that in this unit they will practise ways of talking about places and transport. Encourage students to choose a couple of expressions in the strip that look interesting and to find out more about them.

You might need to explain some of the following expressions:

- A *crossroads* is where two streets cross.
- A *roundabout* is a central space at a road crossing which cars must go round in a circle.
- If something is *miles away*, it is far away. For example: *I don't want to walk there. It's miles away.*
- If you say *It'll be quicker by train*, you mean that the fastest way to get somewhere is by train. We can also say *It'll be quicker by bus/car* or *It'll be quicker walking.*
- If you have got *no sense of direction*, you are not good at finding your way around. For example: *I'm always getting lost. I've got no sense of direction.*
- If you say *They've introduced a charge*, you usually mean that some authority, like the government, has decided to make people pay for a service. For example: *They've introduced a £5 charge for crossing the bridge.*
- If the government *privatises* something, they sell off a state-owned industry or company to private buyers. For example: *They privatised a lot of industries in the eighties.*
- If something is *state-run*, the government manages it. For example: *All public transport is state-run here.*
- *Peak hours* are the times when most people are travelling to work in the morning and from work in the evening, so train and bus fares are usually higher. For example: *It's £10 during peak hours, but only £6 off-peak.*
- If you *book* something *in advance*, you make a reservation for it before you need it. For example: *You have to book the ferry at least six days in advance.*
- If you *get off at the wrong stop*, you get off a bus at a stop where you didn't mean to get off. For example: *Sorry I'm late. I got off at the wrong stop and had to walk over a mile here.*
- You might say *Excuse me!* when you accidentally bump into someone, or want them to move out of your way. For example: *Excuse me. I'm getting off here.*

Remind students to record any of the expressions they like in their notebooks and to take note when they see similar expressions throughout the unit.

Use the language strip later on in this unit for a small group task. Here are some possibilities:

- Students choose expressions that are questions (e.g. *Do you know where she lives?*) and come up with a possible response (e.g. *I think she lives in Oak Road*). Then they can choose expressions that are responses (e.g. *I got off at the wrong stop*) and come up with possible prompts (e.g. *Why are you so late?*).
- Students find those expressions that are probably to do with cars (e.g. *I couldn't find a parking space*) and those that are probably about public transport (e.g. *We'd better get the bus*).
- Students find all the expressions that contain a comparative (e.g. *It'll be cheaper if you book in advance).*

Lead in

One way to lead in is to point out the title of the unit, *Getting around*, and brainstorm a list of different ways people use to get around. For example: *by bus, by train, by bike, on the underground, on foot, on the monorail* etc. You can then ask students to talk about different cities or towns using the following pattern:
The best way to get around (St Petersburg) is (by underground).

Conversation

1 Using vocabulary: around town

The focus of this activity is to work on some vocabulary that can be useful when giving directions. You can ask students to work on the matching task in pairs, and then go through the answers. As you do so, you could also write up one or two collocations for some of the places. For example:
stop at the traffic lights
go round the roundabout
look out for a sign
cross the bridge
walk through the subway

You may need to explain the following:

- A *monument* is structure that commemorates a person or event.
- A *mosque* is a place of worship for Muslims.
- In Britain a *subway* is a tunnel under a road for pedestrians, whereas in the US it is an underground train system.

Answers

A a subway B a roundabout C a monument
D a crossing E a mosque

Explain the second task, making sure students understand *landmark*. Then ask them to discuss in pairs, or do the task as a class. You could write the following sentence starters on the board to help:
There are a few/several/a lot of … in my town.
There aren't any/many …
There's a famous (bridge) called (the Bridge of Sighs).
There's the (Royal Palace).

2 Asking for directions (1)

You could introduce this activity by asking students the following questions:
Have you ever asked for directions in English?
Have you ever given directions in English?
Have you ever had any difficulties understanding or being understood? What did you do?

Explain to students that they are going to hear a tourist asking several people for directions to a place called The Gagosian. Read the two questions and then play the recording. Get students to compare their answers in pairs.

Answers

The Gagosian is an art gallery. The people aren't exactly sure, but it's down past the park somewhere.

Next, read the 12 expressions aloud and play the recording again while students tick the ones they hear. Play the recording one more time or ask students to read the tapescript on page 155. You may need to explain the following expressions in the conversation:

- *What's that?* is an informal way of asking someone to repeat what they have just said.
- *I'm not from round here myself* implies you don't know the area very well because you don't live there.

In the list of expressions, point out that we can say *down the road, along the road* or sometimes *up the road*, especially if the road is rising from where the speaker is. Also point out that if you say *You can't miss it* about a place, you mean it is very easy to see when you get to the general area.

Answers

Excuse me, could you help me?
Do you know if this is the way to The Gagosian?
I'm sorry. I'm not from round here myself.
I don't really know the area.
It's down there somewhere.
Ask someone else when you get there.

Explain the translation task and, if possible, get students who share the same language to compare their translations.

3 Pronunciation: sentence stress

Explain that in English the important content words in a sentence are usually stressed. If a word is made up of more than one syllable, then usually one syllable in the word is stressed. Point out the two examples in the Coursebook and read them aloud a couple of times so students can hear which parts are stressed. You could also write the two examples on the board and draw a wavy line above each of them to show how the voice rises on the stressed syllables.

Ask students to work on marking the stress in the remaining questions individually or in pairs. It might be a good idea to ask them to use pencil so they can make any changes if necessary. Remind them that they can use their dictionaries to help find the stress of individual words. Play the recording or read out the tapescript on page 155. Pause after each one and maybe rewind a little to let students hear it again. Ask them to tell you which sounds are stressed and then get them to practise saying the complete expression. Finish up by asking them to read the conversation in groups of two or three.

Answers

1. Excuse me, could you help me?
2. I'm looking for a gallery called The Gagosian.
3. Do you know if this is the way to The Gagosian?
4. I'm sorry. I'm not from round here myself.
5. I don't really know the area.
6. Ask this lady here.
7. It's down there somewhere.
8. It's just past the bridge on the right.
9. Follow the signs to the city centre.
10. Just keep going straight on down this road until you get to some traffic lights. Then turn right.
11. It's along that road on your left. You can't miss it.
12. Ask someone else when you get there.

4 Practice

This activity gives students the opportunity to practise some of the language from the conversation. Draw their attention to the map and check that they know what is being shown by asking questions like:
Where are the traffic lights?
Can you find the bridge? Which road does it go over?

You may want to model an example with a student first before pairs of students ask each other. To extend this activity, get pairs of students to ask each other about places near where they are studying. For example:
Could you help me? I'm looking for The University Bookshop.

5 Asking for directions (2)

Before playing the second part of the conversation, ask students to think of two possible problems the tourist might have. Ask them to tell you their suggestions and reformulate any if necessary. Tell them to listen to see if any of their suggestions were right and play the recording before asking them to compare their answers in pairs.

Answers

The Gagosian is actually miles away, near Oxford Circus. The tourist has to get the 214 bus to get there.

Play the recording again while students follow the tapescript on page 155. Ask them to underline any expressions they want to remember or ask about. You may want to point out the following:

You're best taking a bus.
cross over to the other side of the main road
ask the driver to let you off at …

Talk about **Real English: miles.** Ask students to translate some of the *miles* expressions into their own language and record them in their notebooks. You may then want to get them to practise reading the conversation in pairs using the tapescript.

For further practice, you could write just the key words of the conversation on the board, like the conversation in **Unit 4**, and ask students to try to remember as much of the conversation as possible.

6 Speaking

Make sure students understand the expression a *good/bad sense of direction.* Ask them to use it about any of the people in the conversations they just heard. For example:
The person in the second conversation probably had a good sense of direction.

Give students a model for answering the second question by talking about a time you got lost. Encourage them to ask you further questions as well. Ask them to remember any expressions you used to help tell the story. Write the expressions on the board so students can use some in their own stories if they want to.

7 Using grammar: indirect questions

Ask students if they remember how the tourist first asked for directions to The Gagosian (*Do you know if this is the way to The Gagosian?*). Then go through the explanation and the examples in the Coursebook. Make sure students notice that yes/no questions use *if* in the indirect form. Some students may want to use question form word order in the indirect questions, so make sure they notice that there is no inversion of the subject.

Ask students to write the eight questions individually. Monitor and check they are getting the word order right as well as any -s endings.

Answers

1. if there is a post office near here?
2. if he has got any brothers or sisters?
3. if she is coming tonight?
4. if she lives near here?
5. how old he is?
6. where he is from?
7. what she does for a living?
8. where the toilets are?

Model the pronunciation of these questions and then ask students to practise asking each other. They can reply appropriately. For example:

A: Do you know if there's a post office near here?
B: Yes. It's just down this road, on the right. You can't miss it.

8 Practice

Before students ask each other, you may want to elicit different kinds of things they could ask about and write them on the board. For example: how old they are, where they live, how long they have been studying English etc. Write up some other expressions they can use when they don't know the answer. For example:
I've no idea.
I'm not sure.

Encourage students to add a follow-up comment, as in the examples.

As an extension get pairs of students to write five indirect questions about you. They can then ask another group. For example:
A: Do you know what her favourite colour is?
B: I think it's blue.

Finish up by letting students ask you the questions to see who got the most answers right. Refer students to G21 of the **Grammar commentary** on page 168, which they can read either in class or as homework.

Reading

1 Using vocabulary: *How long does it take you to get to work?*

This activity helps students talk about travelling to work (or school). Point out the question *How long does it take you to get to work?* Explain that we often use *it* and *take* when we want to know how long someone spends doing something. Then ask students to complete the sentences **1–6** individually before comparing their answers with a partner. Make sure they notice the pattern in the answer:
it (usually/only) takes (me) ...

Here are some follow-up questions to ask as you go through the answers:
What's the opposite of 'on a good day'? (on a bad day)
What do you think happens on a 'bad day'? (there's a lot of traffic, there's an accident)
How many trains does the person in **2** *take to work? (three)*
Apart from trains, what other forms of transport can we change? (buses, planes)
What is the opposite of 'it comes late'? (it comes on time)
Are the buses/trains reliable in your town?
What kind of problems happen on the underground (a breakdown, a bomb threat, a strike)

Answers

1. traffic 2. trains 3. cycle 4. close 5. late
6. underground

For the second task, you could get students to ask about school instead of work. Ask them to wander around asking several people. Then finish up by asking who has the longest journey to get to work/school.

If you want more practice with this pattern, elicit some alternative questions starting *How long does it take you to (get ready in the morning/eat breakfast/do the homework)?* Students then ask each other.

2 Before you read

To help students with ideas for this task, ask them to look at the pictures on page 79. Elicit what the pictures show (*a congestion charge, a traffic jam, road works*). Then ask them to work in pairs on their lists. Go around and help with vocabulary if necessary. After students have compared their lists with another pair, ask them to tell you their suggestions and write the three lists on the board, reformulating any expressions if necessary. Students can then discuss which form of transport is best. Write some sentence starters on the board to help. For example:
I think (driving) is the best way because ...
It's better to (drive) because ...

3 While you read (It drives me mad!)

Point out the title *It drives me mad!* Explain that if something drives you mad, it annoys you very much. Ask students to tell you what drives them mad (e.g. buses arriving late, the way people drive). Then get them to read the article to see which things from their lists in **2 Before you read** the writer mentions. Ask students to compare their answers with a partner.

Alternatively, use this as a listening task first. Play the recording while students listen with the text covered. Then ask pairs of students to compare their answers before they read the article.

Answers

Cycling to work
Good things: you can cycle past traffic jams; it keeps you fit.
Bad things (according to Kate): it's dangerous; you get hot and sweaty; it's hard and boring.

Driving
Bad things: sometimes it's slower because there are traffic jams, road works or accidents; sometimes it's hard to find a parking space; some places charge for driving into the centre of town.

Public Transport
Good things: it's relaxing because you can read, listen to your Walkman, write letters, watch people, make friends or sleep.

Finish up by reading the article aloud or playing the recording while students follow along. As they do so, ask them to underline any expressions they want to remember or ask about. You may need to explain some of the following expressions:

- We use *more or less* to mean *approximately* or *nearly.* For example: *I live more or less a mile from here, I'm more or less finished.*
- If you say *all you can do is* something, you mean that it is the only thing you can do. For example: *There's an accident blocking the bridge. All we can do is wait until they clear it.*
- We sometimes use *(daylight) robbery* when we think we are being charged too much for something. For example: *£5 for a cup of coffee? That's daylight robbery!*

4 Vocabulary focus

This activity focuses on some useful collocations from the article. Ask students to work on the matching task individually before comparing their answers with a partner and trying to remember what was said in the article. Ask them to reread the article to check if they were right.

Answers

1. b. 2. c. 3. d. 4. a. 5. f. 6. g. 7. h. 8. e.

On public transport, you can listen to your Walkman.
Kate sometimes arrives at work later because she can't find a parking space.
She has never actually had an accident or fallen off her bike.
The council have promised to spend the money they make on improving public transport.
She prefers to go on the bus.
She shares a flat with Kate, a friend from work.
The council say the £5 congestion charge will cut pollution.
They often arrive at work around the same time.

For further practice you could also ask students to think of one or two alternative collocations for each of the verbs. For example:
listen to the radio
fall off your chair
find work
improve your fitness
go on a trip
share the cost
cut taxes
arrive home

5 Speaking

Before students discuss these questions in small groups, write some collocations and expressions on the board. For example:
The traffic is usually terrible/awful/really heavy/very light.
The pollution is really bad.
I (don't) think it's a good idea because …
I don't think it'll help. They should … instead.
I think they should also …

6 Using grammar: comparatives

Before doing this activity, revise the formation of comparatives. For example, ask students to make statements comparing cycling, driving or public transport based on information from the article. For example:
Public transport is more relaxing than going in the car.
Driving to work is sometimes slower than cycling.

Go through the two examples as a class. Let students hear how the two conversations are said, especially how *it'll* is pronounced. Then ask them to complete **1–3** individually before comparing their answers with a partner. You could then get them to practise asking and answering these questions in pairs.

Answers

1. a. It'll be cheaper
1. b. It'll be quicker
1. c. It'll be nicer
2. a. It'll be more relaxing
2. b. It'll be more exciting
2. c. It'll be better
3. a. It'll be easier
3. b. It'll be cooler
3. c. It'll be cheaper

For the second task, revise the use of *or shall we* to offer an alternative. Then ask students to complete the three responses. They can compare their answers by asking each other the questions. Finish up by inviting a few students to share their responses with the rest of the class. As an extension, get students to write three more choice questions using the pattern *Do you want to … or shall we … ?* They can then go around asking other students, who can respond with *Let's* and a comparative structure.

Listening

1 Trains!

Use the questions in the Coursebook to introduce the topic of trains. You can provide students with a model answer for the second question by talking about a personal experience. For example:
About 20 years ago I went by train from Ostende in Belgium to Moscow. It took about three days, so we had sleepers. We didn't get much sleep because the beds were hard and we kept getting woken up by the police whenever we crossed the border, but it was really exciting travelling through all those countries. The conductors were really friendly and they kept bringing us tea.

Before students read the text, ask them what they know about travelling by train in Britain. Then ask them to read the text, or read it aloud as they follow along. You could also ask a few follow-up questions to test their comprehension. For example:
Has privatisation made it easier to travel by train?
When are fares more expensive?
What do you have to do to get the cheapest ticket?

Point out and explain the following expressions in the text:
buy a ticket on-line
travel on peak days/at peak hours
get a day return/single
book in advance
buy your ticket on the day

Then ask students to discuss the three questions in pairs or small groups.

2 Before you listen

Elicit from students what each of the photos shows and use this as a way to teach some vocabulary like *a car rental, rent a car, on a platform, bus driver, ticket counter.* Then read the sentences **1–6** aloud while students match them to the corresponding photo.

Answers

1. A 2. D 3. B 4. C 5. B 6. D

As you go through the answers, elicit possible responses. For example:

1. Get off at Oxford Circus.
2. One hundred and seventy pounds? That's ridiculous!
3. I'd like a medium sized one.
4. Yes. The train will be here any minute.
5. Yes, but you have to pay extra for personal property insurance.
6. Tomorrow.

3 Role play

By role-playing the situations before they listen to the conversations, students become aware of the kind of language they need. This gives them a purpose for listening in the next activity. Give them time to prepare and go around helping with vocabulary if necessary. Ask them to role-play the two conversations in pairs. Then explain that they will now hear four conversations based on similar situations.

4 While you listen

Explain the matching task and play the recording. Ask students to compare their answers with a partner. Then play the recording again as students listen for what the problems are.

Answers

1. C 2. D 3. B 4. A

Answers

1. The person is on the wrong platform.
2. The price of the ticket is expensive.
3. The cheapest class of car is not available.

Ask students to read the tapescript on page 156. You could also play the recording again as they follow along. Before students tell their partner about the expressions they underlined, you may need to explain the following:

- If a ticket is *not valid before* a certain time, you can only use it after that time.
- If something is *the next cheapest*, it is not the cheapest but the second cheapest.
- You say *I'll take it* to mean that you will buy or accept something. For example: *Fifty pounds return? OK. I'll take it, I suppose.*

Finish up by asking the same pairs of students from **3 Role play** to role-play their conversations again. This time you can ask the pairs to perform for another group.

Point out the **Real English note: sir / madam / mate / love**. You may want to explain that there are actually a lot of informal regional variations in Britain. For example, some alternatives to *love* include *pet* and *dear.* Also, a female assistant can call a man *love* and in some areas even a male assistant will sometimes call a man *dear* or *love*.

5 Key words: *right* and *wrong*

This activity focuses on several common expressions with the words *right* and *wrong*. Ask students to complete the conversations individually before comparing their answers with a partner. Here are some extra questions to ask as you go through the answers:

In what other situations can you be on the wrong side? (driving on the wrong side of the road, fighting on the wrong side)

What would you say in **2** *if you were travelling by train? (I got off at the wrong station.)*

What do you say or do if you ring the wrong number? (You can say, 'I'm sorry. I've got the wrong number,' and then hang up.)

What should the person in **6** *do? (Put the batteries the right way around.)*

In what situations could you say 'I was in the wrong place at the wrong time'? (a traffic accident)

Answers

1. right, wrong 2. wrong 3. wrong 4. right
5. right, wrong 6. wrong, wrong 7. right, right
8. wrong

For the next task make sure students underline the complete expressions and then transfer those they want to remember – along with an equivalent translation – to their notebooks.

Answers

1. Is this the right platform for …
2. I got off at the wrong stop
3. I have the wrong number
4. We're going in the wrong direction
5. is this the right answer
6. use the wrong form
7. there's something wrong with …
8. I put the batteries in the wrong way round
9. I was in the right place at the right time
10. it's the wrong size

6 Speaking

This activity lets students use some of the expressions from **5 Key words: *right* and *wrong***. Talk about some personal experiences first to provide students with a model.

Follow-up

Write up a list of about ten different forms of transport including some not so obvious ones. For example: *bus, horse, monorail, underground, water taxi, ferry, taxi, jeepney, tuk-tuk, rickshaw, tram, minibus*. Then students should individually select four forms of transport according to certain criteria. For example: the ones they would like to travel to work on, the ones that cause the most/least pollution, the ones that would be the most relaxing etc. They can then compare their choices with a partner or a small group.

12 Free time

Unit overview

General topic
Free time activities, football, taking classes, making enquiries.

Conversation
Ed and Frances talk about their interests.

Reading
A football fan explains why she supports Manchester City.

Listening
Mark helps Liugi find out about a photography course.

Language input

- Free time activity vocabulary: *go to see a movie, go to a concert.*
- Adding information: *I went to see this exhibition, Art in Time, at the National Gallery.*
- Adverbs of frequency: *Yes, all the time – I usually go at least three times a week.*
- Expressions for talking about team sports: *Do you support anyone? I can't stand baseball. It's so boring!*
- Superlatives: *She's one of the best players I've ever seen.*
- Verbs with *how to: No-one knew how to do it, I learnt how to surf while I was on holiday.*
- Present simple for timetabled events: *The course lasts for ten weeks, What time does the next coach leave?*

Language strip

You can use the language strip as a way to lead in to the unit. Ask students to quickly look through the strip and find four expressions they can change slightly so that they are true for them (e.g. *I can't stand golf, I learned how to drive last year).* Then ask them to share their ideas with a partner. Explain that in this unit they will practise ways of talking about free time activities. Encourage them to choose a couple of expressions in the strip that look interesting and to find out more about them.

You might need to explain some of the following expressions:

- If you ask *Was it any good?* about something, you want to know what the person thought of it. For example:
  A: I saw the new Jackie Chan movie last night.
  B: Oh yes. Was it any good?
  A: It was OK, I suppose.
- If you *hardly ever* do something, you don't do it very often. For example: *I hardly ever drive any more. It's just too expensive.*
- If you *can't stand* something, you don't like it at all. For example: *I can't stand all this rain. When's it going to stop?*
- If you ask someone *Who do you support?* you want to know which sports team they like. For example:
  A: Who do you support?
  B: Celtic. Why?
- *Photoshop* is software for editing images.
- If someone is a *bad loser,* they get upset if they lose something like a game. For example: *I don't want to play with him. He's a really bad loser.*
- If you are *useless at* something or doing something, you are not good at it. For example: *I'm useless at maths. I hate numbers.*

Remind students to record any of the expressions they like in their notebooks and to take note when they see similar expressions throughout the unit.

Use the language strip later on in this unit for a small group task. Here are some possibilities:

- Students choose expressions that are questions (e.g. *When does that exhibition finish?*) and come up with a possible response (e.g. *At the end of the month*). Then they choose expressions that are responses (e.g. *No, hardly ever*) and come up with possible prompts (e.g. *Do you go skiing often?*).
- Students find those expressions that refer to something in the future (e.g. *I'd like to learn how to use Photoshop*) and those that refer to something in the past (e.g. *It was one of the best films I've ever seen*).

Lead in

Ask students in pairs to think of five examples of free time activities. Then write up their suggestions on the board. Add appropriate collocations and reformulate if necessary. For example:
watch TV
work out in the gym

The list can serve as a resource for when students talk about what they do in their free time in **1 Speaking**.

Conversation

1 Speaking

Use the photo to help students with free time activities vocabulary. Give them appropriate collocations. For example:

see a play

go to a concert

Then read the six questions aloud. You may also want to teach some example responses. For example:

I can't remember exactly. It was ages ago.

Actually, I've never been to one.

Last week, actually.

Five years ago, I think.

Get students to ask each other these questions in pairs. Tell them to continue the conversation by asking each other about other free time activities. For example:

So what do you do in your free time?

Encourage them to keep the conversation going. To finish up, ask students to memorise the six questions and close their Coursebooks. They can then ask you the questions.

2 Talking about your free time

Explain the situation of the conversation and ask students to just listen for what Frances does in her free time. Play the recording, making sure that students cover the text. Get them to discuss their answers in pairs. Remind students to keep the text covered as they do this.

Answers

Frances likes to go to the theatre. She also likes singing and is a member of a drama club.

Play the recording again and ask students to try to fill in each of the gaps as they listen. They should then compare their answers with a partner. Play the recording a third time, but this time pause after each gap. Elicit the missing words and maybe write the complete expression on the board. Model the pronunciation and get students to practise saying it. Play the recording through one more time with students following the completed script.

Answers

1. Was it any good? 2. a lot 3. hardly ever
4. kind of things 5. are you any good
6. that good 7. in your free time

Ask students to read the completed conversation in pairs.

3 Vocabulary focus

Explain the translation task and, if possible, ask students who share the same language to compare their translations. Encourage them to record any expressions they want to remember – along with the translation – in their notebooks. You may need to explain that we often say *I'm not that good* when someone asks if we are good at something and we want to say that we are OK, but not very good. Sometimes we use it when we just want to be modest. Explain that we sometimes use *that* to mean *very*. For example:

A: *Do you want to go by bus or shall we take a taxi?*

B: *Let's take a taxi. It's not that expensive and it'll be quicker.*

4 Role play

Let students read the conversation one more time before they do the role play. Stress that they don't need to remember the exact words. To help, you could write some key words on the board, as in **Unit 4**. When students continue the conversation, encourage them to use some of the expressions from **3 Vocabulary focus**. For example:

What kind of things do you (cook/make/paint)?

When they have finished, get them to do the role play again, but this time they change roles.

5 Pronunciation: adding information

Read through the explanation with the class. Then model the pronunciation of the example a couple of times. Play the recording once all the way through while students listen. Tell them to underline the words that are stressed and to put a slash (/) where there is a pause. Then play the recording again, pausing after each sentence so students can practise repeating. If students ask, *Leeds Castle* is a castle in Kent, not in Leeds Yorkshire.

Answers

1. I WENT to SEE this exhibition, *ART in TIME*, at the NATional GALLery.
2. I STAYed in and WATCHed this PROgramme, *WILD at SEA*, about DOLphins.
3. I STAYed in. I'm READing this BOOK, *The YaKUza*, about the JAPanese MAFia.
4. I WENT to this new REStaurant, TIto's, in MARket STREET.
5. We WENT on a DAY TRIP to this PLACE, LEEDS CAstle, with the SCHOOL.
6. I WENT to my kaRAte CLASS at this SPORTS CENtre, the SoBELL, near my HOUSE.

Then ask students to complete the conversations. You may need to point out the following:

- We sometimes use the expression *I've seen better things/ones* when we explain that something was not that good.
- If something is *impressive*, you are impressed with it. You think it is very good because it is very beautiful, large, artistic etc. For example: *Have you seen the new bridge yet? It's very impressive. It's over a mile long.*

Finish up by asking students to practise reading the conversations in pairs.

Answers

1. I stayed in. I'm reading this book, *The Yakuza*, about the Japanese mafia.
2. I went to this new restaurant, Tito's, in Market Street.
3. I went to my karate class at this sports centre, The Sobell, near my house.
4. I stayed in and watched this programme, *Wild at Sea*, about dolphins.
5. I went to see this exhibition, *Art in Time*, at the National Gallery.
6. We went on a day trip to this place, Leeds Castle, with the school.

6 Practice

Before students complete these sentences, go over some of the different ways they can end the sentence, for example, by saying what it was about, who it was with, where it was, who it was by etc. Model an example with one student before getting pairs of students to ask each other. You may want to ask them to do the task again, but this time with a different partner.

7 Using grammar: expressions of frequency

Introduce this activity by asking students if they remember how often Frances and Ed go to the theatre (*Frances goes quite often, maybe once or twice a month, but Ed hardly ever goes*). Then read the explanation in the Coursebook. Point out that the four examples are in descending order of frequency. Point out and explain the following patterns in the examples:

once/twice/three times a + period of time

once or twice/two or three times a + period of time

once every + period of time

Make sure students notice the expression *at least*. Ask them to make sentences that are true for them using *at least*. They can use the following patterns:

It takes me at least … to …

There were at least … people at the last … I went to.

I want to earn at least … a … by the time I'm …

Ask students to complete the six conversations. Tell them to cover the four examples before they do this. They can then uncover the examples and check their answers.

Answers

1. time, at, a 2. often, every 3. hardly
4. that, maybe 5. all, usually, least, day
6. ever, remember, time

Make sure students notice how all the questions use *a lot*. Model and practise the pronunciation of the questions before students ask each other in pairs. Encourage them to ask follow-up questions too. For example:

What are you reading at the moment?

Where do you usually go?

Where was the last place you went to?

What was the last thing you saw?

Do you have a favourite place?

What kind of programmes do you like watching?

Refer students to G22 of the **Grammar commentary** on page 168, which they can read either in class or as homework.

Reading

1 Using vocabulary: team sports

Use the matching task to make sure students know the names of the team sports. You could also use follow-up questions like the following:

Have you ever played … ?

Have you ever seen a … game?

Do you know how many people are on a … team?

Do you know the name of a famous … competition?

Which countries are good at … ?

Answers

1. E 2. F 3. D 4. B 5. C 6. A

Talk about **Real English: football**. Your students might be interested to know that several different games are called *football,* depending on which country you are in and which game you prefer. For example, all the following are sometimes called *football*: *rugby, American football, Australian Rules football and Gaelic football.*

Explain the second task and ask students to complete the sentences. Tell them that they can include any sport, not just those in the pictures. Go around and help with vocabulary if necessary. You may need to explain that some sports don't collocate with *play*. For example:

do karate

do athletics

However, these are often not team sports. You could also mention that we can use some of the expressions to talk about teams too. For example:
I can't stand Arsenal. They're so boring!

After students have talked about their choices in pairs, find out what the most and least popular sport in the class was.

2 Typical questions

This activity focuses on some useful vocabulary for asking about team sports as well as leading into the reading activity. Go through the explanation, explaining that a *fan* is someone who really likes something, not just a sports team. Teach students the pattern *I'm a really big … fan* and give them some examples:
I'm a really big country music fan.
I'm a really big fan of Michael Caine.

Students can then tell each other who or what they are fans of, using the same pattern.

When students have completed the sentences, go through the answers explaining that a *rival* is a person, team or company who is your main competition because they are as good or as big as you, or, especially in sports, are from the same area. You might also need to give some possible answers to the question *How're your team doing at the moment?* For example:
They're doing really well. They're second from top.
They're rubbish this season. They've only won one game.

Then get students to find a new partner and ask each other these questions. They can start off like this:
A: *Do you follow any kind of team sport?*
B: *Yes. I really like … .*
A: *Really? Do you support anyone?*

Answers

1. support 2. Why 3. favourite 4. team
5. rivals 6. see

3 While you read (The other team in Manchester)

Lead in to the reading task by asking students to tell you what British football teams they have heard of, who their famous players are, how well they are doing etc. Then explain that they are going to read about a fan of a certain British team. They should read to find out the answers to the six questions in **2 Typical questions**.

When students have finished reading, ask them to compare their answers with a partner. Encourage them to use the expressions in the questions to make true sentences about the writer. For example:
She supports Manchester City.

Alternatively, use this as a listening task first. Play the recording, while students listen with the text covered. Then ask them to compare their answers with a partner before they read the article.

Answers

1. She supports Manchester City.
2. She was born in Manchester, and her dad supported Manchester City.
3. Her favourite player ever is Mike 'Buzzer' Summerbee.
4. Manchester City aren't doing as well as Manchester United.
5. Manchester United are their local rivals.
6. She goes and sees Manchester City all the time.

Finish up by reading the article aloud or playing the recording while students follow along. As they do so, ask them to underline any expressions they find interesting or want to ask about. You may need to explain the following expressions:

- If something is *part of who you are*, it is something important that affects your ideas, behaviour or personality (e.g. your religion, where you grew up, your family background).
- In Britain, if a team wins the FA cup and the Premiership, they win the *double*.
- If you are a *good loser*, you don't get upset if you lose something. The opposite is a *bad loser*.
- If something or someone is *perfect for* you, it or they really suit you. For example: *Don't they look great together? They're perfect for each other.*

You may also need to explain about the English Football Association. There are four professional divisions, the top one being the Premiership. If a team ends up at the bottom of a division, they go down – or are relegated – to the division below. If a team ends up at the top of a division, they go up – or are promoted – to the division above. If they end up at the top of the Premiership division, they win the Premiership. The Champions League and the Football Association (FA) Cup are knockout competitions. The team that finished top in each of the European leagues in the previous season compete for the Champions League, while all English and Welsh teams compete for the FA Cup. The finals of each competition are played at the end of the season in May.

4 Speaking

Get students to discuss these questions in small groups. You could also feed in other questions as necessary and develop the activity into a class discussion. For example:
Is there a team that wins everything in your country?
Are there any big rivalries between fans? Are there sometimes problems?

Are you a good loser? Do you ever get upset if you lose or your team loses?

5 Using grammar: superlatives

Introduce this activity by asking students to suggest names of teams that could complete these sentences:
I think … are the best football team in my country.
In my country … fans think they're the best.

Then point out that *best* is the superlative form of *good*. Explain that we use the superlative form when we want to say something is better, bigger etc. than anything else and that the superlative form is usually preceded by *the*. Ask students to tell you the superlative form of *bad* (*the worst*).

Go through the example with students, explaining that this pattern with *ever* and the present perfect is very common in English. When students have completed the sentences, play the recording so they can check their answers. You may need to explain that if you think something or someone is *useless*, you don't think it or they are good. If you think something is *disgusting*, you think it tastes, smells or looks really bad.

Answers

1. best 2. worst 3. worst 4. best 5. worst 6. best

Play the recording again so students can mark the stress. Then play the recording one more time, pausing after each sentence so students can repeat, following the same stress pattern.

Answers

1. She's one of the BEST players I've EVER seen. She's BRILLiant!
2. He's one of the WORST players I've EVER seen. He's USEless!
3. It was one of the WORST places I've EVER been to. It was AWful!
4. It was one of the BEST places I've EVER been to. It was REALLy BEAUtiful.
5. It was one of the WORST things I've EVER eaten. It was disGUSting!
6. It was one of the BEST things I've EVER eaten. It was deLIcious!

Before students do the personalisation task, point out that we can often add *in my life,* as in the example. Finish up by inviting a few students to tell you some of their sentences. You could then get them to ask you questions using a similar structure:
What/Who is/was one of the best/worst … you've ever … ?

One way to introduce the rule about the formation of superlatives is to write up some gapped expressions on the board and ask pairs of students to discuss how they should be completed. For example:
He hates spending money. He always orders the … thing on the menu.
I hate taking my brother out to dinner. I always have to pay and he always orders the … thing on the menu.
My wedding day was the … time of my life.

Students can then read the guidelines in the Coursebook to see if they were right. Ask them to complete sentences **1–7** individually and compare their answers with a partner. As you check students' answers, ask a few follow-up questions, focusing on some of the other expressions. For example:
What are some other ways to stay fit? (swim every day, work out in a gym)
What do you think the person in **3** *does all day? (sits around and watches TV)*
What is the opposite of 'the easiest game we've ever had'? (the hardest game we've ever had)
How can you change **5** *to be the opposite? (She's one of the most uptight/nervous people I've ever met. She worries about everything.)*

You may need to explain that *Wimbledon* is a tennis competition held in England, *Liechtenstein* is a small country in Europe between Austria and Switzerland and *Machu Picchu* is a ruined Inca city high up in the mountains in Peru.

Answers

1. fittest 2. youngest 3. laziest 4. easiest 5. most relaxed 6. most interesting 7. most beautiful

6 Practice

You may want to answer some of these questions yourself first to provide students with a model. Remind students about the meaning of *close* in **5**. As an extension, ask them to write five questions of their own using some of the following patterns:
Who's the … person you know?
Who's one of the … people you've ever met?
What's one of the … things you've ever done?
What's the … place you've ever been to?

Then ask students to wander around asking each other their questions. Finish up by referring them to G23 of the **Grammar commentary** on page 168, which they can read either in class or as homework.

Listening

1 Using vocabulary: *I'm thinking of*

Remind students of this structure from **Unit 3**. Then ask them to do the matching task. You may need to explain that although *course*, *class* and *lesson* are similar, there are some slight differences in meaning:

- A *course* is a series of lessons over a certain period of time in a certain subject.
- A *class* could be one or more lessons. We tend to use *class* when there is a group of students (e.g. *an aerobics class*).
- We tend to use *lesson* when there is only one student (e.g. *a piano lesson*).

An easier difference to see, however, is that these words collocate with different verbs. Encourage students to choose a couple of examples with each of these words and record them in their notebooks. Ask students to describe what they see in the photos. Get them to tell you about the photos by saying *I'm thinking of taking (guitar lessons)*.

Also point out the following collocations in the sentences:
set up (my own) website
have basic conversations
develop (my own) pictures
do (Thai/Chinese) dishes
play (my favourite) songs
get fitter

Answers

1. c. 2. d. 3. b. 4. a. 5. f. 6. e.

Ask students to test each other on the follow-up comments, and then get them to say if they would like to do any of these or any other courses, lessons or classes. Point out the use of *I'd like*. Explain that *'d* is short for *would* and that *'d like* is used to express something that you wish for in the future.

2 While you listen

Explain the situation of the conversation and ask students to just listen for the answers to the two questions. Play the recording and ask them to compare their answers with a partner. Then play the recording again as they follow the tapescript on page 156. Encourage them to underline any expressions they want to remember or ask you about. You may want to point out the following:
It (the magazine) tells you/doesn't say …
It's good for my English
Is it just about … or do they … ?
Would you like me to phone for you?
Pass me (the magazine),

Answers

Luigi is thinking of doing a photography course because his teacher said it will be good for his English and that he will meet other people.

3 Know how to

In this activity students see some common verbs that are often followed by *how to*: *know, show, learn* and *teach*. You could introduce this by asking students which one word completes the following sentences:
Do you know … to drive?
Can you show me … to use your mobile?
My mother taught me … to play the piano.
I learned … to swim when I was three.

Then go over the examples in the Coursebook and ask students to complete the sentences individually before comparing their answers with a partner. As you go through the answers, ask them follow-up questions. For example:
Does anyone know how to surf? Are you any good?
Do you know how to play tennis? How often do you play?

Here are some additional questions to ask:
What else could you learn while you're on holiday? (scuba diving, how to say something in another language)
What else can you boil? (vegetables, water for tea)
What do you have to do when you want to leave a campsite? (take the tent down, pack the tent away)

Answers

1. how to surf
2. how to get
3. how to make, how to do
4. how to serve
5. how to boil
6. how to put up
7. how to fight

Introduce the personalisation task by telling students three things you would like to learn how to do. Then ask them:
Does anyone know how to … ?
Can you show/teach me how to do it?

Ask students to wander around asking each other the same questions.

4 Before you listen

Explain the situation of the second part of the conversation and ask pairs of students to write the four questions. Then invite a few students to share their suggestions. Write them on the board and reformulate them if necessary.

5 While you listen

Explain the task and play the recording. Ask students to compare their answers with a partner. Then play the recording again so they can add anything they missed.

Answers

The course teaches you how to develop photos as well as take them. You don't need any previous experience. The price includes all of the materials. The course starts on Thursday and is from six until eight. The course lasts ten weeks. There are only two or three places left.

6 Vocabulary

Students can work on this activity individually and then compare their answers with a partner. Play the recording so they can check their answers. Then ask them to listen again as they follow the tapescript on page 157. You may need to explain that *enquire about* is often used in formal situations like a telephone conversation when you want to get some information. You could reinforce the language from the activity by getting pairs of students to test each other. One person reads the sentence, saying *blank* for the gap. The other person, with their Coursebook closed, tries to remember the missing word and says the complete expression.

Answers

1. help 2. enquire 3. previous 4. put, through
5. absolute 6. include 7. lasts 8. places

7 Using grammar: present simple for the future

You could introduce this grammar structure by writing the two examples from the Coursebook on the board but with the verbs gapped. Students close their books and try to remember how to complete them. Then you can go through the explanation as a class. Ask students to complete the eight sentences individually. Go around and make sure they are getting the right forms, particularly for the third person singular. Here are some more questions to ask as you go through the answers:

How else can you get to the airport (a friend gives you a lift, by bus)

What kind of thing can you usually see in an exhibition? (paintings, photographs, sculpture)

What's the difference between a coach and a bus? (A coach travels longer distances between cities, while a bus usually travels within a certain area.)

Talk about **Real English: arrive**. Explain that we can also use *get in* without mentioning the place. For extra practice, get students to ask each other some questions. For example:

When does your flight get in?

When does your train get in?

What time do you get in tomorrow?

Answers

1. leaves
2. do you arrive
3. starts
4. does the match start
5. does your train arrive
6. lasts
7. does that exhibition at the Town Hall end
8. does the next coach leave

8 Role play

Explain the task and ask students to work in pairs. Go around and help with any vocabulary problems. For example, explain that if you *pay a deposit*, you pay some money to reserve something until you can pay the full amount. Give students time to prepare and add that they can also look at the tapescript of the conversation on page 157. When they have finished the two conversations, you could ask them to repeat the role play with another partner.

Follow-up

Give students a list of about ten superlative expressions to complete. For example:

... is the best football team in my country.

... is one of the easiest things to learn.

... is the hardest thing I've ever done.

... is one of the best ways to spend your free time.

... is the most famous person I've met.

Students can then tell each other what they wrote in small groups.

Review: Units 9-12

Most of these exercises should be done in pairs or small groups.

1 Act or draw

Get students to read through the list individually first. Then ask them in turns to draw or act out the five words or expressions they have chosen. Next, they should ask their partner about any of the words or expressions they are not sure of.

2 Grammar

Answers

1. the fittest
2. easier
3. where the Grand Hotel is
4. gets into, leaves
5. I'll have
6. tore, fell down
7. any
8. I'd like

3 Opposites

Answers

1. in advance
2. off peak
3. overcharged
4. well done
5. stale
6. hard-working
7. miles away
8. alive
9. tiny

4 Questions and answers

Answers

1. b. 2. c. 3. e. 4. a. 5. d. 6. j. 7. g. 8. i.
9. f. 10. h.

5 What can you remember?

When the class have finished working in groups of four, invite a few students to tell you what they remember.

6 Verb collocations

Answers

1. throw 2. hurt 3. set up 4. follow 5. make
6. cut 7. last 8. cost 9. put 10. introduce

Examples of other collocations

1. (throw) a ball
2. (hurt) your feelings
3. (set up) a meeting
4. (follow) me home
5. (make) the coffee stronger
6. (cut) the grass
7. (last) till the end of the week
8. (cost) too much
9. (put) your books away
10. (introduce) myself

7 Look back and check

Ask students to choose one of the activities. You could then get them to do the other one on another day.

8 Expressions

Answers

1. eye
2. split
3. sweet
4. thing
5. finish
6. mixed
7. common
8. hear
9. round
10. seen

9 Vocabulary quiz

Answers

1. Answers will vary.
2. Lose weight. (although there some other diets).
3. To a waiter, 10–15% (depending on the country).
4. Possible answers: You can fry, boil or scramble them.
5. A play is a story performed by actors in a theatre; a musical is a play or film with many songs; an opera is a story that is sung by opera singers in an opera house.
6. Madam.
7. Die of.
8. Possible answers: Road works, an accident.
9. They come on time.
10. Possible answers: The wrong train, the wrong answer, the wrong time.
11. Got better.
12. *We both like it* means there are two of us, while *we all like it* means there are more than two.
13. Possible answers: Software, music.
14. Beat.
15. No.
16. Possible answers: Delete, send.

Pronunciation

1 Contrastive stress

Answers

1. your 2. yours 3. mine 4. my 5. them
6. He

a. It's not <u>you</u>. It's <u>me</u>.
b. It's not <u>yours</u>. It's <u>mine</u>.
c. It wasn't <u>me</u>. It was <u>him</u>.

You could say *It's not you. It's me* when you are explaining why you want to break up with your boyfriend or girlfriend. You could say *It's not yours. It's mine* when you see someone with one of your things. You could say *It wasn't me. It was him* when someone thinks you have done something wrong but another person really did it.

2 Consonant sounds: /l/ and /r/

Model and practise the sounds. Ask students if they can hear the difference. Then model the examples. Ask students to work in pairs saying them to each other.

3 Difficult sounds: consonant clusters

If students have difficulty with any of these, get them to lengthen the sound of the first consonant. They can also clearly say the second consonant so that someone listening can hear whether it is /r/ or /l/.

13 Places to stay

Unit overview

General topic
Staying at places on holiday, staying with friends.

Conversation
Anton tries to book a room at a hotel.

Reading
Five people talk about the best place where they have ever stayed on holiday.

Listening
Kasia is staying with her friend Jeremy and is getting ready to go out.

Language input

- Vocabulary to describe places where you stay: *We rented a villa up in the mountains, The room looked out over the beach.*
- First conditionals: *If you wait a second, I'll get a pen; I'll go and get some if you want.*
- Expressions with *hardly any: There are hardly any people on the beach, hardly anyone ever goes there.*
- Answering requests with *as long as: Yes, of course, as long as you're quick; I'm expecting a call.*

Language strip

You can use the language strip as a way to lead in to the unit. Explain to students that in this unit they will practise language connected with staying at different places. Ask them to quickly look through the strip and find those expressions that might be said during a conversation at a hotel reception desk (e.g. *I'd like a twin room for two nights*), those that might be said when describing a holiday (e.g. *We rented a villa in the south of Spain*), and those that might be said between two friends staying together (e.g. *I'll give you a spare key*). Encourage students to choose a couple of expressions in the strip that look interesting and to find out more about them.

You might need to explain some of the following expressions:

- If something is *posh*, it is very formal and usually expensive. We often use it to describe places. For example: *a posh house, a posh restaurant, a posh hotel.* If you describe someone as *posh*, you think they are upper-class. For example: *I'm going to stay with my posh friends this weekend.*
- A *villa* is a largish house, especially in southern Europe, that is often rented out to holiday-makers.
- A *twin room* is a bedroom with two beds in a hotel. Other kinds of room in a hotel include a *double room* – with one large double bed – and a *single room* – with a single bed.
- A *hut* is a small house or building made of wood, grass or mud. For example: *Let's stay in one of those huts on the beach. It'll be cheaper.*
- If there is *hardly any* of something, there is only a very small number or amount. For example: *There's hardly any ice cream left. Who ate it?*
- If a room *looks out over* a place, there is a view of that place from the room. For example: *My bedroom looks out over the park.*
- The *expiry date* of something is the date from which it is no longer usable. For example, you have to give the expiry date for your credit card when you order over the phone or the internet.

Remind students to record any of the expressions they like in their notebooks and to take note when they see similar expressions throughout the unit.

Use the language strip later on in this unit for a small group task. Here are some possibilities:

- Students discuss what these expressions could be referring to: *I'll carry those for you, if you want; It had satellite TV; There were hardly any people there; I don't mind, as long as you're quick.*
- Students find all the expressions that contain a preposition (e.g. *I'd like a twin room for two nights*). Later on, write a list of these expressions on the board, but with the preposition gapped out. Ask students to complete them.
- Students try to find pairs of expressions that might logically go together. For example: *The hotel was really posh; It had satellite TV* or *I'd like a twin room for two nights; If you wait a minute, I'll check on the computer.* They can then explain their choices.

Lead in

One way to lead in is to tell students about a time you went on holiday. Explain where you stayed, what it was like, what you liked or didn't like about it. Encourage them to ask you questions. Then maybe retell the story and ask students to listen and write down any new expressions they hear. Finish up by writing these expressions on the board and go on to **1 Using vocabulary: places to stay**.

Conversation

1 Using vocabulary: places to stay

Follow on from the **Lead in** by asking students, in pairs, to tell each other about the last time they went away and use any of the expressions that you wrote on the board, if appropriate. Invite a couple of students to tell the whole class. Then, in preparation for the next task, brainstorm a list of places where people can stay on holiday. For example: *hotel, villa, bed and breakfast, campsite, hut, caravan, cabin, canal boat* etc. Feed in others and explain any if necessary. Ask questions like the following:

Would you like to stay (in caravan/on a canal boat)?

Has anyone ever stayed (in a cabin in the woods)?

What's good/not so good about staying (in a hotel/bed and breakfast)?

Explain the matching task and ask students to compare their answers with a partner. Make sure they understand a *five-star hotel*. Point out the expression *up in the mountains*. You can then teach them related expressions. For example: *down on the beach* and *down by the lake*. You may need to explain the difference between *rent* and *hire*. Often they are used interchangeably, but *rent* is often used for places where we can stay, or a longer period of time. For example:

We rented a villa for two weeks.

We hired a boat for the afternoon.

As you go through the answers, model each conversation, and at the end ask students to practise the conversations in pairs.

Answers

1. c.   2. d.   3. b.   4. a.   5. e.

Finish up by asking students to tell a different partner about a time they went away, using the conversations as a model.

2 Booking a room in a hotel

Use the photos to do some vocabulary building. Ask students what they see, and teach the corresponding vocabulary. Whenever possible, give some useful collocations. For example:

take the lift to the fourth floor

wait in the lobby

Ask students to imagine they are phoning to book a room in a hotel, and in pairs, to think of three questions they might ask or be asked by the receptionist. Invite them to tell you their ideas and reformulate any if necessary. Then draw their attention to the list of questions. Tell them to quickly look through the list to see if there are any questions that are similar to those they thought of.

Then ask students to look through the list and mark those questions they think are said by the receptionist and those said by the customer. Explain that if a bedroom has an *en-suite bathroom*, it has its own private bathroom attached. Also explain the difference between a *single room* and a *twin room*. Students should then look at the text of the conversation and decide which question goes in which of the gaps **1–10**. They can write in the question, but advise them to use pencil in case they need to change it.

Play the recording and ask students to listen and check if they were right. Pause after each gap and then get them to practise saying it. Make sure they follow the same intonation. Play the recording through one more time with students following the completed script.

Answers

1. When exactly would you be arriving?
2. And what kind of room would you like?
3. So how much would two singles be?
4. And what if we shared a twin room?
5. Is that with an en-suite bathroom?
6. So you'd like one twin room for five nights arriving the 19th and departing the 24th?
7. What kind of card are you paying with?
8. And the number?
9. And what's the expiry date?
10. And your name as it appears on the card?

3 Role play

Explain the task and teach some vocabulary associated with explaining a problem. For example:

I'm afraid there's a problem (with your card).

I'm sorry, but we (don't have any single rooms available for those dates).

You might also want to brainstorm a list of possible problems and teach appropriate expressions. Give students time to prepare and go around helping with vocabulary if necessary. Ask them to role-play the conversation and then get two pairs of students together to do it again for each other.

4 Using grammar: first conditionals

Explain that the conversation continues and Anton asks the receptionist for something else. Ask students to listen for what he asks and play the recording. Get them to compare their answers in pairs. Then play the recording again as they follow the tapescript on page 157. Follow up with a short class discussion about visas. Teach some associated expressions beforehand. For example:

apply for a visa
fill in a visa application
my visa expired
I was denied a visa.
overstayed my visa
get my visa extended

Focus students' attention on the two examples and ask them to complete them with the verbs in brackets. Then ask them to compare their answers with a partner and, if necessary, play the recording again. Check that students know that *'ll* is the short form of *will.*

Answers

1. fax, 'll fax 2. wait, 'll get

Go over the explanation of the first conditional as a class and answer any questions students have. Explain that usually the action in the main clause depends on whether the statement in the *if* clause is true.

You may need to explain the difference between *might, going to, can,* and *will.* We use *might* when we want to show there is only a possibility of something happening, whereas *will* is more definite. We use *going to* when we want to show that we intend to do something (i.e. we have already decided to do it). We use *can* when we want to emphasise that we will only be able to do something when the other thing happens.

Ask students to complete the conversations **1–7** individually and then compare their answers with a partner. Remind them of the negative form *won't.* Tell them to use the short form *'ll.* Point out that *if you want* and *if you like* are very common when we are offering to do something for someone, and that *if (you're sure) you don't mind* is common when we accept an offer.

You may need to explain some of the other expressions in this activity.

- If you *go and see*, you go somewhere to look. For example:
  A: There's supposed to be a great swimming pool here.
  B: Oh right. Let's go down and see.
- We also use *go and see* to mean *visit.* For example:
  I want to go and see my parents this weekend.
- If you *pick someone up*, you go to where they are waiting and drive them somewhere. For example:
  A: Do you want to come to the concert with me?
  B: I'd love to.
  A: Great. I'll pick you up at six then.

Here are some more questions to ask as you go through the answers:
What else do we brush? (my hair, my shoes)
If you found a wallet in a hotel, who would you hand it in to? (the receptionist) How about in a restaurant? (the waiter)
What expression can we use to mean that we drive someone somewhere? (give them a lift, drop them off)
What is the opposite of 'take your bags down'? (take your bags up)
What other verbs could we use with 'bags'? (carry your bags, pack your bags, unpack your bags)
What kind of things do you tell someone if you leave them your details? (your name, phone number)

Answers

1. wait, 'll drive
2. wait, 'll go
3. call, 'll come
4. 'll come, like, 're, 'll be
5. 'll take, like
6. leave, 'll ask
7. 'll do, don't forget, won't be, don't book

Many students have difficulty using the weak form of *will.* Ask students to practise saying *I'll* and *we'll* in isolation before getting them to practise saying the complete expressions. Then ask them to practise reading the conversations in pairs.

5 Practice

Ask students to complete these sentence starters and then share their answers with a partner or in small groups. Point out that *I'll probably* is used when you are not absolutely sure about something. Invite some students to tell you their sentences and write them down in a list, reformulating any if necessary. Use the list later to revise the form of the first conditional by writing up gapped versions of the sentences on the board and asking students to complete them. Finish up by referring students to G24 of the **Grammar commentary** on page 168, which they can read either in class or as homework.

Reading

1 Using vocabulary: hotels

One way to do the first task is to let students read through the list and put a question mark next to anything they don't understand. They then get together with one or two other students to see if anyone can explain the expressions they didn't know. Check that everyone understands by asking a few follow-up questions. For example:
In what places is it important to have air-conditioning?
Why might you call room service?
Where do you usually find a mini-bar?

Then ask students, in pairs or small groups, to talk about the things they like to have or the ones they don't care about. Explain that if you *don't care* if you have something, you don't mind not having it because you don't have strong feelings about it. You can also tell students to add other things not mentioned in the list. For example: *a restaurant, a shuttle service, an en-suite/shared bathroom, a lounge, free breakfast, a free daily newspaper*.

2 Before you read

Check that students know what is shown in each of the photos: *a luxury hotel, a wooden hut, an old-fashioned hotel, a small village, a house on the beach*. You also might want to ask them to guess where each place is located. Teach them the expression *That looks like (France/an American house)*. Give students a minute or so to think about what would be good (or not so good) about staying in each of the places. They can then discuss their choices in pairs or small groups. Provide some additional sentence starters for when they talk about the places they didn't choose. For example:
I wouldn't like to stay there because you couldn't …/you'd have to … .

Finish up by asking which was the most popular choice and why.

3 While you read (The best place I've ever stayed)

Explain the task and ask students to read the text. Then ask them to compare their answers and share their reactions with a partner. Alternatively, use this as a listening task first. Play the recording while students listen with the text covered. Then get pairs of students to compare their answers before they read the article.

Finish up by reading the article aloud or playing the recording while students follow along. As they do so, ask them to underline any expressions they find interesting or want to ask about. You might want to point out some expressions. For example:
I spent my 18th birthday there. (Ask where or how students spent their 18th or 21st birthday.)

I always stay with the same family. (Ask if anyone has been on a holiday when they stayed with a family. Ask how it was and whether they stayed with them again.)

He phoned room service. (Ask if anyone has ever phoned for room service, and if so, what they ordered.)

You may need to explain some of these expressions:

- A *foyer* is the area just inside the entrance to a hotel or other large building.
- *Maine* is a state in the US. It is in the north-east, next to Canada.

Talk about **Real English: Thanksgiving**. Explain that *Thanksgiving* is a big celebration in the US. Ask what days are big celebrations in the students' own countries.

Answers

Katherine b. (a wooden hut)
James d. (a house on a Greek island)
Harry a. (a luxury hotel)
Diana c. (an old-fashioned hotel)
Alan e. (a house in Maine)

4 Using vocabulary: *hardly*

Ask students if they remember the expression of frequency *hardly ever*. Explain that it means *almost never* and that *hardly* means *almost*. Then ask them if they can find two expressions using *hardly* in James's part of the article (*There are hardly any hotels* and *wonderful beaches with hardly any people on them*. Check that students understand the meanings by asking:
Are there no hotels?
Are the beaches completely empty?

Then go through the explanation in the Coursebook.

Before students complete sentences **1–6**, revise countable and uncountable nouns. Ask students which of the words in the list are in the plural form *(cars, people, shops)*. Explain that *hardly any* is followed by either a plural countable noun or an uncountable noun. Here are some possible follow-up questions to ask as you go through the answers:
What other expressions do you know with 'safe' (e.g. *It's not a very safe area, It's not safe to walk by yourself at night.*)

Between what times is 'the middle of the night'? (11:00–3:00)

What kind of things do people do when they have a really relaxing holiday? (lie on the beach, read books, sit by the swimming pool)

When do people usually get paid? (at the end of the week/month, on the 15th of the month)

What other words can we use to describe 'a party'? (a fun party, a great party, a brilliant party)

What are some verbs we can use with 'party'? (go to a party, leave a party, clear up after a party)

Answers

1. crime 2. shops 3. people 4. cars, pollution
5. money 6. experience 7. anyone 8. anything
9. anything 10. anyone

Introduce the last task by talking about a personal experience. Encourage students to ask you questions and then ask pairs of students to talk to each other.

2 Using vocabulary: describing places

This activity helps students visualise the meaning of the expression *looks out over*. It also helps check they understand the meaning of places like *harbour, building site* etc. Students might be hesitant to draw pictures. Do one yourself – the worse the better – and ask them to guess what the place *looks out over*. Then encourage them by saying you are sure they can do a better job themselves.

After students have shown each other their drawings, ask them to talk about the three questions, either in pairs or as a class. Teach some useful expressions. For example:
It's got a great view of …
There's an amazing view of … from …

When students have finished, write up any problems with vocabulary and reformulate them. For example:
~~*My house look over big road.*~~
My house looks out over a main road.

Listening

1 Are you ready?

Use the four questions to lead into this section. Revise the expression *it takes me* + time. Remind students of expressions like *ages, a few minutes, about an hour*. You could get students to wander around and ask the questions to several people before you ask them who takes the longest. Draw their attention to the photos and check that they know what action is being shown:
put on some make-up
dry my hair
get money out of a cash machine

Then go through the list of activities. Check that students understand them. You might want to feed in a few others as well. For example:
brush my hair
wash my hair
put on mascara
check my messages
feed the cat
tidy up my room

This can help students with the pair work task at the end. Ask them to match the activities to either of the conversations **a.** or **b.** Point out that in **a.** *I'll be two seconds* is a very short time.

Answers

Conversation a: 1., 2., 3., 7.
Conversation b: 4., 5., 6., 8.

Demonstrate the memorisation task with a student. Use conversations **a.** and **b.** as models and encourage students to do the same.

2 While you listen

Explain the situation of the conversation and ask students to listen for the answers to the two questions. Play the recording and ask them to compare their answers with a partner. Play the recording again if necessary.

Answers

Kasia still needs to have a shower, iron her clothes and put on some make-up. Tom is just a friend.

3 Comprehension

This activity not only tests students' comprehension of the listening but also focuses on and revises some useful expressions. For example, the pattern *I spent most of the day + -ing*. Draw students' attention to these expressions and encourage them to record those they want to remember in their notebooks. Ask students to correct as many mistakes as they can on their own before comparing their answers with a partner. Then play the recording again or get students to read the tapescript on page 157.

Answers

1. I spent most of the day walking round town.
2. You could lay the table, if you like.
3. Have you got an iron I could use?
4. No, not particularly. I think we might just go to the cinema.
5. Come back whenever you like.
6. Can you make sure both locks on the front door are locked before you go to bed?

You could finish up by asking students to reread the tapescript and underline a couple of expressions they want to remember or want to ask about. You may need to explain a few expressions. For example:

- *Cutlery* is knives, forks and spoons.
- If you *get dressed up*, you put on smart clothes because you are probably going out somewhere.
- If you *are seeing someone*, you are going out on dates with them, i.e. they are your current boyfriend or girlfriend.

4 Speaking

In multinational classes, this activity can be a good opportunity to talk about cultural differences. At the end of the task, if you are a different nationality from your students, explain what would be considered OK in your country. Go through the list of things, explaining any if necessary. Point out and explain the following expressions: *without asking, come and go as (they) please.* Give students some other examples:

You can't leave the classroom without asking.

Do/Did your parents let you come and go as you please?

Before students compare their answers in pairs, write up some sentence starters and expressions to help. For example:

I'd be happy to … because … .

I'd never … . I'd … instead.

I wouldn't … . I'd be afraid they would … .

It's rude to … .

In my country, we expect guests to … .

Go around and monitor, helping with vocabulary if necessary. You could also feed in more questions. For example:

What would you bring as a present?

How late would you stay out?

Would you offer to cook dinner?

5 Using grammar: asking for permission

You could lead into this activity by asking students what they would say to make some of the requests in **4 Speaking**. You can then revise *Do you mind if I … ? Is it OK if I … ? Could I … ?* Then go through the examples in the Coursebook. Check that students understand the meaning by asking questions. For example:

Can A watch a different channel?

What does B have to do at ten o'clock?

How many cups of tea is A going to make?

Students can do the matching task individually before comparing their answers with a partner. You can check the answers by playing the recording. Pause after each request and invite a student to give their answer. Then play the reply so that students can check if they were right. Replay the request and reply again, pausing after each exchange to allow students to repeat. Make sure they are linking *as long as*. Then do the same for the next one. Finish up by asking students to read the conversations, using the tapescript on page 157 in pairs. Ask one person to close their Coursebook and see if they can remember the replies when their partner reads the requests.

Answers

1. d. 2. g. 3. h. 4. a. 5. e. 6. f. 7. c. 8. b.

Here are some further questions to ask about some of the language in this activity:

*How can you change **1** to use the word 'bath'? (have a bath … as long as you don't take all the hot water)*

*What is 'stuff' in **2**?*

What other things can we 'expect'? (a visitor, a parcel, a baby)

What do you have to do if a baby wakes up? (put it back to sleep, feed it, change it, drive it around in the car until it finally falls asleep)

What other verbs can we use with 'music'? (turn the music off, go out and buy some music, go out and hear some music)

*What kind of work do you think the person in **8** needs to do? (finish writing a report, finish some programming, reply to an e-mail)*

6 Practice

Explain the task and ask students to write their variations of the replies **a–h**. Highlight the different patterns on the board to help:

as long as you're quick

as long as you're finished by …

as long as (you) don't …

Then get pairs of students to practise the conversations. You could also write a list of different starters for the replies on the board. Encourage students to use a few different ones.

No, of course not.

No, not at all.

Yes, of course.

Yes, sure.

Yes, no problem.

Finish up by referring students to G25 of the **Grammar commentary** on page 169, which they can read either in class or as homework.

7 Role play

Explain the role play and give students enough time to look back through the unit. You could also throw in some extra ideas. For example: the guest never wants to go out anywhere, the guest has a secret boyfriend/ girlfriend etc. Go around and help students with any language problems. After students act the conversation out for another pair, get them to swap roles and do it again, but for another pair.

Follow-up

For a writing task ask students to imagine they are on holiday somewhere. They should write a postcard from that place. Encourage them to describe what the place they are staying in is like, what the view is like and what they spend their time doing. To help students, bring in some pictures from travel magazines so they can make actual postcards. When they have finished, distribute the postcards around the class or put them on the wall so that students can read each other's cards.

14 What was it like?

Unit overview

General topic
Describing what places and people are like, teaching.

Conversation
Tom tells Mary about his trip to the States.

Reading
Three teachers describe what their jobs are like.

Listening
Eight people describe what different things are like.

Language input

- Expressions for asking and talking about a holiday: *So what was New York like? It rained nearly the whole time we were there.*
- Present perfect questions and their replies: *Have you ever been to Disneyland? No, not yet. Have you?*
- Expressions with *I'd like*: *I'd like to go to China one day. I'm really interested in Chinese culture.*
- Expressions with *have*: *I had a really nice time, I didn't have any breakfast.*
- Asking longer *like* questions: *What was the film on Channel 4 last night like?*

Language strip

You can use the language strip as a way to lead in to the unit. Ask students to look at the title of the unit *What was it like?* Explain that we use *like* when we want someone to describe something. Tell them to quickly look through the strip and find any expressions that could be used to answer the question in the title (e.g. *I got badly sunburnt, It's such an interesting place, It's dreadful!*). Explain that in this unit they will practise ways of asking and answering questions about what different things are like. Encourage them to choose a couple of expressions in the strip that look interesting and to find out more about them.

You might need to explain some of the following expressions:

- *Mali* is in North Africa. It is famous for its music, historic cities and culture.
- If people *go on strike*, they stop work in protest against something. For example: *The bus drivers are going on strike tomorrow, so I'll probably be late.*
- We often ask *What are the hours like?* when we want to know how long the workday is. For example:
  A: *What are the hours like?*
  B: *Not bad. I start at 10:00 and I usually finish around 5:00.*
- We often ask *What's the money like?* when we want to know if someone gets paid well or not. For example:
  A: *And what's the money like?*
  B: *Great. I get £20 an hour and a bonus at the end of each year.*
- If you *have a quiet night in*, you stay at home and relax. For example: *I'm really tired. I think I'll just have a quiet night in and watch TV.*
- If you *have a day off*, you don't go to work or school. For example: *I haven't had a day off work in five years.*
- If something is *dreadful*, it is really bad. For example: *Are you sick or something? You look dreadful.*
- If you describe the *atmosphere* of a place or situation, you are describing the feeling it gives you. For example: *They had a big argument while I was staying there. The atmosphere was really bad for a few days.*
- If you are *jealous*, you wish you could have or do the same thing as someone else. For example: *Salem's going to Jamaica for two weeks? I'm really jealous.*
- If you are *starving*, you are really hungry. For example: *When's dinner? I'm starving.*

Remind students to record any of the expressions they like in their notebooks and to take note when they see similar expressions throughout the unit.

Use the language strip later on in this unit for a small group task. Here are some possibilities:

- Students find those expressions connected with the topic of places (e.g. *It's such an interesting place*) and those connected with the topic of work (e.g. *What are the hours like?*). Some could be both (e.g. *I went there a few years ago on business*).
- Students discuss what *it*, *there* or *they* could refer to in several of the expressions.
- Students choose three or four expressions from the strip and – if necessary – change them to be true about themselves (e.g. *I'd like to try scuba-diving one day*). They can then talk about their choices with a partner.
- Students choose expressions that are questions (e.g. *What's the flat she's moving into like?*) and come up with a possible response (e.g. *It's great. It looks out over the Seine*). Then they choose expressions that are responses (e.g. *It's dreadful!*) and come up with possible prompts (e.g. *What's the food like?*).

Lead in

Tell students either a true or made-up story about a really bad holiday. Include a lot of different things that made it bad. For example, the weather, the people, the food etc. Encourage students to ask you questions. Then put them in pairs. Ask them if they can remember the details of your story. This will provide them with some ideas for **1 Speaking**.

Conversation

1 Speaking

Point out the expression *have a good/bad time* and explain that we can use several adjectives to describe *time* like this. Teach a few example expressions. For example:
How are you? Are you having a good time?
I'm having a great time. How about you?
Did you have a nice time?
I had a hard time finding your flat.

Ask students what kind of time the people in the photos are having. Tell them to explain their decisions. Give them the sentence starter:
I think he's having a bad/good time because ... .

Help with vocabulary and reformulate students' suggestions if necessary. For example:
I think he's having a bad time because he's getting sunburnt.

Explain the second task and go around helping students with the language if necessary. Tell them they can invent a holiday. Then demonstrate with one student. For example:
S: *When did you last go on holiday?*
T: *Last year. In August.*
S: *Really? Where did you go?*
T: *Actually, I went to Iceland.*
S: *Did you have a good time or a bad time?*
T: *We had a great time. The scenery was wonderful, the people were really friendly, and the nightlife was amazing.*

Students should then take it in turns describing their holidays.

2 What was your holiday like?

Explain the situation of the conversation and ask students to just listen for how Tom answers the question. Play the recording, making sure students cover the text. Get them to discuss their answers in pairs. Remind them to keep the text covered as they do this.

Answers

Tom went to the States. He had a great time. New York was an amazing place with a real mixture of people. The food was great too. He had a nice time in Boston. It was quite interesting. He met a lot of his friends' friends. They were really nice and friendly.

Play the recording again and ask students to try to fill in each of the gaps as they listen. They should then compare their answers with a partner. Play the recording a third time, but this time pause after each gap. Elicit the missing words and maybe write the complete expression on the board. Model the pronunciation and ask students to practise saying it. Play the recording through one more time with students following the completed script. Explain that if a place is *lively*, there are a lot of things happening. Ask them to tell you what kind of things make a city *lively*.

Answers

1. for a while 2. I thought 3. whereabouts
4. a couple of days 5. was it like 6. lively place
7. do much 8. and friendly 9. three years ago

Ask students to read the conversation in pairs, continuing from where Mary describes where she went. Point out that the West Coast could include Washington and Oregon, not just California. Then play the second part of the recording. Ask a few questions to check students' understanding. For example:
Whereabouts did Mary go?
Did she have a good time?
What did she do?
What was the weather like?
Which city do you think Mary prefers? Why?
Has Tom been to California before?

Go through the list of expressions. You may need to explain the following:

- If you *haven't seen someone for a while*, you haven't seen them recently.
- If a place has *a real mixture of people*, there are people there from different races, countries, backgrounds, ages etc.
- We say *what a shame* when someone tells us something bad and we want to sympathise with them.

Get students to translate the expressions **1–9** into their own language. If possible, pair up students who speak the same language and ask them to compare their answers and then test each other. If you have a very mixed class, ask one person to test the other by saying the first two or three words of the expression in English. Finish up by playing the conversation one more time and then getting pairs of students to role-play the conversation from memory. This helps them memorise several useful expressions.

3 Using grammar: present perfect questions

Ask students if they can remember the question Tom asked Mary at the end of the first part of the conversation (*Have you ever been to the States?*). Then ask them if they can remember what Mary said (*Yes, I went there about three years ago, but I went to the West Coast*). Remind students that we usually use a past tense when we give details about something we have done. Then go through the explanation in the Coursebook. Read the two example conversations. Point out that *ever* would sound unnatural in the second example because the restaurant is new. You might want to do a little practice by going around the class asking students *Have you (ever) been to Disneyworld?* and getting them to reply using some of the expressions in the examples. You might want to tell students that *Disneyworld* is in Florida and *Disneyland* is in California.

The next task focuses on some common ways to answer *Have you ever … ?* questions. When students have finished doing the task, ask them to compare their answers with a partner. Then check the answers by asking a student a question. For example: *Have you ever been to the States?* Students should then give a reply with the words in the correct order. Model the pronunciation and ask them to repeat it. Finish up by getting pairs of students to test how many they can remember.

Answers

1. (No,) but I'd like to.
2. (No,) what's it like?
3. (No,) I've never really wanted to.
4. (Yes,) I went to Washington last year.
5. (Yes,) I went there three years ago.
6. (Yes,) I went there on holiday last year.
7. (Yes,) I went there on business not long ago.
8. (Yes,) I went there a few years ago to visit a friend of mine.
9. (No,) but I'm actually going there in the summer.
10. (No,) but I'm thinking of going there next year.

4 Practice

Get students in groups to ask each other these questions. Alternatively, ask them to wander around asking lots of people about different places. You could also tell them to write down eight places on a sheet of paper and then try to find at least one person in the class who has been there. They then put a tick next to the place. Finish up by asking who has ticked off the most places. Then refer students to G26 of the **Grammar commentary** on page 169, which they can read either in class or as homework.

5 I'd like to

You could lead in by asking students if there is anyone who hasn't been to Disneyworld – or some other place – but would like to go. Ask them why. Do the same for anyone who has never wanted to go there. Then go through the explanation and examples in the Coursebook. Explain that we use *supposed to* when we have heard or read something about a place or person. For example:

A: Have you met her new boyfriend yet?
B: Not yet, but he's supposed to be really good-looking.

You might want to complete a couple of the sentences **1–8** yourself before students complete the rest. Go around and help if necessary. When they have finished, ask them to read the sentences and memorise as many as they can. They should then get into small groups and tell each other what they wrote. You might want to teach a few follow-up expressions too. For example:

Really? Me too/neither.

So, do/am I.

Really? I've heard that it's …

Reading

1 While you read

This next section is on the topic of teachers. You could lead in by asking questions like the following:
Can you remember your first day at school? What was it like?

Who was your favourite teacher? What was she/he like?

Did you ever have a teacher you didn't like? Why? What was she/he like? What did she/he do?

Then explain to students that they are going to read someone's opinion about teachers in Britain. Point out that they don't have to underline only those things that teachers in their own countries also complain about. For example, they can underline *they don't have computers* if that is true for their country, even though teachers might not necessarily complain about it. You could also read the text aloud as students follow along and underline. Get them to compare their answers with a partner and then invite a few students to share their ideas with the rest of the class. Ask them if they agree or disagree with any of the complaints.

Make sure they notice the two main patterns for *complain*:
They complain about + noun
They complain (that) + clause

2 Speaking

Write some useful patterns on the board to help with the discussion. For example:

They were protesting about …
I'd probably go on strike because …
I'd never go on strike because I'd be afraid of (losing my job).
They always complain that/about …
I usually complain to (my friends) about …

If you wanted to do some more work on complaining, you could write a few situations on the board and ask students if they would complain if this happened to them and what they would say. For example: a waiter brings the wrong order, you are overcharged in a shop, a taxi driver gets lost and then charges you a huge fare, there's a lot of noise coming from the next-door room in your hotel.

3 Reading (What's your life like?)

This activity is a jigsaw reading. Divide the class into three groups: A, B and C. Explain that each group will read about a different teacher. They should read the appropriate article and then answer the questions **1–7**. They can then compare their answers with someone from their group. You could also model the pronunciation of the questions and ask students to alternately ask and answer each other in pairs.

Answers

Text A: Megan

1. England.
2. Coventry. It's in the centre of England.
3. I teach English in a secondary school.
4. It's OK, but it's harder than I expected.
5. I work about 60 hours a week.
6. I get about twenty thousand pounds a year.
7. I sometimes go out to the cinema, but most of the time I just get a video and have a quiet night in.

Text B: Patrick

1. Guinea Bissau
2. Bissau, the capital.
3. I teach English.
4. I really like my job.
5. I work ten hours a day, five or six days a week.
6. I get about £20 a month, which isn't enough to live on.
7. I sit around chatting in the shade. I also work on a farm.

Text C: Olga

1. Latvia.
2. Riga, the capital city.
3. I teach history.
4. It's OK, but most students aren't interested in learning about it. I think teaching English would be better for my future.
5. I work from eight till three.
6. The money is not good. I get $125 a month (which is about £70).
7. I work part-time in the evenings as a barmaid and give private English classes.

4 Role play

Get students into new groups of three: one person from group A, one from group B and one from group C. You might need to have a few groups of four with two people playing the same person, or a few groups of two people. Go through the list of responses, modelling the pronunciation. Focus on the intonation, so that it conveys the appropriate emotion. Then model the conversation starter and ask students to role-play the conversation. When they have finished, invite a couple of groups to do it again for the rest of the class.

Finish up by reading the three articles aloud. Get students to underline any expressions they want to remember or ask about.

Talk about **Real English: have a quiet night in**. Teach the variation *have a great night out.*

5 Key word: *have*

Ask students in pairs if they can think of five expressions that use the word *have*. Some that have appeared so far in this unit include *have a quiet night in, have a good/bad time*. Then explain that English has a lot of expressions that use the verb – as opposed to the auxiliary – *have*. Find the first few expressions together as a class until students get the hang of it.

Answers

1. I had a really nice time.
2. We had a really terrible time.
3. I had something to eat.
4. I didn't have any breakfast.
5. have a quick shower
6. I had the day off.
7. I had a meeting.
8. have dinner
9. I've just had an argument.
10. Have you had any lunch?

Play the recording so students can check their answers. Pause after each expression and ask students to repeat, following the same stress pattern. Get them to record these expressions – along with a translation – in their notebooks.

Then ask students to complete the conversations **1–8**. Point out and explain some of the other common expressions as you go through the answers. For example:

I'm starving
It's a shame …
He can be so stupid sometimes.
don't ask
Everything that could possibly go wrong went wrong!
it went on till eight

Answers

1. I didn't have any breakfast
2. I had a really nice time
3. Have you had any lunch, I had something to eat
4. I had the day off
5. I've just had an argument
6. We had a really terrible time
7. I had a meeting
8. have dinner, have a quick shower

Finish up by asking students to practise the conversations in pairs. Then get them to think of alternative endings for each one. For example:
A: Are you hungry?
B: No, I'm OK. I had something to eat before I got here. But I'm a bit thirsty. Could I have some water?

6 Speaking

Go through the questions, explaining any vocabulary and maybe giving your own answers so that students have a model. Alternatively, wait till students have finished discussing in pairs and ask them to guess what they think you will say in answer to these questions. Then answer the questions yourself. Ask if anyone guessed correctly.

Listening

1 Before you listen

Focus students' attention on the pictures on page 102. Ask students what they can see in each picture. Then add some follow-up questions and feed in some relevant vocabulary. For example:
*What kind of film do you think **1** is?*
*What kind of person is the boy in **3**? How old do you think he is?*
*What kind of music do you think they're playing in **5**?*

Then ask students to match the questions with the pictures.

Answers

a. 3. b. 8. c. 5. d. 4. e. 7. f. 6. g. 1. h. 2.

Model the example conversation and then ask students to practise asking and answering the questions.

2 While you listen

Explain the task and play the recording. Pause after each conversation to give students time to write down the question. Then get them to compare their answers. Play the recording again while students follow the tapescript on page 158. Encourage them to underline any expressions they want to remember. You may need to explain the following:

- If you describe something or someone as *ideal*, you think it or they are the best choice. For example: *I think she'll be ideal for the job.*
- If something is *lovely*, it is very nice. For example: *It's got a lovely view of the beach, He's got a lovely smile.*
- If you describe something or someone as *smart*, you think it or they are clever. For example: *That was a smart decision.*
- A *venue* is a place where an event like a concert, competition or conference is held. For example: *They haven't decided on the venue for next year's conference yet.*

Ask students to think of other places, apart from a hotel, that we might describe as *family-run (a restaurant, a company)*. Ask them what other nouns we can use after *it was a waste of … (time, space, energy)*. You could also ask them to go back and find all the examples of the present perfect.

Answers

1. e. (What's the area you live in like?)
2. h. (What's the food in that Moroccan restaurant like?)
3. d. (What was Italy like?)
4. g. (What was that film you saw the other day like?)
5. a. (What's your brother like?)
6. c. (What was the concert like?)
7. f. (What's that course you're doing like?)
8. b. (What's your new flat like?)

Get students to ask each other the questions and make up their own answers. Demonstrate with one student first.

3 Pronunciation: the food, the wine, everything!

Ask students if they can remember what the speaker said about Italy. Then go through the explanation in the Coursebook. Play the recording once all the way through while students just listen. Ask them to listen for how the voice goes up and down. Then play the recording again, pausing after each sentence and getting students to repeat. Make sure they are following the stress and intonation pattern.

To help students with the task, you could elicit some questions with the pattern *What was … like?* For example: your old school, the place you grew up, the last movie you saw.

Students then ask each other these questions. Tell them they can make up answers if they like.

4 Using grammar: asking longer questions

Lead in by asking a student *What was the film like?* They should look confused and say *What film?* Then explain that we often add details explaining which thing we are asking about. For example:
What was the film you saw last night like?

Explain the matching task. When students have finished, ask them to compare their answers with a partner. Point out that some of the sentences are in the present and some in the past.

You might want to point out that some of the missing parts use *that* or *who*. Explain that we use these relative pronouns when they stand for the subject of the verb that follows them. For example: *the restaurant that does East African food.* Ask students what *that* stands for (*the restaurant*). When the relative pronoun stands for the object of the verb, it is often omitted. For example: *the film (that) you went to see.* Ask students what the subject is (*you*) and what the object of *see* is (*the film*).

As you go through the answers, ask some follow-up questions. For example:
Where do you go to see a film? (a cinema)

Where else could the guy in **2** *live? (downstairs from you, across the hall from you)*

What kind of company lets you book holidays? (a travel agent, a tour company)

How many different ways can you book a holiday? (over the phone, on-line, in person)

What usually happens at a wedding reception? What happens before and after a wedding reception? (you get married, you go on honeymoon)

Answers

1. e. 2. c. 3. f. 4. d. 5. g. 6. b. 7. a.

Remind students that *awful* means *very bad* and then ask them to complete the sentences **1–7**. As you check the answers, model the pronunciation and get students to repeat. Check that they know what is being described in each one.

Answers

1. Great (a restaurant)
2. Great (a hotel)
3. Awful (a film)
4. Great (a person)
5. Awful (an area)
6. Great (a company)
7. Awful (a party)

Then model the two example conversations and get students to practise asking each other the questions **1–7** of the first activity.

6 Free practice

Explain the task and ask students to write their four questions. Tell them to try to use longer questions. Go around and help. They can then either ask their partner or go around asking several students their questions. Finish up by referring them to G27 of the **Grammar commentary** on page 169, which they can read either in class or as homework.

7 Can you remember?

Explain the task and ask students in pairs to decide on a country. They can then reread the conversation on page 98. Also encourage them to use some of the expressions from the other activities. When they have finished, put two pairs of students together and ask partners to switch roles and act out their conversation for the other pair.

Follow-up

Each student writes a list of five things to describe. For example: a holiday, their younger sister, their last teacher, their parents, their old job, their flat, the town they were born in. Give students five minutes to think of the vocabulary they need to describe each thing. Then put them in groups of three. One person begins by describing the first thing on their list but using *it, he, she* or *they*. The other members of the group try to guess what is being described. Do a couple of examples with students first before they do it themselves.

15 What's on?

Unit overview

General topic
Television and cinema.

Conversation
Ian and Jo discuss which film they want to see.

Reading
Tonight's TV schedule.

Listening
Leroy books tickets for a concert.

Language input
- Film vocabulary: *a horror film, a comedy.*
- Asking questions about films and TV programmes: *What time's it on? Who's in it?*
- Vocabulary for describing who people are: *a TV personality, a writer, a film star.*
- Vocabulary to talk about problems: *The show's completely sold out.*
- Passives: *The film was written by John Hodge, The book was made into a film.*

Language strip

You can use the language strip as a way to lead in to the unit. Explain to students that in this unit they will practise talking about TV and movies, and problems. Ask them to find those expressions connected with TV (e.g. *Who's in it?*) and those connected with problems (e.g. *My bag's been stolen!*). Encourage them to choose a couple of expressions in the strip that look interesting and to find out more about them.

You might need to explain some of the following expressions:

- If we ask *Where's it on?* we are usually taking about a film at a cinema. If we are talking about a film on TV we say *What's it on?*
- A *TV personality* is someone who is famous for being on TV. A *sports personality* is someone who is a famous sports person.
- A *contestant* is someone who takes part in a competition like a game show or quiz on TV. For example: *My brother was a contestant on a quiz show once, but he didn't win anything.*
- A *chat show* is a TV show where a few famous people are interviewed. For example: *Michael Jackson is going to be on that new chat show tonight.*
- A *soap opera* is a short drama that is shown on TV, usually several times a week. Soap operas usually last many years. Sometimes we just say the *soap*. For example: *I love watching the soaps. I buy all the TV magazines and read about the actors too.*
- *Sitcom* stands for *situation comedy*. This is usually a 30-minute comedy programme, usually to do with a family or a workplace. For example:
  A: What's on tonight?
  B: Nothing much. Just chat shows and sitcoms.
- If you *missed an episode*, you didn't see part of a TV series. For example: *Don't miss the final episode. It's supposed to be really funny.*
- If something is *under-rated*, most people don't recognise how good it actually is. For example: *I think English wine is very under-rated. It actually is very good and cheap.*
- If something is *sold out*, there are no tickets left because they have all been bought. For example: *The game sold out two weeks ago, but a friend of mine has a spare ticket.*
- If your *card is rejected*, it means that your credit card isn't accepted because you gave the wrong number, it has expired, or you are over your limit.

Remind students to record any of the expressions they like in their notebooks and to take note when they see similar expressions throughout the unit.

Use the language strip later on in this unit for a small group task. Here are some possibilities:
- Students choose three or four expressions from the strip and – if necessary – change them to be true about themselves (e.g. *My favourite soap opera's on every Friday*). They can then talk about their choices with a partner.
- Students find all the expressions with prepositions (e.g. *Who's in it? I've got cable at home*). Then later, write the expressions on the board but gap the prepositions. Ask students if they can remember what is missing.
- Students find all the expressions that use an apostrophe (e.g. *It's a very under-rated film, My bag's been stolen!*) and make sure they know what letters it is replacing. They should then practise saying the phrases linking the words where necessary.

Lead in

Ask students to tell you about the last film they saw at a cinema, on video or DVD, on a plane or on TV. Ask them what it was called, what kind of film it was, and whether they liked it or not. Alternatively, you could just lead in by focusing students' attention on the pictures and doing the first activity.

Conversation

1 Speaking

Ask students to match up the types of movie with the photos and then discuss the three questions as a class. You could also elicit or give students a few other types of film. For example: *a musical, a thriller, an animated film*. Ask students if they ever watch them. If you want students to talk about films with certain actors or by certain directors, you could also revise the expression *I like anything with (Sean Penn) in; I like anything by (John Sayles).*

Answers

1. E. 2. D. 3. B. 4. A. 5. C.

2 Arranging to go to the cinema

Explain the situation of the conversation and ask students to just listen for the answers to the two questions. Play the recording, making sure they cover the text. Get them to discuss the answers in pairs. Remind them to keep the text covered as they do this.

Answers

They are going to see *City of Dreams*, a French film about some Algerians growing up in Paris. The film starts at 8:15, so they'll meet at the cinema around 8:00.

Play the recording again and ask students to try to fill in each of the gaps as they listen. They should then compare their answers with a partner. Play the recording a third time, but this time pause after each gap. Elicit the missing words and maybe write the complete expression on the board. Model the pronunciation and have the class practise saying it. Play the recording through one more time with students following the completed script.

Answers

1. nothing planned 2. Have you seen
3. neither do I 4. What's it about 5. where's it on
6. something to eat 7. around eight

Ask students to read the conversation in pairs using the tapescript on page 159. Remind them to try and follow the stress and phrasing as indicated. For extra practice let students look at the conversation again and memorise as much as they can. Write a few key words on the board for each line of dialogue, and then ask pairs of students to have the conversation.

You may want to point out the expression *It's OK, but it's not brilliant*. Ask students if they can make similar expressions about other things or people. For example: *Ibiza's OK, but it's not brilliant.*

3 Using vocabulary: questions

Lead in by writing the name of a film you think your students won't know. Tell them that you really recommend this film. This should prompt them to ask you what it is about, who the actors are, if it is on video etc. Reformulate students' questions if necessary. For example:
S: ~~*Who is actor?*~~
T: (writing) *Who's in it?*

Then explain the matching task and ask students to complete the sentences individually before they compare their answers with a partner.

Answers

1. What's on? 2. Who's in it? 3. Where's it on?
4. What time's it on? 5. What's it about?
6. Who's it by?

Model and practise the pronunciation of the questions as well as the following patterns:
I'm thinking of going to the cinema/to see …
Do you want to come?
I haven't heard of it/that one.

4 Practice

Go through the explanation and model and practise the examples. Ask students to give you examples of what *that* could refer to in each one. Point out that *that sounds fine* could refer to an arrangement to meet at a certain time and place.

Talk about **Real English: That sounds good**. Point out that *Sounds good* is an example of ellipsis, which is common in informal conversation. You can model the example conversation and get students to practise saying the short conversation before they practise the ones in **3 Using vocabulary: questions**.

5 Further practice

This activity lets students personalise the language by talking about films they would like to see. For a little variation teach the following conversation starter too: *I'm thinking of renting … . Do you want to watch it?*

6 Using vocabulary: describing who people are

Explain the task and go through the list explaining that an *artist* could be a painter or a sculptor. In a multinational class suggest that students think of the most famous person from their country. They can then get together with someone from another country and talk about their choices.

For the last task, after modelling and practising the example conversation, elicit or give some examples of follow-up questions to ask. For a singer like Curtis Mayfield you could ask the following:
What kind of songs did he sing?
What are some of his most famous songs?
Do you have any of his CDs?

Reading

1 Using vocabulary: What's on TV?

Lead in by brainstorming a list of different kinds of TV programmes. As students make suggestions, reformulate and explain any if necessary. Then you can use the matching task to reinforce students' understanding and teach some associated vocabulary. As you go through the answers, you may need to explain the following.

- If someone *hosts* a game show, they are usually in charge. You may also want to teach the expression *host a party*.
- *The Simpsons* is an American cartoon series that is primarily aimed at adults.
- If a film or programme is a *classic*, it is old and quite famous.

Answers

1. e. 2. a. 3. c. 4. b. 5. d. 6. h. 7. g. 8. i. 9. f. 10. j.

Give students a few minutes to memorise the sentences **1–10**. Then do one example with the class before asking students to test each other in pairs. This task helps them memorise the following patterns:
there's a … on later I'd like to watch
… is on later
I have to watch it
I'd like to watch … later

2 Speaking

Introduce this activity by telling students your answers to the questions. Use this opportunity to model useful language. Write some helpful expressions on the board for students to use when they discuss in pairs or groups. For example:
I usually/hardly ever watch …
They have too many commercials.
They don't have any commercials.
One of my favourite programmes is … . Have you seen it?

3 While you read

Ask students where they usually get information about what is on TV (e.g. *the newspaper, a special TV magazine*). Then explain the task. Point out that they should quickly look at the titles of the programmes to see if any look interesting. They can then read in more detail about those that do. Suggest that they put a tick next to the programmes they definitely want to watch.

Then ask students to compare their choices with a partner. When they have finished, ask them to tell you if they had similar choices. Give them a few expressions to help. For example:
We both like (comedies)/watching (films).
We both like the same things.
… likes (sitcoms), but I can't stand them.

You could also use the TV guide for some quick scanning exercises. For example, ask students to find all the sitcoms, documentaries, or history programmes.

4 Speaking

Go through the list of expressions, explaining that a *variety programme* is one that has people doing different things: singing, comedy, magic etc. You may need to talk a little bit about *reality shows* (e.g. *Big Brother*) if students are unfamiliar with them.

Talk about **Real English: over-rated**. Ask students to tell you about anything or anyone who is over-rated or under-rated. For example:
Bruce Willis is often under-rated, but he's actually a really good actor. Did you see him in 'Pulp Fiction'?

5 Role play

Explain the task and tell students to use the TV guide on page 107, or alternatively, bring in the TV guide from a newspaper or magazine for that day. You may be able to get some TV guides from different English-speaking countries off the internet. Then groups of students could role-play being in different countries.

Give students a few minutes to look back through some of the activities and find any language they want to use. Then give them a conversation opener to get them started. For example:
A: *I'm exhausted. I just want to have a quiet night in and watch TV. Is there anything good on tonight?*
B: *Well there's … on later. It's supposed to be good.*

Listening

1 Using vocabulary: problems

Discuss questions **1–3** as a class. You could also feed in more questions. For example:

Did you pay a service charge?

What is good about booking on-line? Are there any disadvantages?

Do you prefer booking on-line or over the telephone?

Then lead in to the topic by asking students to brainstorm some problems people might have when they book things. Use the photos on page 108 to help generate ideas. For example:

They don't accept American Express.

My card was stolen.

Ask students to discuss the problems **1–6** in pairs. Here are some follow-up questions to ask when they have finished:

Why do you think the concert sold out? (the artist is very popular)

When is a show cancelled? (when the performer is ill, when the performer hasn't arrived)

What would you do if they didn't have the seats you wanted? (ask for different seats, ask about another night)

For what reasons are credit cards rejected? (you are over your limit, the card has been reported stolen)

2 While you listen

Explain the listening task, making sure students understand *box office*. Then play the recording. Get students, in pairs, to tell each other what problems Leroy had.

Answers

The show is completely sold out for Saturday evening. The seats upstairs are more expensive than the ones downstairs.

3 Comprehension check

Get students to work together to complete as much of the form as they can. Then play the recording so they can fill in what they are missing. Ask students these questions to elicit the answers:

What's his first name?

How many tickets does he want?

What row does he want?

What's his credit card number?

What's the expiry date?

Where does he live?

Then get students to ask each other these questions in pairs. You might also want to do a bit of work on how we say credit card and telephone numbers, focusing on intonation. Write a few more examples on the board and ask students to practise saying them.

Answers

Name: Leroy (Jones)
Number of tickets: 2
Row: S
Card number: (4926-)8631(-6231-)9221
Expiry date: 04/07
Address: 14 (Beechwood Park) E 17

4 Speaking

Read the questions out loud. Ask students what people usually see at a theatre (*a play*). Also give students *the bulkhead seats* as an alternative for **2**. You might want to tell students your answers for **1–3** before they discuss their answers with a partner. You could then turn questions **4** and **5** into a class discussion. Depending on the experience and needs of your students, you could talk about strategies for helping yourself be understood and for understanding the other person. For example, speaking slowly and clearly or asking the other person to repeat what they said.

5 Using grammar: passives

Students often have problems with passive structures, both with their form and their use. Students may drop the *be* part of the form (e.g. ~~*the show cancelled*~~) or they may use a passive when an active form is correct (e.g. ~~*the film was begun at 8:00*~~). In some languages inanimate things like *a film* don't take active verbs.

The first task focuses on recognising the passive. Ask students to explain their choices. They may recognise the form or they may recognise that the 'subject' is not the 'doer' of the verb.

Answers

's been cancelled
was written

Go through the explanations and examples with students. Stress that one of the main reasons we use the passive is for the 'object' of the verb to become more important. You could also give students another use – when we want to shift responsibility. For example, I might say, *The dinner was burnt* if I don't want to admit it was my fault. Ask students to look back at sentences **1–3** in **1 Using vocabulary: problems** on page 109 and tell you which use a passive and why they think it is used.

Go over the explanation of the form of the passive. Revise the past participle and ask which tense they have met in the Coursebook uses this form (*the present perfect*). Ask students to underline the passive part of the verb in the four examples and then ask if they recognise which tenses are used.

Answers

is collected: present simple
is being fixed: present continuous
was built: past simple
has been stolen: present perfect simple

For extra practice write up some examples of the passive from the unit, but gap parts of the verb phrase. Ask students what is missing. For example:
It's a great film. … directed by Luis Buñuel.
My boss was … for stealing money.

Finish by asking students to find the passives in sentences **1–12** individually before comparing their answers with a partner. Tell them to be careful of *'s* because it could be *has* or *is*. Here are some follow-up questions to ask:

Why are flights delayed? (the weather, security, engine problems)

What other kinds of transport can we catch? (the bus, a plane)

How is the person in ***5*** *getting home from the airport? (probably by car)*

What happens if someone is caught without a ticket? (they pay a fine)

What is the person in ***11*** *talking about? (a restaurant, a flight)*

What are some differences between a show, a film and a concert? (e.g. *you see a film at a cinema, you listen to a concert in a concert hall, and you watch a show at a theatre*)

Answers

1., 2., 5., 6., 7., 9., 11.

6 Practice

Ask students to complete the sentences individually and then compare their answers with a partner. In this activity they also focus on collocations. Point these out and tell students one or two other collocations. For example:
my credit card was rejected (stolen)
his books have been translated into English (made into films)
be invited to a wedding (go to a wedding)

Make sure students understand *close down* and *knock down*. Ask what else can be *closed down* (*a factory, a school)*. Note that *close down* is often used in the active. For example:
The factory is closing down at the end of the month.

Answers

1. wasn't cleaned
2. are made
3. been closed down, be knocked down
4. was rejected
5. been translated
6. being repaired
7. been invited
8. 's directed

Finish up by referring students to G28 of the **Grammar commentary** on page 169, which they can read either in class or as homework.

7 Speaking

Use these questions to practise some of the language from **6 Practice**. Get students to ask each other in groups. You may want to answer a few of the questions yourself first. Alternatively, ask students to close their Coursebooks and try to remember the questions to ask you.

Follow-up

Divide the class into two groups: A and B. Tell students in A to come up with a list of ten famous people and students in group B to come up with a list of ten famous films. Explain that the films and people should be familiar to everyone in the class. Ask one person in each group to write down the names on a piece of paper. Give them about five minutes to do this. Ask each group to give you their paper and write the two lists on the board. Then tell students in group A that they have to choose the three films they would most like to see from list B, and students in group B that they have to choose the three people they would most like to meet from list A. Ask students to discuss in pairs first of all. After a few minutes, get students together in their groups. Tell them they must decide, as a group, on the top three people and films. Give them about five more minutes to do this. Then ask each group to explain their choices.

16 Telephoning

Unit overview

General topic
Telephoning.

Conversation
Paola calls Jenny to ask if she knows somewhere cheap to stay when she comes to London.

Reading
Three people describe an experience they have had on the phone.

Listening
Four conversations about mobiles.

Language input
- Expressions with *phone*: *make a couple of quick phone calls, phone in sick.*
- Ways to explain why someone can't come to the phone: *Sorry, she's just gone out to lunch.*
- Adjectives ending with *-ed* or *-ing*: *It was really embarrassing, I was so embarrassed.*
- Reporting what people say: *Alan told me to tell you, Allan was telling me about ... .*

Language strip

You can use the language strip as a way to lead in to the unit. Explain to students that in this unit they will practise language connected with telephoning. Ask them to quickly look through the list and find those expressions that are probably said on the phone to someone else (e.g. *Do you want to leave a message?*) and those that are just referring to telephoning or phones (e.g. *I had my phone stolen*). Encourage students to choose a couple of expressions in the strip that look interesting and to find out more about them.

You might need to explain some of the following expressions:

- If you *phone in sick*, you call your place of work and say that you are sick and won't be coming in to work. For example: *You should just phone in sick and stay home in bed.*
- If you *give someone a ring*, you call them on the phone. For example: *Give me a ring tonight and we'll decide where to go.*
- You might need to *change your number* if someone keeps calling you and you don't want them to. For example: *I had to change my number because I kept getting calls for the pizza restaurant on the corner.*
- If you do something *straightaway*, you do it immediately. For example: *You have to leave straightway if you want to catch the 6:00 bus.*
- If you *swap* something, you exchange something with another person. For example: *Marie, can you swap places with Gil?*

Remind students to record any of the expressions they like in their notebooks and to take note when they see similar expressions throughout the unit.

Use the language strip later on in this unit for a small group task. Here are some possibilities:
- Pairs of students write a conversation that contains four or five of the expressions. They then act it out for another pair.
- Students find all the expressions that contain *to* (e.g. *I'm going to phone in sick, I need to recharge the battery*).
- Students choose three or four expressions from the strip and then ask a partner an information question about each one. For example: *Why did she have to change her number? Where was his phone stolen?* Their partner then makes up an answer.

Lead in

Write the word *phone* on the board. Ask students in pairs to think of five things you can do with a phone. Then invite students to tell you their suggestions. You will probably have the obvious answers like *answer, pick up* and *put down* but you might also get verbs like *drop, bug* or *disconnect*. Reformulate students' suggestions if necessary. Explain that *phone* is both a verb and a noun, and is used in many expressions. Then do the first activity.

Conversation

1 Key word: *phone*

Explain the task and ask students to complete the sentences on their own and compare their answers with a partner. As you go through the answers, ask a few follow-up questions. For example:
*Think of two alternative endings for **1**: I just need to ... . (go to the toilet, tidy up)*
What else can you book over the phone? (a holiday, a room in a hotel)
What else do we look up? (a word in a dictionary, an address)
What other things can teenagers spend hours doing? (sitting in their room, listening to music, surfing the internet)

Answers

1. make 2. phone 3. book 4. put 5. sell
6. look up 7. spends 8. answered

Ask students to underline the complete expressions and tell them to spend a few minutes memorising them. Then they can test each other in pairs. One person reads the sentences but says *blank* for the missing word. Their partner, with their Coursebook closed, says the completed expression. Finish up by asking students what they think the situation in **8** is. You can teach the expression *have an affair.*

2 Speaking

These questions practise some of the language from **1 Key word: *phone***. Read the questions aloud and then give your answers to one or two of them. This provides students with a model. For example:
In my family my husband spends the longest on the phone. He loves talking. He rings his friends every day. He never calls me, though.

Here are some extra questions to feed in if you wish:
What do people say when they answer the phone in English?
Do you like chatting on the phone?
How often do you give your friends a ring?
Do you prefer to book things over the phone or over the internet?
Do you ever buy phone cards? Are they worth it?

Talk about **Real English: give you a ring**. We can also use *ring* as a verb with the same meaning:
I'll ring you tomorrow.
Ring me at home.

For some extra practice, get students in pairs. Write the following on the board:
I'll call you ...
I'll give you a ring …
I'll ring you …

Tell students to write down five time phrases that refer to the near future (e.g. *later, tomorrow night, this afternoon, in two days, at the end of the week*). They can then drill each other using the time phrases and the patterns on the board:
A: later tonight
B: I'll ring you later tonight.

3 Answering the phone (1)

Use the questions to lead in to the listening task. If you want to focus on messages on answer machines, ask students if they usually leave messages on answering machines or just hang up, and if they have ever left messages in English. Ask them in pairs to write a message in English for their own answering machine (e.g. *I'm not here at the moment, so please leave a message*). Encourage them to be creative. They can then practise telling it to each other.

Explain the situation of the conversation and ask students first of all to just listen and not worry about writing anything. Then maybe ask a couple of comprehension questions. For example:
Where's Jenny gone?
When's she coming back?

Ask students to try and fill in as much as they remember of the conversation on their own. They can then work in pairs. Play the recording one more time so they can fill in anything they missed. To check the answers, call on a student to say each whole sentence. Then model the pronunciation and ask students to practise saying it. Students can then practise reading the conversation in pairs.

Answers

L: Hello.
P: Hi. Is (Jenny) there(?)
L: I'm afraid (not). She's gone out shopping.
P: Oh right. When will she be (back?)
L: (She'll probably) be about an hour. Do you want to leave a (message?)
P: No, it's all right. (I'll) just call back later.

4 Answering the phone (2)

Point out that Lara said *I'm afraid not* when Paola asked if Jenny was there. Explain that we often use this expression or *I'm sorry* when we explain why someone is not there or can't come to the phone. Ask students to think of another reason why Jenny couldn't come to the phone (*she was at work*). Explain that they will now see some similar conversations with several different reasons. Ask them to complete the sentences. As they do so, encourage them to notice any patterns. The focus of the next activity will be on some of these patterns.

Answers

1. for lunch, an hour
2. off sick, a couple of days
3. on holiday, next week
4. his day off, around half eight
5. in the shower, ten minutes
6. closed, between ten and four

Ask students to tell you which conversations probably take place in an office *(all except **5**).* Then get pairs of students to think of some more reasons why someone can't come to the phone – maybe three at home and three at work. For example:

He's putting the baby to sleep.
She's in the middle of dinner.
He's on the other line.
She's in a meeting.

Ask students to practise reading the conversation in pairs.

5 Grammar questions

These questions draw students' attention to the function and meaning of some of the grammatical patterns in the conversation. Ask these questions to the whole class and ask students to explain their answers. You may need to explain that *normally* means *usually*. Ask some follow-up questions too. For example:
When do you normally get up?
What do you normally eat for breakfast?
What time do people in offices normally start work?

Check that students understand *by seven*. Ask if the person is expected before seven or after (*before seven*).

Answers

You would use *I'd like to speak to X, please* when you phone an office and *Is X there?* when you phone a friend's house.

1. c. 2. b. 3. a.

6 Practice

One way to do this activity is to ask each student to write down either *home* or *office* and a name (e.g. *Antonia, Mr Gold*) on a slip of paper. They should then use this information as a basis for their conversation. For example:
(home)
A: *Is Antonia in?*
B: *I'm sorry. She's at school at the moment.*
A: *When will she be back?*
B: *She's normally back by five.*
A: *Thanks. I'll try then.*

When each student has had their conversation, they exchange slips and find a new partner. They then have another conversation based on their new slip. Get students to do this for several minutes. You could also take part in this activity.

7 Talking on the phone

Tell students that Paola phones back and talks to Jenny. Ask them to guess some reasons why Paola is phoning. Then play the recording. Get them to compare their answers with a partner. You could feed in a few more comprehension questions too. For example:
Has Paola met Jenny before?
When does she want to visit London?
Is Paola going to call back?

Answers

Paola is phoning Jenny because she wants her to recommend somewhere cheap to stay when she visits London. Jenny has a spare room and invites Paola to stay with her.

8 Word check

Ask students to complete as many of the sentences as they can. Then play the recording again so they can fill in anything they missed. As you go through the answers, check that they understand the expressions. You may need to explain the following:

- If you have got a *spare room*, you have an extra bedroom.
- If you say *it's no trouble*, you are happy to do something. For example:
  A: *Thanks for picking me up at the airport last night.*
  B: *Oh, it was no trouble.*

Point out **3** as a good example of how we can change the 'tense' of verbs to be more polite. The continuous is used (*wondering* instead of *wonder*), the past is used instead of the present (*I was wondering* instead of *I'm wondering*) and *could* is used instead of *can*.

Answers

1. same 2. told 3. wondering 4. recommend
5. spare 6. trouble 7. time 8. nearer 9. say
10. offer

Students can then use the ten expressions to help them remember the conversation. When they have finished, play the recording one more time as they read the tapescript on page 159. They can then practise the conversation again from memory. Finish up by asking students to translate the complete expressions.

For more practice ask students some follow-up questions focusing on some of the language. For example:
Can anyone recommend somewhere cheap to eat/stay in ... ?
Are you still friends with anyone you went to the same school with?
Do you have a spare room in your house? What do you normally use it for?

Reading

1 Before you read

Make sure students understand the adjectives in the box. Elicit or give them examples of an embarrassing, funny, annoying or horrible situation. For example: forgetting the name of my best friend's husband, going to work dressed as a monkey, being interrupted in the middle of dinner by people phoning up to try and sell things, finding a dead rat in the kitchen. Ask students which is stronger, *horrible* or *annoying*. Then ask them to complete the four sentences.

Answers

1. It was really funny!
2. It was really embarrassing!
3. It was really horrible!
4. It was really annoying!

Introduce the personalisation task by telling students about an embarrassing, annoying, funny or horrible event in your life. Write any helpful expressions you used on the board. Then get students in pairs or small groups to tell each other their stories. Finish up by inviting a few students to tell their stories to the whole class.

2 While you read (Telephone stories)

Ask students to think of two reasons in pairs and invite them to share their ideas with the whole class. Then explain the reading task. When students have finished, get them to compare their answers with a partner. Alternatively, use this as a listening task first. Play the recording while students listen with the text covered. Pause just before the last word of each story and get them to shout out the missing word.

Answers

Jiang: embarrassing
Emilie: horrible
Rebecca: annoying

As a variation, use this as a jigsaw reading. Get students in groups of three. Each person reads a different story and completes the missing word. They then retell the story they read to the other people in their group.

Finish up by reading the three stories aloud or playing the recording while students follow along. As they do so, ask them to underline any expressions they find interesting or want to ask about. You may want to point out the following telephone expressions:
it was in the middle of the night
sorry to phone you so late
I called (my mum) by mistake
we swapped telephone numbers
I had to change my number
talk(ing) really loudly on (his) mobile

You may need to explain some of these expressions as well:

- If you *take the hint*, you understand what someone has suggested indirectly that you do. For example: *I wish you'd take the hint and give me a lift to the airport.*
- If you *keep on doing* something, you continue to do it. For example: *I really wanted the tickets, so I kept on calling and I finally got through.*
- If you *take no notice*, you ignore something. For example: *Take no notice of Helen. She thinks she's always right, but she isn't.*
- If you *text* someone, you send them a text message on a mobile phone.

3 Speaking

Ask students to discus these questions in pairs or small groups. Write some useful expressions and sentence starters on the board. For example:
I had a similar experience (a few years ago/last week).
It went off in the middle of (class/the film).
I only use it for emergencies.
I only give out my home number to my closest friends.
I was getting too many calls/e-mails from … .
I was getting too many junk e-mails.

Ask students if they ever eavesdrop on people having conversations on their mobiles. Point out that if they have the opportunity, listening to these conversations in English is good practice, and they will hear a lot of common expressions.

4 Texting

Introduce the activity by asking students the questions. Explain that texting is very popular in the UK. Get students to work in pairs on the task. Explain that they should say the names of individual letters or numbers to find the word. For example, *I* could stand for *eye*, *P* could be *pea* etc.

Answers

1. Thanks for the information.
2. It's up to you.
3. See you tomorrow.
4. It's easy.
5. Can you do it as soon as possible?
6. See you tonight.
7. Are you OK?
8. See you later.
9. Great news.
10. Mind your own business.

Point out that these are all very common expressions. You may need to explain the following:

- We use *it's up to you* when we want the other person to decide because we don't have a particularly strong opinion about it.
- We say *mind your own business* to tell someone that they shouldn't ask about our private life.

Ask students to practise saying these expressions until they can say them comfortably. For further practice, get students to write a mini-conversation using several of these unabbreviated expressions.

5 Word check

This activity reinforces some of the expressions from the reading task. Ask students to work on their own and then compare their answers with a partner. They should then find similar expressions in the reading text. Encourage them to record those they want to remember in their notebooks.

Answers

1. on 2. in the middle of the 3. line 4. hung
5. dialled 6. swapped

Here are some additional questions you could ask:
What could you say if you can't hear someone on the other end of the line? (Could you speak up? Can I call you back? I can't hear you.)

What could you say in English if someone called you by mistake? (Sorry. You've got the wrong number; Sorry. There's no-one here by that name.)

What else could people in the class swap? (places, books, papers)

6 Writing

Ask students to work on the writing task in a group. Then get them to share their ideas with another group. As an alternative or follow-up, ask students to write one of the following conversations: between Jiang and his girlfriend when he next calls her; between Emilie and the guy when they went out together; one of the stupid conversations the guy on the train had on his mobile. Students can then act out the conversations for another group.

7 Using vocabulary: adjectives ending with *-ed* or *-ing*

This is often a confusing area of English. Although it is good to know the rules for when we use the two forms, encourage students to learn and record examples of these adjectives in larger chunks. Start off by asking them to remember Jiang's story. Then write the following on the board and ask students in pairs to discuss how to complete them:
It was really embarrass…
I was so embarrass…

Go through the explanation in the Coursebook. Explain that usually the *-ed* form describes how we feel, whereas the *-ing* form describes what causes us to feel that way. You might want to reinforce this by writing the following on the board and asking students in pairs to complete them:
Rebecca was really annoy… with the guy on the train.
The guy on the train was really annoy… .

Then go through the next four examples. Explain that if something is *shocking*, it surprises or upsets you very much. Ask students to complete the sentences **1–8** and then compare their answers with a partner. Here are some questions to ask as you go through the answers:
What do you think the talk was about? (e.g. *accountancy, Europe's greatest roundabouts*)

Why do you think the person's excited about going to San Francisco? (e.g. *It's a lively city, She's never been abroad before.*)

Why might the person in **4** *be annoyed?* (e.g. *He kept calling her 'Shirley' when her name is really Claire.*)

What do you think the person in **6** *is describing?* (e.g. *being in a plane making an emergency landing*)

Why might the guy in **7** *be very interesting? What does he do?* (e.g. *He's a bodyguard for famous people.*)

What do you think the situation in **8** *might be?* (e.g. *in a police station after the person's passport was stolen*)

Answers

1. boring 2. excited 3. interested 4. annoyed
5. exciting 6. frightening 7. interesting
8. annoying

For extra practice, get students to test each other in pairs. One person reads the sentences but says *blank* for the missing word. Their partner, with their Coursebook closed, says the completed expression.

Finish up by discussing the three questions as a class or in small groups. You may want to lead in by telling students a personal story first. While students are talking, you could feed in some more questions. For example:
What is the most exciting place you've ever visited? Why? What did you do?

Who's the most interesting person you've ever met?

Is there anything you're really excited about?

Later, you could revise some of the language by writing one column of five sentence starters and one column of five endings on the board. Students then have to match them up. For example:
Column 1:
I heard some shocking …

I had a tiring ...
I've just heard an interesting ...
She's got a really annoying ...
That was one of the most frightening ...
Column 2:
story.
news.
habit.
films.
day.

You could also write sentence starters and endings on slips of paper, one for each student. Give each student a slip of paper and then ask them to find their matching partner.

Listening

1 Using grammar: reporting what people say

Students may have learned some 'rules' of reported speech, such as changing the tense of the verb, changing *here* to *there* etc. However, there are often times when we report what someone has said with different patterns. In this activity students practise different patterns with *tell.*

Introduce this activity by asking students to memorise and then role-play Paola and Jenny's conversation. Then go through the explanation and examples in the Coursebook. Tell students to underline each of the patterns:
told me to say ...
told me to tell you ...
told me to ask you if ...
was telling me about ...

Explain that we often use *tell* with a person (i.e. *told me* and *tell you*), and that we use *if* with *ask* when reporting a yes/no question. Also, explain that we use *was telling me about* when the person talked in more detail. Ask students to think about the difference between *he was telling me about your new car* with *he told me you got a new car.* Then ask students to complete the sentences with correct forms of the verbs.

Answers

1. tell 2. tell 3. ask 4. say 5. telling 6. say 7. ask 8. telling 9. say 10. tell 11. telling 12. telling

Finish up by referring students to G29 of the **Grammar commentary** on page 169, which they can read either in class or as homework.

2 Pronunciation

Play the recording and ask students first to just listen for which words are stressed. Then play it again so they can mark the stressed words. Ask them to compare their answers with the tapescript on page 160, or just play the recording one more time, pausing after each sentence and getting students to repeat it.

3 Practice

Ask students what Paola will say to Fernanda (*Jenny told me to say hi*). Then explain the task. Get students to complete the conversations and then compare their answers with a partner. Point out that we often use *by the way* when we want to start a different topic of conversation. For **2**, you could also teach the expression *... told me to wish you luck.*

Answers

1. me to say
2. me to say
3. me (that) you're going
4. me to tell you
5. me to ask you if you could

Ask students to practise reading the conversations in pairs. You could then do some extra practice by writing a list of expressions on several slips of paper. For example:
thanks for the party
don't forget to bring that CD

Then get students to form a big circle. Join the circle. Give the student on your left a slip of paper. They should report the expression on the paper to the person on their left. For example:
Alan told me to say thanks for the party.

They then pass on the slip to this person, who in turn, reports to the person on their left and so on. Keep feeding in slips to the student on your left until the whole circle is involved. When the slips return to you, take them out of circulation. Finish when the last slip gets back to you.

4 Further practice

Use the photos to introduce this activity. Ask students to tell you what they see and ask if anyone has ever gone to hospital in an ambulance or won a prize. Then explain the task. Ask students to sit down with a partner and tell them something interesting. Then ask them to get up and tell other students what they were told. Write some responses on the board to help the conversation. For example:
Really? That sounds interesting/terrible.
Really? I can't believe it.

5 While you listen

Explain the task and then read the choices for each of the conversations. Play the recording and ask students to compare their answers with a partner. Play the recording again if necessary.

Answers

1. b. 2. c. 3. b. 4. c.

Then play the recording again while students follow the tapescript on page 160. As they listen, ask them to underline any expressions they are interested in or want to ask about. You might want to draw students' attention to the following responses:

what a shame

that's terrible

what a pain

Wow! That's amazing!

You may need to explain the following:

- *Straight* means *directly*. For example: *When I get paid, I put half of my money straight into my savings account.*
- If you *don't bother* doing something, you don't do it because it is too much trouble. For example: *Don't bother ringing me when you get in. I'll be asleep, anyway.*
- *Tesco's* is a British supermarket chain.
- *Fourth Generation* refers to the fourth major advance in a product.

You could also follow up with some discussion questions. For example:

Have you ever turned up so late your friends had already left?

How long would you normally wait for a friend?

Would you ever buy a mobile phone like Takashi's?

6 Vocabulary focus

When students have completed the collocations, ask them, in pairs, to use them to remember what happened in the conversations. Then follow up by asking them some extra questions to discuss in pairs. For example:

Think of two reasons why you might have to contact someone.

Think of two different ways to complete this expression 'I tried calling her but … '.

Do you usually try to sort out problems straightaway?

Where do you normally leave your mobile or your keys when you are at home?

What are two more verbs we can use with photos? (develop, enlarge)

What other things do we need to recharge batteries for? (a laptop, a car)

What are two more things you can miss? (my flight, my family)

Answers

a. contact (Conversation 2)
b. try (Conversation 3)
c. sort out (Conversation 4)
d. leave (Conversation 2)
e. take (Conversation 4)
f. recharge (Conversation 1)
g. go (Conversation 3)
h. miss (Conversation 1)

7 Speaking: talking about crimes

Ask students if they can remember what happened to Kenny's phone. They can then tell each other. Then point out the two patterns:

have something + past participle

somebody tried to …

Ask which pattern is used to say something was actually stolen. Go through the list of crimes, explaining any vocabulary as students tick any that have happened to them. Then ask them to tell a partner. You may want to get them to tell the story again to another partner. Explain that repeating it in this way improves their telling of their story.

Follow-up

Ask students in pairs to choose one of the situations from **7 Speaking: talking about crimes**. They should write a telephone conversation between the person and the police, a friend or a relative. Encourage them to look back through the unit to find language they want to use. Then ask them to practise the conversation in pairs. Finally, they can act it out for another pair.

Review: Units 13-16

Most of these exercises should be done in pairs or small groups.

1 Act or draw

Get students to read through the list individually first. Then ask them in turns to draw or act out the five words or expressions they have chosen. Next, they should ask their partner about any of the words or expressions they are not sure of.

2 Tenses

Answers

1. I travelled
2. I'm actually going
3. I change, I'll call you
4. I can finish it, arrive
5. I translate
6. has been delayed
7. is being decorated
8. She's normally here

3 Grammar

Answers

1. not, as
2. be, is, ago
3. say
4. such
5. like, everything
6. hardly, sounds
7. had, a
8. there/in, out, 'll

4 Questions and answers

Answers

1. d. 2. a. 3. e. 4. c. 5. b. 6. g. 7. f. 8. j.
9. h. 10. i.

5 What can you remember?

When students have finished working in groups of four, invite a few students to tell you what they remember.

6 Verb collocations

Answers

1. answer 2. have 3. lock 4. look out over
5. complain 6. miss 7. take 8. watch
9. sit 10. stay

Examples of other collocations:

1. (answer) the door
2. (have) a headache
3. (lock) the windows
4. (look out over) the lake
5. (complain) about the noise
6. (miss) my family
7. (take) the train
8. (watch) the news
9. (sit) at the back
10. (stay) in bed

7 Look back and check

Ask students to choose one of the activities. You could then get them to do the other one on another day.

8 Expressions

Answers

1. miles
2. mean
3. seconds
4. shame
5. ask
6. told
7. hand
8. jealous
9. same
10. went

9 Vocabulary quiz

Answers

1. Boats.
2. Your hair.
3. Being in the sun.
4. Because they're old or dangerous.
5. No.
6. One.
7. Your name, the card number, the expiry date.
8. Stay at home.
9. About a film, a book, a play, an album, a concert/performance.
10. Recharge the batteries.
11. In your home. When you go out.
12. He/She writes books.
13. Buy tickets.
14. Possible answers: A film, a ride at a park.
15. Possible answers: To get higher wages, to protest against losing their jobs.
16. Yes.

Pronunciation

1 Contrastive stress

Answers

1. tomorrow
2. eleven
3. the main exit
4. foot
5. train

2 Vowel sounds

Model and practise the sounds. Ask students if they can hear the difference. Point out that some of them are long vowels.

Answers

1. visa
2. pollution
3. worst
4. harbour
5. morning
6. passport
7. the train journey
8. she teaches Greek
9. use your computer
10. boring sports course

3 Problem sounds: /b/ and /v/, /t/ and /θ/

Model and practise the sounds. Ask students if they can hear the difference. Then model the expressions before asking students to practise saying them.

17 Accidents

Unit overview

General topic
Talking about accidents, apologising.

Conversation
Ruth helps David, who has just fallen.

Reading
Six people describe an accident that happened to them.

Listening
Two conversations involving accidents.

Language input
- Expressions for talking about health problems: *have it X-rayed, it might need stitches.*
- Expressions for describing accidents: *I tripped, I hit my head.*
- Past continuous and past simple: *I was running back outside and I tripped on a step.*
- Expressions for apologising for accidents: *I'm really sorry, I can be so clumsy sometimes.*
- Offers with *I'll* and *Let me*: *I'll pay to have it cleaned, Let me get a cloth.*

Language strip

You can use the language strip as a way to lead in to the unit. Ask students to quickly look through the strip and find any expressions they could say or could once have said about themselves. For example, perhaps once they had to have stitches. Explain that in this unit they will practise ways of talking about accidents. Encourage them to choose a couple of expressions in the strip that look interesting and to find out more about them.

You might need to explain some of the following expressions:
- If you say *You should have that looked at*, you are advising someone to go and see a nurse or doctor to check for injury or some other problem. For example: *You should have that looked at. It looks very red.*
- If part of your body is *bruised*, it has a mark on it because you hit or knocked it. For example: *What happened? Your leg's all bruised.*
- If you *have to have stitches*, you have a bad cut that needs to be sewn together. For example: *That looks bad. I think you'll have to have stitches.*
- If you *have fillings*, you had small holes in your teeth and they needed to be filled. For example: *I had to have a filling every time I went to the dentist's when I was a kid.*
- If you *have a scar*, you have a mark on your skin where you were once injured. For example: *You'll recognise him. He's got a scar on his cheek.*
- If you are *clumsy*, you aren't very careful and you often break things. For example: *He's so clumsy. I never let him help in the kitchen.*
- If you say *Let me call you a taxi*, you are offering to phone for a taxi for the other person.

Remind students to record any of the expressions they like in their notebooks and to take note when they see similar expressions throughout the unit.

Use the language strip later on in this unit for a small group task. Here are some possibilities:
- Students find those expressions that are probably said by the person who had the accident (e.g. *I fell off a horse*) and those that are probably said by the person they are talking to (e.g. *Can you bend it at all?*).
- Students discuss what *it* or *that* might refer to in several of the expressions.
- Students find the expressions that contain common verbs like *give, have, put, fall, call*. Later, write the expressions on the board but gap out the verb. Ask students in pairs to complete the expressions.

Lead in

One way to lead in is to write *accident* on the board. Tell students that two common adjective collocations for this noun are *serious* and *minor*. Ask students in pairs to think of three examples of *serious accidents* and three examples of *minor accidents*. Then get them to share their suggestions. Reformulate any if necessary. You could also ask students if they have heard or seen any other collocations or expressions with *accident*. For example:
by accident
a traffic accident
have an accident
it was an accident

Then go on to **1 Talking about what's wrong with you**.

Conversation

1 Talking about what's wrong with you

If possible introduce this activity by telling students about a time when you – or someone you know – saw an accident. Encourage them to ask you questions. Then get them to tell their own story in pairs or small groups. Invite a couple of students to share their story with the rest of the class.

Focus students' attention on the picture and tell them to cover the conversation. Ask a series of questions to elicit some ideas for when students make up the conversation. For example:
What has just happened? (Elicit *He's just fallen down the steps.*)
Why do you think he fell down the steps?
How does the man feel?
What's the woman doing?
What do you think she's going to do next?

Then ask pairs of students to have the conversation they think the man and the woman are having.

Explain that you are going to play the actual conversation. Tell students to keep the text covered. Ask them to just listen to see if their conversation was similar to the one on the recording. Then explain the completion task. Play the recording again and ask students to try to fill in each of the gaps as they listen. They should then compare their answers with a partner. Play the recording a third time, but this time pause after each gap. Elicit the missing words and maybe write the complete expression on the board. Model the pronunciation and get students to practise saying it. Play the recording through one more time with students following the completed script.

Answers

1. are you all right 2. Are you sure 3. stand up all right 4. Maybe you should 5. It might be 6. have it X-rayed 7. get you a cab 8. appreciate it

Ask students to read the completed conversation in pairs. Then ask them to underline any expressions they want to remember. Encourage them to transfer these into their notebooks. You may need to explain the following expressions:

- If you have a *nasty fall* or *bite*, it looks bad and might be serious.
- If you *trip*, you hit your foot on something and fall or nearly fall.
- We often say *I appreciate it* when someone has offered to do something for us. For example:
  A: Can I give you a hand tidying up?
  B: Yes, thanks. I appreciate it.

2 Grammar questions

The first questions focus on two modal auxiliaries from the conversation. When students have found the two expressions, write the following pattern on the board:
You should … . It might be … .

Elicit a way to complete the pattern. For example:
You should see a nurse. It might be infected.

Practise the pronunciation with the class. Then ask students in pairs to think of two more examples. Get them to practise saying their examples. You could also point out the related expression *It's probably just …* .

Answers

a. you should b. it might be

Ask students about the expression *should have it X-rayed.* You might need to teach them *technician* or *radiologist* to help them answer the question. Get them to tell you what part of speech *X-rayed* is (a past participle). Remind them that the passive uses the past participle too. Explain that we use expressions like this when we want someone to do something for us. We don't need to mention who the person is because it is obvious who they are, or it is not relevant. Give students some more examples:
I'm having my hair cut.
I've just had my ears pierced.
You should have your tyres checked before you leave.

3 Using vocabulary: health problems

This activity focuses on useful vocabulary for describing health problems. Ask students to look at the photos on page 120 and get them to do the matching activity. Ask a few follow-up questions as you check their answers. For example:
Has anyone had stitches before? What happened? How many did you have? Do you still have a scar?
When do we use bandages? What's the difference between a bandage and a plaster?
What do we put cream on?
What are some things that can give you a rash?
What should you do if you have a rash?
What happens before you have a filling? What can't you do after you have a filling? When was the last time you had a filling?
Why do people have X-rays?

Answers

1. B 2. A 3. D 4. F 5. C 6. E

4 Practice

This activity gives students contexts for the vocabulary from **3 Using vocabulary: health problems**. Encourage students to record the expressions they want to remember in their notebooks. Remind them to record complete expressions, not just single words. Go through the choices in the box, explaining that *checked out* is similar to *looked at,* but we might use it when it might not be possible to tell if something is OK just by looking at it. For example, it is not usually possible to tell if someone has a temperature just by looking at them. Then ask students to complete the conversations individually before comparing their answers with a partner.

Answers

1. have it looked at, stitches, a bandage
2. have it X-rayed, broken, bruised
3. have it looked at, filling, an appointment
4. have it looked at, red, cream
5. have a check-up, nothing, worrying

Ask students to practise reading the conversations in pairs. Point out the following useful expressions and write them on the board:

Are you all right?
Maybe you should ...
It might need/be ...
You might need to ...
I just need to ...
No, it'll be all right. It's probably just ...
Yes, maybe you're right.

Ask students what tense B uses a lot (the present perfect). Explain that we often use this tense when we want to explain why we are not all right. Get students to memorise the suggestions. Then they can take it in turns asking each other if they are all right. As an alternative write some problems – or draw pictures representing the problems – on slips of paper. Give each student a slip and ask them to go around the class asking other people *Are you all right?* They can use the problem on their slip to answer. They then exchange slips and have a new conversation about the new problem with another student.

5 Vocabulary: describing accidents

You could draw a picture on the board of someone slipping on a banana skin. Then ask *What happened?* to elicit *She slipped on a banana skin.* Rub out the banana skin and ask students to tell you what else can cause people to slip. You will probably get suggestions like *ice, water, a polished floor.* Then focus students' attention on the box. Explain that they will see different collocations for these common verbs. Ask them to work on this task individually and then compare their answers with a partner. As you go through the answers, explain any vocabulary if necessary.

Answers

1. slipped 2. fell over 3. hit 4. broke 5. tripped
6. had it 7. cut 8. put 9. fell off 10. got bitten

Tell students to spend two minutes looking back at the collocations. They can then test each other in pairs. One person reads the list of collocations and the other tries to remember the verb. For extra practice ask students to choose four different expressions and have conversations like the ones in **4 Practice**. For example:

A: *Are you all right? What happened?*
B: *I've just got bitten by a dog.*
A: *Oh no. You should go straight to the hospital and have it looked at. I think you'll need to have stitches and an injection.*
B: *Oh right. I probably should.*

6 Vocabulary: in hospital

Ask the class if anyone has ever had an accident like falling down stairs or banging their head, and had to go to the doctor's. If they have, ask them to remember what questions they were asked. If they haven't, ask them to guess what questions a doctor might ask. Then explain the reordering task. As you go through the answers, practise the pronunciation of the questions, paying attention to the stress and intonation. Explain that we often use *at all* at the end of questions for emphasis – to ask if there is any possibility that what we are asking is indeed the case.

Answers

1. What seems to be the problem?
2. How did it happen?
3. Does this hurt at all?
4. Can you stand up?
5. Can you lift your arm?
6. Can you bend it at all?
7. Did you hit your head at all?

Finish up by asking students to role-play the conversation between David in **1 Talking about what's wrong with you**, and a doctor. Alternatively, they can choose one of the other problems from **4 Practice** or **5 Vocabulary: describing accidents**. Write some useful answers to some of the doctor's questions on the board. For example:

It hurts a lot.
Yes, but it's painful.
Yes, a little, but it hurts.
Yes, but it's a little sore.

Reading

1 Before you read

Focus students' attention on the photos on page 122. Ask them what each place is (*a club, a rugby pitch, the seaside, steps, a swimming pool, a road which slopes*). Ask them why each place could be dangerous. For example:
There're lots of people.
There's deep water.
There's a steep slope.

Then get pairs of students to discuss examples of accidents that could happen in each place. Invite them to tell you their suggestions and reformulate their responses, feeding in appropriate vocabulary. For example:
You could drown.
You could knock yourself out.
You could get electrocuted.
You could get crushed.

2 While you read (It really hurt!)

Ask students to read the six stories to see if any of their guesses were right. Alternatively, use this as a listening task first. Play the recording while students listen with the text covered. Then they read the article. You can play the recording again as they read along. You could also do this as a jigsaw activity. Divide the class into groups of three. Each person reads two stories. They then tell the other members of the group what happened. You may need to explain the following:

- If someone is *showing off*, they are trying to impress other people by showing that they can do something. It is often a negative expression.
- A *wound* is a usually a serious injury where your skin is broken and there is a deep cut or hole. Ask students what could cause wounds (*a gun, a knife, something sharp*).

3 Comprehension

Go through the choices, explaining any vocabulary if necessary. Ask students which choice indicates the worst accident (*sound really nasty*) and which the least serious (*don't sound that bad*). Remind them that *that* can mean *very*. Let them think about the stories and then get them in small groups or pairs to tell each other what they think. Encourage them to explain why they think so.

Answers

Probable answers:
Chris's sounds really nasty, Zeynep's was probably just bad luck, and Barney's was really stupid.

4 Word check

This activity focuses on several expressions from the reading task. Ask students to complete as many as they can on their own before comparing their answers with a partner. They should then look back at the reading text to check if they are right. As you go through the answers, model and practise the pronunciation of the expressions. Students may have difficulties with some endings (e.g. *slipped* and *tripped*) or with individual words (e.g. *injection* and *stitches*).

Answers

1. blood 2. slipped 3. hurt 4. tripped 5. stitches, scar 6. screaming 7. injection

Get students in pairs or small groups to discuss the three questions at the end. You could also ask them to think of three different things you need an injection for. Then invite them to share their ideas with the class. Here are some possibilities:
You could slip on a banana skin, some mud or some water.
You could trip over a cable, someone's leg, a tree root.
You can hurt your back falling down, doing exercise, just bending over.
You sometimes need an injection when you have a filling, a vaccination, or an operation.

Finish up by asking students who had the funniest or most unusual thing.

5 Using grammar: past simple and past continuous

Choose an example of the past simple with the past continuous from the reading text and write it on the board, but gap out some parts. For example:
I … dancing and … a great time, but then I … over on a drink.

Ask students to complete the missing words. Then ask them to find two similar patterns (*was* + *-ing* and past simple) from the reading text. Go through the explanation in the text and then ask students the two questions.

Answers

1. The running started first.
2. The running lasted longer.

Explain that we often use the past continuous in a story to provide the background – what was happening at the time – and the past simple for the action we want to focus on – in this case the accident. We choose the continuous form because we want to show that the action was in progress and that it was interrupted by the action in the past simple. You could represent this visually on the board with a line and a cross. For example:

Ask students to do the matching task. As you go through the answers, ask a few follow-up questions. For example:

*Why do you think the person in **1** was drilling a hole? (to put a picture up)*

What sometimes happens when you cut onions? (you cry)

*Where was the light in **3**? (on the ceiling)*

What could you do if you knocked three teeth out? (get some false teeth)

What are you doing if you 'mess about with' something? (playing with it, not using it for what it's normally used for)

*What other words could you replace 'coffee' with in **6**? (tea, soup)*

Answers

1. e. 2. d. 3. c. 4. f. 5. b. 6. a.

6 Practice

This activity reinforces the form of the past simple and past continuous while also giving students some good examples of collocations like *banged my head, was cleaning the windows.*

Ask students to complete the sentences on their own and then compare their answers with a partner. Go through the answers. Point out that the time expression *the other day* is often used with the past continuous to give the background to a story. You may need to explain the following:

- If something *goes* a colour, it becomes that colour. For example: *Some people go red when they're embarrassed.*
- We can use the word *nail* for the thing we hammer into something and also for the part of our body at the end of our fingers and toes.

Answers

1. was crossing, tripped, banged, got
2. was pouring, knocked, went, burnt
3. was driving, ran, hit, killed, was
4. was cleaning, fell, hurt
5. was fixing, banged, hurt, went

Ask students to read through the five situations again. Then write the following key words on the board:

1. road, tripped, pavement, head
2. tea, arm, hand
3. home, dog, awful
4. windows, ladder, back
5. floor, hammer, nail

Ask students to close their Coursebooks and in pairs try to retell the stories using the key words. You may want to do the first one together as an example. Students can then do the same for the six stories in the reading text by just using the photos on page 122. Finish up by referring students to G30 of the **Grammar commentary** on page 169, which they can read either in class or as homework.

7 Free practice

Introduce this activity by telling students about an accident that happened to you – or someone you know. Before telling it, explain and model the examples of responses. Encourage students to use some of these as you tell the story. Then give them enough time to prepare their own stories and go around helping with vocabulary. Students can either tell their stories in pairs or small groups, or wander around telling different people.

Listening

1 Apologising

Explain that we can use *accident* to describe when someone gets hurt, and that we also use it to describe a mistake when something gets broken or damaged. Remind students of the expression *by accident.* Point out the photo on page 124. Tell students that what they see is an example of an *accident.* Ask students what you usually do if you break or damage something accidentally to elicit *you apologise.* Explain that when we apologise, we often explain why something happened or offer to do something. Then explain the matching task.

Ask students to work on this on their own or in pairs. As you go through the answers, model the pronunciation and check students' understanding by asking questions. For example:

What does 'it' / 'one' refer to?
Where do you think they are?
What do you think has just happened?

Answers

A: 1., 5., 6., 7., 10., (11.,) 12., 14., 15.
B: 2., 3., 4., 8., 9., (11.,) 13., 16.

It was an accident could be said by either person, depending on the intonation.

2 While you listen

Explain the task and play the recording. Ask students to compare their answers with a partner. Then play the recording again so they can check.

Answers

Conversation 1

I'm really sorry.
I don't know what I was doing.
It just slipped from my (fingers).
I'm afraid you'll have to pay for it.
It was an accident!
Forget about it.
Don't worry about it!
It was partly my fault.

Conversation 2

Let me get a cloth.
Don't worry about it!
I'll pay to get it cleaned.
Don't be silly! It's fine.
Forget about it.
I can be so clumsy sometimes.
Don't worry about it!
I'm really sorry.

3 Comprehension

Explain the task and let students work through it on their own. You may want to read both reports aloud as students listen and read. Then ask students to compare their answers with a partner. Play the recording again or play the recording while students read the tapescript so they can check their answers.

Answers

Conversation 1

We went to look for a present for Anna's birthday.
I picked up a vase and it slipped through my fingers.
The vase cost £80.
The shop assistant made me buy it.
The shop assistant wasn't very nice about it.
Jenny offered to pay half.

Report 2

I spilt wine.
It was quite an old dress.
There were just a couple of spots.
Lisa was OK about it.
I offered to pay to have it cleaned but she said it would just come out in the wash.

4 Speaking

This activity gives students a chance to share their reactions to the conversations. Go through the list of choices, explaining any vocabulary if necessary. Point out that in **2. c.**, you would just pretend that the jumper was old. Ask students to discuss in pairs or small groups. Then as a class go through each choice and ask how many students chose it. Finish up by getting students to discuss the remaining questions. Explain the following:

- If we *bump into* someone, we accidentally knock into them.
- If we *get rid of a stain,* we make the stain go away.

Write some expressions on the board to help with the last question. For example:
(White wine) gets rid of (red wine) stains.
You can use (white wine) on (red wine) stains.
There's something called … , which is good for stains.

5 Role play

Explain the task and go through the six situations. Answers will vary, but some obviously refer to a specific situation. For example:

1. I'm afraid you'll have to pay for it.
2. Let me get a cloth.
5. It's OK. I need to get a new one anyway.
6. I'll pay to get it cleaned.

Ask students to work with a new partner for the role play. Finish up by inviting a few pairs of students to act out their role play for the rest of the class. For a slight variation ask them to do a few role plays where one of the people isn't very nice about the accident. You could teach the expressions *you shouldn't (have).* For example:
You shouldn't drink red wine and wear a white shirt.
You shouldn't have left your glasses on the sofa.

6 Using grammar: *will*

Students may think we just use *will* when we want to talk about the future. Explain, however, that we often use *will* to show we are happy or willing to do something, and so we often use it to make offers. Ask students to find an example in **1 Apologising** on page 124 (*I'll pay to get it cleaned*).

Ask students to complete the offers and then play the recording so they can check their answers. Pause before each expression and invite a student to tell you their answer. Then play the expression. Get students to repeat it, making sure they use the reduced form. Explain that we often use *I'll have a look* to mean we will check something to make sure it is working, or to see what is wrong with it.

Answers

1. call 2. show 3. help 4. have 5. carry
6. show 7. clean 8. save 9. pay 10. ask

Finish up by referring students to G31 of the **Grammar commentary** on page 170, which they can read either in class or as homework.

7 Speaking

This activity helps students see how the expressions can be used. You could either ask students to do this in pairs or together as a class. The ones that you could use in class are:

I'll show you where to go.
I'll help you move it, if you like.
I'll take a look.
I'll show you how to do it, if you like.
I'll save you a seat.

8 Practice

Ask students to write their examples and go around helping and checking. For extra practice, get them to work in pairs and write six three-line mini conversations based on the expressions. For example:

A: *My flight leaves at 7:00 in the morning.*
B: *I'll give you a lift, if you want.*
A: *Really? Are you sure? We'll probably have to leave at 4:30.*

Talk about **Real English: Let me**. Model the pronunciation of the examples and get students to practise them. Explain that we often use the reduced pronunciation /ˈlemiː/. However, we sometimes stress *me*. For example, we might say *Let ME pay*, stressing the *me*. Explain that we might use *Let me* to offer to help someone off with their coat or to open the door.

9 Further practice

Ask students to work on this on their own or in pairs. As you go through the answers, get them to tell you a couple of situations when you might use the phrase *Let me*.

Answers

Let me could replace *I'll* in 2., 3., 5., 6., 7., 9. and 11.

Ask students to practise these offers in pairs. Explain that we use *I can manage* when we think we can do something difficult ourselves. For example:

A: *I'll help you clean up, if you like.*
B: *No, it's OK. I think I can manage. It's not that dirty.*

Follow-up

Write *The unluckiest day of my life* on the board. Ask students if they ever have days when everything seems to go wrong. Ask them to imagine they once had a very unlucky day. In pairs, they should make up a story about that day. Give them time to go back through the unit finding helpful language. You could ask them to write their story and then ask them to read each other's. Alternatively, they could just go around the class and tell it to different people. In either case, give them a starter. For example:

I'll never forget April 13th. It was the unluckiest day of my life. It all started in the morning. I was …

Finish up by asking who had the best story.

18 Problems

Unit overview

General topic
Explaining and sorting out problems.

Conversation
Tony tells Adriana that he's lost his passport.

Reading
Joining the wrong queue.

Listening
Three conversations about problems with machines.

Language input
- Expressions for sorting out problems: *I've had my bag stolen, so I need to report it to the police and cancel all my credit cards.*
- Present perfect questions to make suggestions: *Have you tried changing the batteries? Have you been back there to see if anyone's handed it in?*
- Expressions with *sort out*: *It'll sort itself out, I need to sort out some papers.*
- Expressions with *must*: *Listen, I must go or I'll be late.*
- Expressions for describing problems with machines: *It's making a funny noise, The photocopier has broken down again.*

Language strip

You can use the language strip as a way to lead in to the unit. Explain to students that in this unit they will practise ways of talking about problems. Ask them to quickly look through the strip and find expressions that could be said about a problem (e.g. *I've got a problem with my landlord, I need to get it fixed*). Encourage students to choose a couple of expressions in the strip that look interesting and to find out more about them.

You might need to explain some of the following expressions:
- A *landlord* is the person who owns the flat or house that you are renting.
- If you say a problem *will sort itself out*, you think the problem will be solved or go away by itself. For example: *Don't worry about that problem at work. It'll sort itself out eventually.*
- If something *makes a funny noise*, there is a strange noise coming from it. For example:
  A: My computer's making this funny squeaking noise.
  B: It's probably the mouse.
- If you lose your credit or bank cards, you need to *cancel them* so no-one can use them.
- If something or someone is a *pain*, it or they are really annoying. For example: *It's a real pain visiting my in-laws every month. They live miles away. We waste most of the weekend just trying to get there.*
- If you *sort out some things for something*, you get things ready for something later. For example: *I'll see you downstairs. I've just got to sort some things out for class tomorrow.*
- If you *jump the queue*, you go ahead of people who are waiting in front of you in the queue. For example: *They always let the tourists jump the queue.*
- If you *save a place for someone in the queue*, you let them rejoin their original position in the queue after they leave for a short time. For example: *Can you save my place in the queue? I'm just going to the toilet.*
- *A cashpoint* is an automatic machine where you can get money out of or put money into your bank account. For example: *Is there a cashpoint around here? I've only got a couple of euros.*
- You might say *Oh well, never mind* when you think something is not important enough to worry about. For example:
  A: I'm afraid I've broken your torch.
  B: Oh well, never mind. It was only a cheap one. I've got two more at home.
- If something is *leaking*, liquid is coming out of it. For example: *Look at your shirt. I think your pen's leaking.*

Remind students to record any of the expressions they like in their notebooks and to take note when they see similar expressions throughout the unit.

Use the language strip later on in this unit for a small group task. Here are some possibilities:
- Students find those expressions with a verb in the present perfect (e.g. *Have you cancelled your cards?*) and those with a verb in the past simple (e.g. *He jumped the queue!*).
- Students discuss what *it* might refer to in several of the expressions (e.g. *I need to get it fixed*).

Lead in

Start by thinking of a problem, for example, your coffee maker is broken. Write the word *problem* on the board. Then write the following collocations around it:
a big problem
a serious problem
I've got a problem with my …
sort out the problem

Tell students that you have a problem and they should try and guess what the problem is by asking you *yes/no* questions, using some of the collocations on the board. For example:

S: *Is it a big problem?*

T: *Well, it's a big problem for me.*

S: *Have you got a problem with a part of your body?*

T: *No.*

S: *Is it easy to sort out this problem?*

T: *Yes, I just need to buy a replacement.*

S: *So it's a problem with some kind of machine?*

Let students keep on asking you until they guess. Give hints if necessary. For example: *It's a problem with something in the kitchen. I can't have something in the morning because of it.*

Conversation

1 Speaking

Focus students' attention on the words in the box. Ask what these objects are. Ask students in pairs to think of at least two problems you could have with each object. Encourage them to use their dictionaries if necessary. After a couple of minutes, ask them to tell you their suggestions. Write them on the board and reformulate any if necessary. This is a chance for you to teach or revise vocabulary like *the strap's broken, it's been rejected, it's expired, there's no sound* etc. Finish up by getting students to discuss the questions at the end in pairs. If they have never had a problem with any of these things, ask them to talk about something similar, like a TV, computer or a driving licence. Tell them to start like this: *I once had a problem with my …*

2 Using vocabulary: sorting out problems

If you haven't done so already, explain that when we *sort out problems,* we solve them. As an example, ask students how they would sort out one of the problems they suggested in **1 Speaking**. For example: *What would you do if your passport was stolen?*

Then get students to do the matching task on their own and compare their answers with a partner. Here are some questions to ask as you go through the answers:

What else could you report to the police? (someone following you, a suspicious bag)

What's the opposite of 'get some money out'? (put some money in)

In **4** *do you think the person will have to buy a new one? Why not? (It's still under guarantee.)*

What kind of things do you think the guy in **6** *is doing? (saying bad things about people, being unhelpful)*

Answers

1. e. 2. a. 3. b. 4. f. 5. c. 6. d.

Point out the pattern in the endings: *so I need to … and …* . Model the pronunciation of the completed sentences and ask students to spend a minute memorising the endings. They can then test each other in pairs. One person reads the beginning of the sentence and the other person tries to remember the ending.

3 Problems on holiday

Before explaining the listening task, ask students in pairs to think of three problems you might have on holiday. For example, you might get food poisoning, have your travellers' cheques stolen, get lost etc. Then play the recording. Ask students to listen for the answers to the two questions. Make sure they cover the text before they listen. Then get them to compare their answers in pairs. Remind them to keep the text covered as they do this.

Answers

Tony has lost his passport. He is going to try to get a temporary replacement from the Embassy.

Play the recording again and ask students to try to fill in each of the gaps as they listen. They should then compare their answers with a partner. Play the recording a third time, but this time pause after each gap. Elicit the missing words and maybe write the complete expression on the board. Model the pronunciation and have the class practise saying it. Play the recording through one more time with students following the completed script. You may want to ask students to practise reading the conversation in pairs.

Answers

1. I've lost my passport 2. having it 3. handed it in 4. How annoying 5. I must go 6. sort it all out

Talk about **Real English: It's a real pain**. Ask students to tell you some things they think are a pain. You could explain that we sometimes use it about people too. For example:

A: *How's Kevin doing?*

B: *He's being a real pain at the moment. He just sits in front of the TV all day and never helps me.*

To help with the second task, ask students to look back at the completed conversation and underline any expressions they think they could use. For example:

Oh no!

The last time I remember having it was …

How annoying!

Yes, it's a real pain.

Well, good luck. I hope you sort it all out.

4 Using grammar: present perfect questions

In this activity students see another contextualised use of the present perfect. Introduce it by asking students if they can remember what Adriana suggested when Tony told her about his passport. Ask them to underline the expression in the conversation. Then go through the explanation in the Coursebook and give examples.

Before students do the completion task, you may want to quickly revise the formation of the present perfect. You should explain that many of the verbs in the task have irregular past participles. As you go through the answers, ask students questions to focus on and check their understanding of some of the expressions. For example:

What causes an upset stomach? (eating food that's gone bad, a stomach bug)

What happens to batteries eventually? (they die, they run out)

What can we take for a headache? (aspirin, paracetamol)

What kind of cards do people keep in their wallets? (credit cards, bank cards, name cards) What else do they keep in their wallets? (money, photos, bus passes)

What else can be 'fully booked'? (a train, a flight)

Answers

1. Have you been
2. Have you tried
3. Have you reported
4. Have you taken
5. Have you looked
6. Have you rung up and cancelled
7. Have you talked
8. Have you tried

Get students to match the questions and the answers. You may want to ask some questions to exploit some of the language in the answers. For example:

Think of two other ways of completing this pattern: 'I picked … up from … '. (e.g. him … the airport, some bread … the supermarket)

What other machines could 'play slowly'? (a VCR, a DVD player, a cassette player)

Who else can you make an appointment to see? (a bank manager, a dentist, a hairdresser)

You may need to explain that we sometimes refer to a police station as *the station* and that if something *doesn't have any effect*, it doesn't cause any change in something. For example:

I talked to him about his behaviour, but it had no effect. He's still rude all the time.

Answers

a. 5. b. 2. c. 1. d. 3. e. 8. f. 4. g. 6. h. 7.

5 5 Grammar questions

These questions help students form guidelines on when to use the three forms. If they see examples in context, it is a lot easier for them to understand why we choose the different forms. When students find the examples, make sure they don't confuse a past simple form with a past participle form. Ask them to discuss the three questions with a partner and then go over the answers together as a class. Point out the time expressions that are used with the examples.

Answers

a. Yes, I picked them up from there this morning; Yes, I bought some new ones yesterday; Yes, I had an aspirin earlier; Yes, I did it this morning.
b. Not yet, I'm going to go to the station this afternoon.
c. I'll do it now; Maybe I'll do it after the next class.

1. The past simple is used in the *Yes* answers. It refers to something you did before.
2. *Will* + verb is used when you are making a decision now. The answers begin with *That's/It's a good idea.* This shows that you hadn't thought of it before.
3. *Going to* + verb is used to show you have already decided. The answer starts with *Not yet. Yet* implies that you intend to do it in the future.

Finish up by referring students to G26 of the **Grammar commentary** on page 169, which they can read either in class or as homework.

6 Role play

Read the four conversation starters out loud. Explain that we often use the expressions *I'm finding … (really) difficult* or *I'm finding it (really) difficult to …* when we describe difficulties we are having. You may want to elicit a couple of example suggestions for each problem before students role-play the conversations. For example:

Have you checked in lost property?

Have you seen anyone about it?

Have you talked to the bank about it?

Have you asked the teacher for help?

Explain the task and when students are ready, put them in pairs. One person closes their Coursebook while the other just looks at the conversations **1–8** in **4 Using grammar: present perfect questions.** You might want to do an example with students when they change roles so they can see how to continue the conversation. For example:

S: *I've got an upset stomach. I've had it for a couple of days now.*

T: *Have you been to the doctor about it?*

S: *Not yet, but I've made an appointment for this evening.*

T: *How are you getting there? Do you need a lift?*

S: *Oh thanks. That'd be great. My appointment's at 6:00.*

7 Key word: *sort out*

You may want to find the first one or two expressions together as a class before students work on their own. Then ask them to compare their answers with a partner. Play the recording so they can check their answers. Pause after each expression and get students to repeat it, following the same stress pattern. Ask them to record these expressions – along with a translation – in their notebooks.

Answers

1. Did you sort out your problem with the passport?
2. I need to sort out some papers.
3. I need to sort out my things to take.
4. It'll sort itself out.
5. I need to sort out this dirty washing.
6. I'm trying to sort out my holiday.
7. Have you sorted out a visa?
8. He needs to sort his life out.
9. I'm just going to sort out the house.
10. I still haven't sorted out that problem with my computer.

In expressions 1., 4., 8. and 10. *sort out* means *find an answer to a problem*. In expressions 2., 3., 5., 6., 7. and 9. *sort out* means *organise or tidy things*.

Check students' understanding of these expressions by asking questions. For example:

*What kind of problems could there be in **1, 4, 8** and **10**?*

*In **3**, where is the person going and what things do they need?*

What do you do when you sort out the dirty washing/the house?

What kind of things do you need to sort out for a holiday?

Finish up by asking students to discuss the questions at the end in pairs or as a class.

Reading

1 Speaking

Focus students' attention on the photograph on page 128. Elicit the word *queue* by asking what the people are doing. Then ask questions to give students examples of collocations with *queue*. For example:

What are they queuing up for?

Is it a long queue or a short queue?

Who's at the front of the queue?

Who's at the back of the queue?

Read aloud the four questions in the Coursebook and ask students to discuss in pairs or small groups. You could also feed in some more questions. For example:

What's bad about queuing? Is there anything good about queuing?

What do people queue up for in your country that they don't queue up for in some other countries?

What things do you think people should queue up for, but they don't?

What things do you think people shouldn't have to queue up for, but they do?

What do you do while you're waiting in a queue? Do you ever talk to people?

2 Before you read

Read through the list of collocations and as you do so, ask a few questions to help students think of possible connections with queuing. For example:

Who introduces laws? Why are laws introduced?

In what places do you have to key in your PIN?

Where do you pay cheques into your account?

Where can you usually find cashpoints?

Ask students to spend a minute thinking and then put them in pairs to come up with a possible scenario. Invite a couple of pairs of students to share their ideas with the rest of the class.

3 While you read (The queue)

Ask students to read the article to see how much they guessed correctly. Then read the text aloud or play the recording as students follow along. Alternatively, use it as a listening task first by playing the recording while students listen with the text covered. Then they can read the article. You can play the recording again while they do this. You might want to ask a few quick comprehension questions when they have finished. For example:

Did she miss the bus?

Does she think all queues are fair? Why/Why not?

Does she think all queues are bad?

4 After you read

This activity further checks students' comprehension of the article. Make sure students work with a different partner from the one they worked with in **2 Before you read.** You could also give them a model of how to explain any differences by writing the following on the board:

I thought it was going to be about ... but it was actually about ...

I thought it was going to be (inside a post office) but it was actually (outside a bank).

I thought he was going to (catch the bus) but he actually (missed it).

Answers

get some money out of the cashpoint
catch my bus into town
join a queue
make the right decision
key in your personal identity number
pay some cheques into your account
introduce a new law
save my place in a queue

5 Word check

Ask students to complete as many sentences as they can from memory. Then get them to compare their answers with a partner before they look back at the article to check if they are right. As you go through the answers, ask a few questions to check that they understand the meaning of the expressions. For example:
In what other situations could you say 'Oh well, never mind'? (Someone broke something you don't really care about.)

What can you say when you give someone something of theirs you've just picked up? (Here you are, There you go, You dropped this.)

You say they 'looked at me as if I was an alien' when you act in a way or say something that other people don't think is normal. What are some other situations when you could use this expression?

What are some situations where people are treated 'unequally'?

Answers

1. that 2. mind 3. picked 4. alien 5. equally
6. sale

6 Speaking

Discuss the first question together as a class. Tell students which group you think you belong to and maybe tell them a story to illustrate it. You could also further the discussion by asking if anyone has any strategies for choosing the best queue to join. For example:
In a supermarket I always choose the queue with more men because they've forgotten half of what they need and they never have any coupons for the cashier to worry about.

Then go through the list of groups **1–8** and ask students to write down two more divisions. Get them to discuss the ten divisions either in pairs or small groups. Here are some more examples if students are having difficulty thinking of any or if you want to add a few more:
People who drink tea in the morning and people who drink coffee.
Smokers and non-smokers.
Mac users and PC users.
Vegetarians and meat eaters.

Write some helpful expressions on the board too, especially for students who don't identify with either group. For example:
I've got a (dog) but I actually prefer (cats).
I like both/neither of them.
I belong to neither/both.

Finish up by asking students how many belong to each group.

7 Using grammar: *must*

Ask students if they can remember how Tony let Adriana know that he wanted to finish the conversation. Ask them to find the expression he used on page 126. Then go through the example and explanation in the Coursebook. Explain that we can also use these kinds of expressions even if they are not true. We often use them on the phone too. For example:
Listen, I must go. There's someone at the door.

Ask students to do the matching task. Point out that they should think about collocations when they are answering. For example, ask what things we *miss*. When you have gone through the answers, discuss the last question as a class.

Answers

1. e. 2. f. 3. b. 4. a. 5. g. 6. d. 7. h. 8. c.

As a follow-up, ask pairs of students to think of an alternative ending for **1–5**. For example:
Listen, I must go or I'll be in trouble.

Finish up by referring students to G33 of the **Grammar commentary** on page 170, which they can read either in class or as homework.

8 Pronunciation: *must*

Play the recording once all the way through while students just listen. Then play the recording again, but this time pause after each sentence and ask them to repeat it. For extra practice get them to take turns testing each other in pairs. One person reads the beginnings and their partner tries to remember the endings.

2 Practice

Demonstrate an example with a student first. For example:

S: *Hi, how are you? I haven't seen you for ages.*
T: *Oh hello, Benny. I'm fine. I've been really busy at work, though.*
S: *Oh right. I heard you got promoted.*
T: *That's right. Listen, I must go. I've got lots of work to do this afternoon.*
S: *Oh, OK. It was nice talking to you. Maybe we can go out for a drink sometime?*
T: *Yes, that'd be nice. Give me a ring at the weekend.*

Then ask students to go around having similar conversations with at least four or five other students.

Listening

1 Using vocabulary: machines and technology

Focus students' attention on the photos on page 130 and get them to do the matching task. As you go through the answers, ask a few follow-up questions to build up some associated vocabulary. For example:
What does a (microwave) do?
What can you do with a (palmtop)?
What can go wrong with a (laptop)?

Answers

1. F 2. E 3. A 4. G 5. B 6. D 7. H 8. C

Ask students to complete the sentences individually and then compare their answers with a partner. As you go through the answers, explain that *some food from yesterday* means *some food that was cooked yesterday* (e.g. *yesterday's dinner*). You could also teach some variations on the pattern *it was* + adjective *of* … . For example:
it was nice of (him)
it was really good of (her)
it was really (nasty) of (them)

You can ask follow-up questions focusing on some of the language in the sentences. For example:
What do you do after you wash up the plates? (dry them, leave them to drain)
What do you do after you take the clothes out of the washing machine? (put them in the dryer, hang them up outside)
How much would it cost me to travel from … to … by bus/train?
How much would it cost me to stay in … ?
What is the opposite of 'small and light'? (big and heavy)
What is the opposite of 'really looking forward to it'? (dreading it, really not looking forward to it)

Answers

1. dishwasher 2. washing machine 3. microwave 4. Walkman 5. palmtop 6. laptop 7. DVD player 8. camcorder

For some extra practice ask students in pairs to think of a follow-up comment for each sentence or conversation. For example:
1. *OK. How do you open it?*
2. *How much is that going to cost?*

You might also want to point out the phrasal verbs *wash up* and *heat up*.

2 Speaking

Read through the questions and write the following patterns and expressions on the board:
I haven't got a … but I want to get one.
I've had my … for … months/years.
I've got a (Toshiba).
It's brand new.
I've never had any problems with it.

Then ask students to discuss the questions in pairs or small groups.

3 While you listen

If you haven't done so already, elicit some problems someone might have with each of the things in the photos. Write students' suggestions on the board and reformulate any if necessary. Then play the recording. Ask students to listen if any of the problems were mentioned. When checking what machine each conversation was about, ask which expressions helped them decide. Then ask students in pairs to tell each other how much they can remember. Play the recording one more time as they follow along with the tapescript on page 161. Encourage them to underline any expressions they want to remember or ask about and to record those they want to remember in their notebooks.

Answers

Conversation 1:	A camcorder. The red light doesn't come on and the film comes out looking strange. It probably needs cleaning.
Conversation 2:	A washing machine. It's making a funny noise and it's leaking.
Conversation 3:	A DVD player. It doesn't work at all.

4 Using vocabulary: problems with machines

Ask students to do the completion task individually. As you check their answers, explain that if something *keeps* doing something, it does it often. You could also ask a few follow-up questions. For example:
What could be wrong with the camcorder? (It doesn't record, The film is out of focus.)
What happens when a computer crashes? (It stops working, shuts down or reboots.)
What causes a computer to crash? (usually a software problem)
How can you tell if oil is leaking? (There's oil underneath the car.)
Who is 'they' in **5**? *(the people in charge of the office equipment)*

Answers

1. working properly 2. a funny noise 3. crashing
4. leaking somewhere 5. it fixed

The next task helps students with collocations. As students discuss the questions, go around listening and checking. Then ask them to tell you their suggestions. Encourage them to record any that are new for them in their notebooks.

Answers

Possible answers:
1. a radio, a TV, a tap
2. heat, a radio, music
3. a cup, a teapot, a washing machine
4. a computer, a car, a telephone
5. a toilet, a public phone, a cashpoint
6. a Walkman, a torch, a remote control

5 Role play

Read the expressions aloud as students mark them with C or S. Then check students' understanding of the expressions by asking a few questions. For example:
What is on a receipt? Why do you need one?
If you say, 'Can I leave it with you?' do you want to come back and get it?
How about if you say, 'I'll leave it'? Do you want to keep it?
If you say, 'I can't promise anything', are you certain you'll be able to do it?
If something is still covered by the guarantee, do you need to pay to have it fixed?
If something will be ready by the weekend, can you pick it up on Thursday?

Answers

1. S 2. C 3. C 4. C 5. S 6. S 7. S
8. C 9. S 10. S

Ask students to translate the expressions and, if possible, compare their translations with someone who speaks the same language. Then explain the role play. You could also suggest students read the tapescript of the three conversations on page 161 again. Get them to work in pairs writing out the conversation. Go around and help. Ask them to practise reading their conversation a couple of times. Then ask them to memorise as much of it as they can and role-play the conversation. Finish up by getting two pairs of students together and getting them to act out the role play for each other.

6 Using vocabulary: *I couldn't live without it*

Start off by explaining the expression *I couldn't live without it*. Use the photos on page 130 to ask *Could you live without a (dishwasher)?* Then go through the list of objects in the box. Make sure students know what they are. Ask a few questions. For example:
What do you use a scanner for?
Where would you normally find an electronic personal organiser?

Give students a few minutes to think, and then ask them to share their ideas in small groups. You could finish up with a class discussion on technology by asking some more questions. For example:
Are there any other things not listed in the box that we can't live without?
Do we really need all this technology?
What technology helps you learn English? What technology doesn't help you much?
What do you think is the greatest invention?

Follow-up

Write the following on the board and ask students to complete them with their own ideas.
I'm always having problems with my …
I've never had any problems with my …
I don't want a … . It causes too many problems.
If I have problems, I always try to …
My biggest problem at the moment is …
The biggest problem facing my country is …
… is a serious problem at the moment.
The biggest problem in the world is …

Then get them in small groups to explain their ideas.

19 Money

Unit overview

General topic
Money, banks and comparing prices.

Conversation
Tim has left his wallet at home, so Bob lends him some money.

Reading
Eight things to hate about banks.

Listening
Four conversations about problems with money.

Language input

- Expressions with *money* and *time*: *He doesn't spend much money on me, I spend most of my time watching TV, I think buying CDs and music is a waste of money.*
- Making and responding to offers: *Do you want me to open the window? Would you mind?*
- Useful expressions in banks: *I'd like to open a new account, I'd like to take out a loan.*
- Comparing prices: *Everything is much cheaper in my country than it is here.*
- Expressions with *pay*: *How shall we pay the bill? Can I pay in dollars?*

Language strip

You can use the language strip as a way to lead in to the unit. Ask students to quickly look through the strip and find any expressions they have heard or seen before and any they think they have used before or will use in the future. Explain that in this unit they will practise ways of talking about money. Encourage them to choose a couple of expressions in the strip that look interesting and to find out more about them.

You might need to explain some of the following expressions:

- If you ask someone *Have you got that £10 you owe me?* you are asking them to pay back the £10 that you lent them. For example:
  A: Have you got that £10 you owe me?
  B: Oh yes. Sorry. Here you are.
- You say *Would you mind?* when someone has offered to do something for you and you want to accept their offer, but at the same time, you want to make sure that it is not too much trouble for them. For example:
  A: You can borrow my car if you like.
  B: Would you mind?
  A: Not at all. I trust you.
- If you think something is *a waste of time*, you think it is not worth doing. For example: *Don't go on the guided tour. It's a waste of time.*
- If someone *charges a commission*, they add an extra charge for providing a service. For example: *If you cash those travellers' cheques in that bank over there, they won't charge you a commission.*
- If your job gives you *sick pay*, you are paid even if you are sick and take time off work. For example: *I get three weeks' paid holiday and 20 days sick pay per year.*
- If you are *in debt*, you owe money. For example: *You're always in debt. You really should try and get out of it.*
- If someone is *well off*, they have a lot of money. For example: *I think he's quite well off. He lives in a big house that looks out over the lake.*

Remind students to record any of the expressions they like in their notebooks and to take note when they see similar expressions throughout the unit.

Use the language strip later on in this unit for a small group task. Here are some possibilities:

- Students find those expressions connected with work (e.g. *Do you get any sick pay?*) and those connected with banks (e.g. *Can I change this into dollars, please?*).
- Students find those expressions that are probably said to a friend (e.g. *Have you got that £10 you owe me?*) and those that are probably said to a stranger (e.g. *I'd like to pay this into my account, please).*
- Students discuss what *it*, *some*, or *this* could refer to in several of the expressions.

Lead in

You could use the questions in the first activity to lead in to the topic of money.

Conversation

1 Speaking

In this pre-listening task students practise using some expressions associated with money. Read the four questions aloud and check that students understand the expressions by asking questions. For example:
Who wouldn't lend you money if you asked them, a mean person or a generous one?

Who would probably leave a big tip, a mean person or a generous one?

Why might we need to borrow money from someone?
Where do people save money?

Then get them to ask and answer the questions in groups. You could feed in other questions that practise some money collocations too. For example:
Do you like spending money?
Do you often worry about money?
Do you ever wish you had more money? What would you do with it?
Do you ever give people money on the street?

Students often have problems with *borrow* and *lend,* so talk about **Real English: borrow / lend**. For further practice write the following gapped expressions on the board and ask students which word, *borrow* or *lend,* is missing:
Could I ... a couple of pounds?
You could ... my car if you like.
I'll ... you some money if you like.
Can I ... your stapler for a minute?
Don't ... her any money. You'll never get it back.
I'll ... you my pen if I can ... your dictionary.

2 Borrowing money

Focus students' attention on the picture. Ask what they think is happening and why one of the men looks worried. Then explain the situation of the conversation and ask students to just listen for the answer to the question. Play the recording, making sure they cover the text. Get them to discuss the answers in pairs. Remind them to keep the text covered as they do this. You could also ask a couple of extra comprehension questions. For example:
What is Tim doing at two? (He's meeting someone.)
How much does Bob lend him? (30 euros)
When is Tim going to pay Bob back? (next week)

Answers

Tim needs to borrow money because he has left his wallet at home.

Play the recording again and ask students to try to fill in each of the gaps as they listen. They should then compare their answers with a partner. Play the recording a third time, but this time pause after each gap. Elicit the missing words and maybe write the complete expression on the board. Model the pronunciation and get students to practise saying it. Play the recording through one more time with students following the completed script.

Answers

1. for a coffee 2. How about 3. matter
4. I'll pay for 5. lend you some 6. of course not
7. enough 8. the cash machine 9. you are
10. no hurry

3 Pronunciation

Go through the explanation of which words we normally stress and model the example. You could point out that if you just said the stressed words, for example, *OK WHERE WANT GO,* your meaning would probably be clear. Ask students to go through the conversation in pairs underlining the words they think are stressed. Encourage them to use pencil in case they need to change their answers. Then play the recording so they can check their answers. They can compare their answers with the tapescript on page 162.

Before students practise reading the tapescript, remind them how we give words stress in English: we make the stressed syllables longer, a little higher, clearer and louder. Demonstrate with a couple of lines. If your students tend to give each word the same stress, give them each a rubber band to stretch out on the stressed words. You might want to play the recording again, stopping after each line so they can repeat it, following the same pronunciation. They can then read the conversation in pairs.

4 Vocabulary: *time* and *money*

Go through the explanation and ask students to complete the sentences on their own and then compare their answers with a partner. As you go through the answers, ask them to underline the complete expressions, for example, *He doesn't spend much money on me,* and record those they want to remember in their notebooks. You may need to explain that if you do something *just in time*, you do it right before the time when it would be too late. For example:
I caught the bus just in time.

Answers

1. money 2. time 3. money 4. time 5. time
6. money 7. money 8. time, time 9. time
10. money

Before students work on the personalisation task, tell them which sentences are true for you. Add details to explain. For example:
My parents didn't spend much time with me when I was younger. My dad was in the army and my mother had her own business. My younger brother and I went to a boarding school and we only came home for the holidays.

You may want to give students some more examples of collocations that *time* and *money* share. For example:
run out of time/money
save time/money
I don't have much time/money left

5 Using grammar: making and responding to offers

Ask students if they can remember how Bob offered to lend Tim some money. Ask them to find the expression in the conversation on page 132 (*Well, do you want me to lend you some?*). Explain that this is a common way of making an offer to a friend. Then ask how Tim responded to the offer (*Would you mind?*). Explain that we use this expression when we want to make sure it is not too much trouble. Remind students of the expressions *Would you mind …* and *I don't mind …* , and that we respond to questions with *mind* with *no* when it isn't a problem and we are happy to do it.

Get students to put the two conversations in order. In **Conversation 1** students may think *That's OK* is the answer to *Is cheese OK?* Explain that we use *That's OK* or *That's all right* to respond to *Thank you* or *Thanks* as a more informal alternative to *You're welcome*. When students have reordered the conversations, read them out so they can check their answers. Then read them again, but pause after each line so students can repeat. Focus on how *Do you want me to … ?* is linked and the intonation of *That's OK*. Finish up by asking students to read the conversations in pairs.

Answers

Conversation 1: 1. e. 2. c. 3. b. 4. a. 5. f. 6. d.
Conversation 2: 1. c. 2. e. 3. b. 4. f. 5. a. 6. d.

6 Practice

Ask students to complete the offers on their own. Go around the class and help if necessary. Make sure students aren't omitting *to*. Invite a few students to tell you their suggestions so you can check. Then do an example with one of the students before they have the conversations in pairs. That way they will have an idea of how to continue the conversation. For example:

S: It's a bit cold in here.
T: Do you want me to turn the heat up?
S: Would you mind?
T: No, of course not, but remember to turn it down before you go to bed.
S: OK. I'm not going to stay up for long.

Finish up by referring students to G34 of the **Grammar commentary** on page 170, which they can read either in class or as homework.

Reading

1 Vocabulary: banks

Lead in by asking students a few questions about banks. For example:
What are the biggest banks in your country? Are any run by the government?
How often do you go into a bank? What for?
Do you usually get money from cash machines or do you go inside?
Do you ever do on-line banking?

Then ask students to complete the expressions on their own before comparing their answers with a partner. As you go through the answers, encourage them to record any expressions they want to remember in their notebooks.

Answers

1. a new account 2. account 3. banks 4. a loan 5. my credit card 6. make 7. change 8. transfer 9. pay 10. apply for

After students have discussed why the people want to do these things, invite a few students to share their suggestions with the class. Reformulate any suggestions if necessary. You could also ask additional questions. For example:
What do you need to open a new account for?
Is it easy to get a credit card?
When do people usually get their first credit card?

You could also do some extra work on the verbs in this task by asking students in pairs to think of two more things that you can *open*, *take out*, *cancel*, and *apply for*.

2 While you read (Eight things I hate about banks)

Go through the list of expressions in the box and check that students understand them by asking a few questions. For example:
Which expression describes the extra money I have to pay on top of a loan? (interest)
Which expression describes the extra money the bank wants for a service like changing money? (a commission)
What might you have to do before you're served in a bank? (queue)
Who serves you in a bank? (a cashier)
What things do you need to fill in forms for? (to apply for a credit card, to take out a loan)
What do you get when you cash a cheque? (the amount of the cheque in cash)

Explain to students that they are going to read an article about banks. Ask them in pairs to think of three good things and three bad things about banks. Then get them to read the article and see if any of the bad things they thought of were mentioned. They should also mark those points they agree with, disagree with and don't understand. Then read the article aloud or play the recording as students follow. Alternatively, use it as a listening task first by playing the recording while students listen with the text covered. Then they can read the article. You can play the recording again while they do this.

You could do this as a jigsaw activity by dividing the class into four groups. Each group reads two points. They then get together with someone from another group and tell them what they read. The next activity, **3 Comprehension**, can be done in the same groups of four.

3 Comprehension

Go through the example expressions first before getting students in small groups or pairs to compare their answers. Encourage them to explain anything another member of the group doesn't understand. Finish up by asking students to read the article again and underline any expressions they want to remember or ask about. If you want to do some work on 'delexical' verbs, ask students to find all the expressions with *make, get* and *take* (e.g. *make so much money, take a very long time, get paid*).

4 Role play

One way you could do this task is to ask students to close their Coursebooks. Read the conversation out aloud for them, but leave a gap of silence for each missing word. Ask students to write down on a piece of paper what they think is missing. Then ask them to compare their answers with a partner. Next, read the conversation for them again. When you have finished, students open their Coursebooks and do the completion task, seeing if they guessed any of the words. Read the completed conversation for students one more time, so they can check their answers. The focus here is on how the expressions sound.

Answers

change, cash, ID, fill in, sign

Ask students to take turns reading the conversation in pairs. You may want to do an example with one student first before they have their own conversations using the questions in **1 Vocabulary: banks**.

Listening

1 While you listen

Focus students' attention on the photos on page 136. Ask how old they think each person is, what they are doing, and where they are going or have been. Then elicit different money problems the people might have. This is a chance to revise some expressions like *her credit card was rejected, she didn't get a promotion* etc. Write students' suggestions on the board and reformulate them if necessary. You could teach the expression *shopaholic* to refer to the woman in photo 3.

Play the recording for students, but before they complete the sentences, make sure they understand *can't afford*. Give a couple of examples:
I can't afford to live in the city.
I'd like to get a new computer, but I can't afford it at the moment.

Students can compare their answers with a partner. Then choose a few students to tell you their answers.

Answers

1. (He can't afford to) go out (because) he only gets £15 pocket money a week.
2. (She can't afford to) live by herself or drive a car (because) she hasn't had a pay rise in five years and she only gets seven euros an hour. (She also can't afford to take time off to go to interviews for another job.)
3. (She can't afford to) go on holiday (because) she's in debt.
4. (He can't afford to) stay in the UK much longer (because) everything is so expensive in London.

2 Word check

Ask students to work on this task in pairs, completing as much as they can. Point out that each space represents one word or contraction (e.g. *he's, it's, I'm* etc.). Then play the recording again so they can fill in anything they missed. Check that they understand some of these expressions:
What do you fill shelves in a supermarket with? (cans, boxes)
What things can you buy in a fancy designer shop? Are they usually expensive? What are some names of fancy designer shops you know?

Explain that *fairly* means *quite*. For example:
I'm fairly sure she's coming, but I haven't spoken to her for a week and her plans may have changed.

Answers

1. It's so (Conversation 1)
2. filling shelves in (Conversation 1)
3. to work (Conversation 2)
4. to go to (Conversation 2)
5. fancy, shop (Conversation 3)
6. in (Conversation 3)
7. cost about six (Conversation 4)
8. fairly, to here (Conversation 4)

For extra practice give students a few minutes to memorise the expressions. Then they can test each other in pairs. One person reads the given words. Their partner tries to remember the complete expression. Finish up by playing the recording again while students follow the tapescript on page 162. As they do so, encourage them to underline any expressions they want to remember and record them in their notebooks.

3 Speaking

This activity gives students a chance to react to the conversations. Explain that if you *feel sorry for* someone, you sympathise with them because something bad has happened to them or they are in a bad situation. For example:
I feel sorry for Gina. She has to go in to work on Saturday.

Talk about your own answers to questions **2** and **3** before asking students to discuss in pairs or small groups.

4 Using grammar: comparing prices

If your students are studying abroad, ask them if they think their own country is cheaper or more expensive. Ask them to tell you what things, for example, food, clothes etc. are cheaper or more expensive. If your students are in their own country, ask them what things a visitor might find more expensive. Explain that in this activity they will practise ways of describing these kinds of differences. Before they do the matching task, you may want to quickly remind them of the guidelines for forming comparatives.

As you go though the answers you may need to explain a few things:

- We often use *I mean* to add an explanation to what we have just said.
- *A pint* is a common way of referring to a pint of beer. We can also use *a half* for *half a pint*.
- We can use a length of time with words like *ride*, *trip*, *flight* and *journey* to say how long it takes. For example: *a three-hour flight, an all-day trip*.
- *Much* is used to emphasise the comparison (*much cheaper*). Ask what the opposite would be (*much more expensive*).
- The following expressions are used for approximations: *two pounds or so, about sixty pence, around ten pounds, thirty or forty pence*.

For extra practice ask students to use some of these expressions to tell you the approximate price of different things in their hometown. For example:
T: How much is a beer?
S: About three euros or so.

Answers

1. a. 2. h. 3. c. 4. d. 5. b. 6. e. 7. g. 8. f.

5 Practice

You might want to check which words in the box complete the two sentence patterns before students talk about the places that were cheaper or more expensive. Ask students how they decided. Ask if we usually make the words that fit with sentence **1** plural (*no*). Explain that when we want to make general statements comparing things, we use the plural form unless the thing is an uncountable noun. You might also want to point out that when we use an *-ing* form (e.g. *watching football, getting your hair cut*), it is singular, even if the noun following it is plural (e.g. *Borrowing books is much more difficult*).

Answers

Sentence 1: chocolate, paper, rice, toothpaste
Sentence 2: clothes, DVDs, hotels, shoes

6 Key word: *pay*

Students may be surprised to learn that *money* is not one of the most typical collocations for *pay*. This activity gives them several common collocations that are. Go through the list saying each expression, and as you do so, tell students to mark those whose meaning they are not sure of with a question mark. Then ask them which ones they would like you to explain. You may need to explain the following:

- Possible answers to *How are you paying?* include *in cash, by cheque, by credit card*.
- If you *pay attention*, you listen or watch something carefully. For example: *Pay attention. I'm only going to tell you this once.*

Ask students to work on the translation task and if possible, get them to compare their ideas with someone who shares the same language. In multi-national classes, where students speak different languages, one person could test the other by saying the first part of each expression. Their partner then tries to remember the complete expression.

7 Practice

Explain the task and ask students to complete the sentences on their own. Then get them to compare their answers with a partner. You may need to explain that if you *split the bill* you each pay half. We can also say *split the cab fare* and *split the cost*.

Answers

1. back, fixed, get 2. shall 3. much
4. into, account 5. How, discount, cash

Ask students to practise reading the conversations in pairs. As a follow-up ask them to practise the conversations again, but this time change the last line and see if they can continue the conversation. For example in **1**:

A: *The cash machine just ate my card and I won't be able to sort it out until the morning.*
B: *OK, there you go.*
A: *Thanks. Come on. I'll buy you a drink.*

8 Speaking

Teach a few expressions to help students talk about bills and getting paid. For example:
I pay my bills on-line/by standing order.
I never/always pay them late.
I pay them just in time/straightaway.
I get paid at the end of the month/on the 15th.

Tell students your answers to the questions before they discuss in pairs or in small groups.

Follow-up

Ask students to think of three things for each of the following categories:
Things that will get cheaper in the future.
Things that will get more expensive in the future.
Things that should be free.
Things that money can't buy.
Things that are a waste of money.
Ways to save money.
Ways to make money quickly and easily.

Then get them in groups to compare their ideas.

20 Society

Unit overview

General topic
Talking about society: the economy, how things have changed.

Conversation
Martin and Alex talk about life back in their countries.

Reading
British males in the seventies, eighties and nineties.

Listening
Marge and Doris complain about young people today.

Language input
- Asking and answering questions starting with *how long*: *How long have you been here? Since Sunday.*
- Expressions for describing the economy: *Inflation is very low, Our currency is very strong.*
- Present continuous and present perfect to talk about change: *Unemployment is falling at the moment, Prices have gone up a lot over the last four years.*
- Expressions to describe young and elderly people: *She never does what she's told, He looks great for his age.*
- Expressions with *used to*: *I used to go out a lot more than I do now, I never used to eat chocolate.*

Language strip

You can use the language strip as a way to lead in to the unit. Point out the title of the unit. Explain that *society* is often used for the way people in a particular area live. We often use it about a country. For example: *British society, French society.* Explain to students that in this unit they will practise ways of talking about society: what things are like and how things have changed. Ask them to quickly look through the strip and find any expressions they could use about their own country (e.g. *The cost of living's really high there*) or about themselves (e.g. *My brother's a vegetarian*). Encourage students to choose a couple of expressions in the strip that look interesting and to find out more about them.

You might need to explain some of the following expressions:
- If something is *in a mess,* it is not in a good state. For example: *Your room's in a mess, The country's in a mess.*
- If the *cost of living is high,* basic things like food, housing, clothes and transport are expensive. For example: *I don't want to study in London. The cost of living's too high.*
- If the *quality of life is great*, people are happy and healthy. For example: *The quality of life there isn't as good as it is in this country.*
- *Inflation* is the rate at which prices increase. For example: *Inflation is going up again.*
- *Racism* is the belief that some people of a different race are inferior.
- *Designer clothes* are made by a fashionable designer. For example: *I can't afford to buy designer clothes any more.*

Remind students to record any of the expressions they like in their notebooks and to take note when they see similar expressions throughout the unit.

Use the language strip later on in this unit for a small group task. Here are some possibilities:
- Students find those expressions that are about bad things (e.g. *The economy is in a mess*) and those that are about good things (e.g. *She gives a lot of money to charity*).
- Students find all the expressions that contain a preposition (e.g. *She looks great for her age*). Later on, write these expressions on the board but with the prepositions gapped out. Students try to remember what preposition is missing.

Lead in

If you used the language strip to introduce the unit, ask students to tell you which expressions they thought were true about their own country. Then, if you come from a different country, tell them which expressions could describe your country. You could also change some expressions so that they are true. (Students will practise talking about their own countries later on in the unit.) For example:
Unemployment is quite high at the moment.

Alternatively, ask students in pairs to think of three things that would make a place good to live in (e.g. *the people, a good economy*) and three things that wouldn't (e.g. *a lot of crime, no jobs*).

Conversation

1 Using grammar: questions with *how long*

You could introduce this activity by writing these two question starters on the board:
How long have you ... ?
How long are you going to ... ?

Ask students to suggest an ending for each one. You may elicit the following:
How long have you been studying English?
How long are you going to stay here?

Ask a few students these questions. You will probably get a few answers with *for*. Explain that we sometimes use short expressions with *for*, *since* or *till* to answer *how long* questions. Explain that we use *since* and *till* with a specific point in time (e.g. *Sunday*) and *for* with a period of time (e.g. *three days*). Then ask students to do the completion task. As you go through the answers, explain that it is helpful to record and remember the complete expressions, for example, *since I was a child*. Make sure students understand that *till* means *up to a point in time,* while *since* means *from a point a time*. You could represent this visually on the board.

Answers

1. Since 2. Till 3. For 4. For 5. Till 6. Since

Once students have tested each other in pairs, get them to work with another partner and ask each other the questions. They can give true answers. For example:
A: *How long have you been here?*
B: *Since ten o'clock.*

Talk about **Real English: till**. Give students a few more examples of expressions with *till*. For example:
You've got till Friday to do your homework.
I slept till ten this morning.
Shop till you drop.

Finish up by referring students to G35 of the **Grammar commentary** on page 170, which they can read either in class or as homework.

2 Talking about life in your country

Explain the situation of the conversation and ask students to just listen for the answers to the two questions. Play the recording, making sure they cover the text. Get them to discuss their answers with a partner. Remind them to keep the text covered as they do this. Ask them where they think the two people are (e.g. *Bali*).

Answers

Alex is travelling. He lost his job and got some money. He is thinking about what to do next. He is going to stay until he gets bored or his money runs out. Martin is there on holiday. He is going home on Friday.

Play the recording again and ask students to try to fill in each of the gaps as they listen. They should then compare their answers with a partner. Play the recording a third time, but this time pause after each gap. Elicit the missing words and maybe write the complete expression on the board. Model the pronunciation and ask students to practise saying it. Play the recording through one more time with students following the completed script.

Answers

1. closed down 2. for a while 3. a bit of a mess
4. something completely different
5. doing quite well 6. the cost of living
7. quality of life 8. not like that 9. run out of

Ask students to underline any expressions they find useful, particularly those they think they might use. Encourage them to transfer these into their notebooks. You might also want to point out the following:
I still haven't decided.
Have you got any idea what you want to do?
I have to get back to work.
I don't have any plans.

Ask students to read the conversation in pairs using the completed script. Follow up by asking them if they have ever felt like moving to a place where they have been on holiday, and if so, why they wanted to.

3 Using vocabulary: the economy

Lead in by asking students the following questions about the conversation:
Is the economy good in Alex's country? (No, it's bad.)
How about in Martin's country? (It was bad, but now it's doing quite well.)

Explain that there are a lot of things that make an economy good or bad. Ask students to suggest a few things (e.g. *jobs, wages, prices*). Then explain the matching task and tell them they will see expressions to describe some of these things. Read through the sentences **1–8**, explaining any vocabulary if necessary. You could also ask whether they think each sentence is about something good or bad. Then get them to do the matching task on their own and compare their answers with a partner.

Answers

1. c. 2. a. 3. g. 4. f. 5. b. 6. h. 7. d. 8. e.

4 Pronunciation: *of*

Go through the explanation and model the first example. Point out that if *of* is followed by a vowel sound, it is pronounced /əv/. For example: *a bit of a*. Play the recording once all the way through so students can just listen. Then play the recording again, pausing after each one so students can repeat.

5 Practice

Explain the first task and ask students to work in pairs. They can then compare their answers with another pair. Go around and help if necessary. Invite a few pairs of students to tell you their answers. Encourage them to record both collocations in their notebooks. For example:
Unemployment is very high.
Unemployment is very low.

Answers

Suggested answers:

1. A lot of people don't have a job. Unemployment is very high.
2. Prices are going up very quickly at the moment. Inflation is very high.
3. The average wage is around £50 a week. Some people earn a lot more and some earn a lot less. Most people's salaries aren't very good.
4. I don't have to give a lot of the money I earn to the government. Tax is very low.
5. Everything is very cheap – even basic things like food and rent. The cost of living is very low.
6. When I go abroad, I can't buy lots of things with the money from my country. Our currency is very weak.
7. The weather is terrible, the people are unfriendly, there's a lot of crime. It's miles from the beach. You have to work really long hours. The quality of life isn't very good.
8. Unemployment is going down, inflation's going down, new factories are opening and new companies are starting up. The economy is doing quite well.

Explain the memorisation task and ask pairs of students to test each other. You could use these summaries later for a quick test. Write gapped expressions on the board and ask students to remember which collocations are missing. For example:
Inflation is very … / … .
The economy is … / … .

6 Further practice

Ask students to discuss the questions in small groups. Go through the examples in the Coursebook. If you haven't done so already, introduce the discussion by talking about your own county/region or another country/region you know well. Encourage students to ask you questions. For example:
Does the government give you money if you're unemployed?
How much tax do you pay?

Encourage them to ask each other questions in their groups.

7 Using grammar: describing changes

You could introduce this activity by asking students to find the expressions Martin used in the conversation on page 138 to describe how the economy is different now. (*the economy's doing quite well at the moment, Prices have gone up a lot over the last few years*). Ask them which expression is in the present perfect and which is in the present continuous. Then go through the explanation and examples in the Coursebook. You could explain that in general, the continuous form often shows that something is unfinished. For example:
I'm still waiting for my visa.

If students ask whether something like *Prices have been going up a lot over the last few years* (i.e. present perfect continuous) is possible, explain that in this situation the perfect expresses that it started in the past and the continuous expresses that you think the change hasn't finished yet.

Ask students to complete the sentences on their own and then compare their answers with a partner. Go around and make sure students are spelling words like *getting* and *has become* correctly. As you go through the answers, ask a few questions. For example:
What is the opposite of 'unemployment is falling'? (unemployment is rising/going up)
What are some examples of children's bad behaviour? (being rude to parents)
What is the opposite of 'worse and worse'? (better and better)
What is the opposite of 'a dangerous place' (a safe place)
What are some examples of racism? (not giving someone a job because of their race)
In what ways might someone have changed over the past ten years? (They're nicer now, They have much shorter hair now.)

Answers

1. is falling 2. is going up 3. has got 4. is getting 5. has become 6. has got 7. has improved 8. 'm working 9. 've changed 10. 've been

Ask students to do the discussion task in pairs or small groups. Finish up by referring them to G36 of the **Grammar commentary** on page 170, which they can read either in class or as homework. For extra practice ask students to complete the following with their own ideas. They can then explain them in pairs or small groups:
I think … is/are getting worse and worse.
I think … is/are getting better and better.
I think … has/have improved a lot over the past several years.
I think … has/have become more expensive over the last few years.
I think … has/have become much cheaper over the last few years.

I think … has/have become much more … over the last few years.

Reading

1 Speaking

Use the photos to introduce this activity. Ask students to describe each man and include details about their clothes, hair etc. Then get them to match the photos to the decades. You could ask students in small groups to talk about what life was like for men in those decades. They should think about men in their own countries, rather than men in Britain. They could use the questions from **3 While you read** below to ask each other.

2 Before you read

Explain the task and ask students to look at the words in the box. Get them to put a question mark next to any they don't understand. Then put students in small groups. If a person understands any words that someone else in their group doesn't, they can explain. Finish up by inviting students to ask about any words they are still not sure of. Use some questions to check their understanding. For example:

What kind of things do people give to charity? (money, books, clothes)

Who goes on strike? (workers) What are some reasons people go on strike? (to get higher wages, to save their jobs)

What are some examples of popular hi-tech toys now? (palmtops)

Where do miners work? (down a mine) What do they do? (get coal, diamonds, gold, copper etc. out of the ground)

What don't you eat if you're a vegetarian? (meat)

Why do people join trade unions? (to protect their jobs, to improve working conditions)

If you wanted to protect the environment, what would you do? (recycle, try to walk more and not use the car)

3 While you read (The changing face of Britain)

This activity is a jigsaw reading. Divide the class into three groups: A, B and C. Explain that each group will read about British men in a different decade. They should read the appropriate text and then answer the questions **1–7**. They can then compare their answers with someone from their group. You could model the pronunciation of the questions and ask students to ask and answer each other in pairs. Go around and help with any cultural or other references:

- The Conservative Party is the right-wing party in Britain. The Conservatives were in power from 1979 until 1997, when the Labour Party won the elections.
- *Phil Collins* is a British singer and musician.
- *Dire Straits* were a British group popular in the late seventies and eighties.
- *World music* is a term to describe music that is not from Western Europe or North America.
- *The stock market* is where stocks and shares are bought and sold.

Answers

Text A

1. They worked in industry
2. They spent a lot of time in the pub and on Saturdays they watched football.
3. They ate typical British food – chips with everything.
4. The text doesn't mention what they listened to. Their children listened to rock music.
5. They thought their wives should stay at home and look after the house and the children.
6. They went on holiday to British seaside towns.
7. Yes. Many belonged to left-wing political groups.

Text B

1. A lot of them wanted to work in business or in the stock market.
2. They liked to wear expensive designer clothes in their free time, and bought hi-tech toys. They played squash or golf and met their girlfriends in wine bars. They listened to music.
3. They liked eating in Japanese sushi restaurants.
4. They listened to Phil Collins and Dire Straits.
5. They had lots of girlfriends and waited longer to get married.
6. They went on holiday to Spain, Greece and the Caribbean.
7. Yes. They voted for the Conservative Party. They didn't like trade unions.

Text C

1. They worked with people or for charities.
2. They went out to Thai or Indian restaurants, or to the cinema. They talked about their feelings, politics and travel plans with their friends.
3. They liked foreign food. Some men were vegetarians.
4. They listened to World music.
5. They had female friends as well as male friends. They had a 'partner' rather than a 'wife'. They helped with the children and around the home.
6. They went on holiday to places in Asia and South America where there weren't many tourists.
7. Yes. They worried about the environment and what was happening to people in other countries.

4 After you read

Get students into new groups of three: one person from group A, one from group B and one from group C. You might need to have a few groups of four with two people who read the same text. Students should then ask each other the questions about the three texts and continue with the three discussion questions. Finish up by asking the groups to share some of their ideas with the rest of the class. You might also want to play the recording of the three texts or read them aloud as students follow along.

5 Word check

Ask students to look at the words in the box and explain any they don't understand. Get them to work individually on the completion task and compare their answers with a partner. They can then look back at the texts to check if they were right. As you go through the answers, you might need to explain the following:

- The Labour Party is traditionally the left-wing party in Britain. A lot of people don't think it is left-wing any more.
- We use *industry* to describe a certain kind of business. For example: *the tourist industry, the steel industry.*

Here are some more questions to ask:

When do men retire in your country? How about women? When do you want to retire?

What happens when workers go on strike? (They stand on picket lines, They go on demonstrations.)

What other words do we use 'ex-' with? (ex-girl/boyfriend, ex-husband, my ex)

Is there anywhere you know like the place in **9***?*

How's the car industry in your country? Where are most of the cars made?

Answers

1. job 2. retire 3. strike 4. successful
5. relationship 6. factories 7. voted 8. politics
9. environment 10. industry

6 Speaking

Tell students your own answers to the questions before they discuss them in pairs or small groups. Feed in some helpful expressions and write them on the board. You might want to include expressions like the following:

There was a general strike.

It went on for nearly a year.

They can't go on strike any more.

They went out of business.

They had to cut back.

They're cutting down lots of trees.

They want to drill for oil.

Listening

1 Using vocabulary: talking about old and young people

Lead in by telling students about two people in your own family. Encourage them to ask you questions. Then get them to talk to another student. Explain that for the oldest person they can talk about a grandparent or an aunt or uncle. Then read each of the sentences aloud as students mark them. Explain any vocabulary if necessary. For example:

- If someone *looks great for their age*, they probably look younger than they really are.
- If someone is *mature for their age*, they act older than they are.
- If someone is *sensible*, they behave in a reasonable way. They don't do things that are silly or dangerous.
- If someone is *losing their memory*, they keep forgetting things.

You could also ask a few checking questions. For example:

If she's almost blind, what can't she do well?

If she's a bit deaf, what can't she do well?

If she uses a stick, what can't she do well?

What kind of things might a person who is very mature for their age do? (have more responsibility, be sensible, talk about adult things)

You could also ask students to tell you which sentences have a positive meaning (3., 7., 8., 9., 10. and 11.).

Answers

1. E 2. E 3. T 4. T 5. T 6. E 7. E 8. T
9. T 10. E 11. T 12. E

Ask students to work with a new partner and tell each other about someone they know. Alternatively, they can use some of the statements to talk about the woman in the photo on page 142.

2 Before you listen

Ask students what older people generally think about younger people in their countries. Ask if they often complain about younger people and if so, elicit a couple of things they complain about. Then explain the situation of the listening. Point out that we use *elderly* as an alternative to *old*. Elicit the first thing that might be said. For example:

They've got too much money and too much free time.

Ask students to work on the rest in pairs. Then invite them to tell you what they wrote. Reformulate any of their suggestions if necessary, feeding in appropriate expressions like *they don't have any manners* etc. Ask students how many they think are true.

3 While you listen

Tell students to listen for the things about young people that are mentioned in the conversation and then play the recording. Ask students in pairs to compare what they heard. You may need to explain the following:

- If someone *has no shame*, they don't care if something they are doing embarrasses other people.
- If someone is *in a rush*, they want to get somewhere or do something quickly.

Answers

Young people nowadays have got no shame.

They swear all the time.

They don't offer to help older people.

They're always in such a rush.

They've got no respect.

You can't tell the difference between boys and girls sometimes.

4 Comprehension check

Make sure students know that the past tense of *swear* is *swore* and that *let someone go first* means *let someone do something before you*. For example:
When I play pool, I always let the other person go first.

Ask students to work on this task on their own and compare their answers with a partner. They should then try to correct any sentences that are false. Play the recording again so they can check their answers.

Answers

1. True
2. False (The young man in the supermarket swore at Marge.)
3. True (She has a bad leg and sometimes uses a stick.)
4. True (She bought some cat food.)
5. False (He swore at her and laughed at her.)
6. False (Marge couldn't tell the difference.)

Finish up by playing the recording of the conversation again while students follow the tapescript on page 163. Ask them to underline any expressions they want to remember or ask about. Encourage them to record some of these in their notebooks.

5 Speaking

Go through the questions and explain any vocabulary. Make sure students remember the meaning of *feel sorry for* and *mind their own business*. Then ask them to discuss these questions in pairs or small groups. You could turn this into a class discussion on the situation for elderly people in their countries. Here are some possible questions to discuss:
Do a lot of elderly people tend to live alone or do they move in with their children?

Do they get pensions from the government? Are they enough to live on?

Do most people respect older people? Is it different from any other countries you know? Are there many elderly politicians in your country?

6 Using grammar: *used to*

Introduce this activity by drawing two columns on the board. Label one *before* and the other *now*. Ask students to remember what Marge and Doris said about what young people were like when they were young and what they are like now. List their ideas in the appropriate columns. Then explain, using the example *we always used to let old people go first*, that we often use *used to* to talk about differences between the past and now. Go through the three examples in the Coursebook, explaining that the negative is often *never used to* and sometimes *didn't use to*. Point out that we use *use* in *didn't use to*, not *used*. Also model the pronunciation of *used to*: /ˈjuːstə/. Then ask students to practise forming statements based on the information in the two columns on the board. For example:
Young people never used to swear.
They used to be more polite.

Explain the matching task. Ask students to work on their own and then compare their answers with a partner. You may need to explain the following:

- A *traditional English Sunday lunch* usually includes roast beef, lamb or pork, roast potatoes and vegetables. Dessert is often apple pie and custard.
- *Passive smoking* means that you yourself do not smoke, but that you breathe in the smoke from other people's cigarettes.
- If someone *starts feeling their age*, they start to think they can't do what younger people do.

Answers

1\. b. 2. a. 3. d. 4. c. 5. g. 6. h. 7. e. 8. f.

Point out the patterns in these structures:
... used to ... , but nowadays ...
... used to ... , but don't/doesn't any more
... used to when I was young

Also point out the two examples of *since*: *since my 40th birthday* and *since she retired*. For extra practice ask students to find any sentences that are true for them or that they can make true. For example:
The trade unions never used to go on strike because it used to be illegal, but nowadays they're always on strike.

7 Practice

For the next task you could ask students to practise saying these expressions, focusing on linking and the pronunciation of *used to*. Then get pairs of students to discuss what happened to cause the change. This is a good opportunity to work on vocabulary. Invite pairs of students to tell the class what they decided and reformulate their suggestions if necessary. Here are some possibilities if students had difficulty with any:

1. I've got two young children.
2. I kept getting speeding tickets and then my licence was taken away.
3. I injured my back and couldn't play any more.
4. I lost my job and had to move into somewhere smaller.
5. I got a job in an office.
6. I got married and had kids.
7. My job became really stressful.
8. I have to go abroad a lot on business.

Finish up by asking who had the funniest or most unusual suggestions.

8 Further practice

Ask students to complete these sentences and then discuss them with a partner. Encourage them to record these personalised examples in their notebooks. Finish up by telling students how you would complete them. Encourage them to ask you questions. Finally refer them to G37 of the **Grammar commentary** on page 170, which they can read either in class or as homework.

Follow-up

Give students a list of things in society that could have changed over the last 20–30 years. For example: fashion, music, attitudes to women, the environment, sport, the economy, politics, food, free-time activities etc. Get them to think about what changes there have been in these areas in their country. Give them time to look back through the unit to find helpful language and to prepare what they want to say. Point out that the patterns with *used to* and the present perfect expressions may be useful. Then ask them to talk about their ideas in small groups.

You could also ask students to do a role play like the conversation on page 138. They could talk about their own countries or pretend to be someone else. For example, one could be an elderly person on holiday and the other a student.

Review: Units 17–20

Most of these exercises should be done in pairs or small groups.

1 Act or draw

Get students to read through the list individually first. Then ask them in turns to draw or act out the five words or expressions they have chosen. Next, they should ask their partner about any of the words or expressions they are not sure of.

2 Tenses

Answers

1. We're staying
2. has gone up
3. I tripped
4. I was cutting, slipped, I cut
5. Have you spoken, I'll talk
6. I'll show you
7. you're going, Let me help you, I'll do it
8. I don't usually, I used to smoke

3 Grammar

Answers

1. make/get, mind, Do/Would, 'm
2. my, should, it, be
3. used, the
4. must, 'll
5. much, than, costs, six

4 Questions and answers

Answers

1. d. 2. a. 3. e. 4. b. 5. c. 6. i. 7. h. 8. f.
9. g. 10. e.

5 What can you remember?

When the class have finished working in groups of four, invite a few students to tell you what they remember.

6 Verb collocations

Answers

1. offer 2. hit 3. lend 4. be covered 5. spend
6. vote 7. run out 8. make 9. take out
10. belong

Examples of other collocations

1. (offer) to help
2. (hit) someone in the face
3. (lend) me your dictionary
4. (be covered) with snow
5. (spend) time with my family
6. (vote) for the Socialists
7. (run out) of time
8. (make) it in time
9. (take out) the rubbish
10. (belong) to a club

7 Look back and check

Ask students to choose one of the activities. You could then get them to do the other one on another day.

8 Expressions

Answers

1. surprised
2. manage
3. plays
4. goes
5. do, promise
6. tell
7. fault
8. Forget
9. paying

9 Vocabulary quiz

Answers

1. No, in a dishwasher.
2. Deaf.
3. If a lot of jobs in your industry were disappearing.
4. *I need to fix it* means that I'll do it myself, while *I need to get it fixed* means someone else will fix it for me.
5. Flowers.
6. You might miss some important information. You might have an accident.
7. Possible answers: a driving licence, a passport.
8. Possible answers: the radio, the heat, the volume.
9. Possible answers: (a loaf of) bread, (a pint of) beer, (a pair of) jeans.
10. A cash machine.
11. When you take out a loan.
12. No.
13. You owe money.
14. Generous.
15. Something nasty.
16. Possible answers: blood, wine. You can wash it or bleach it.

Pronunciation

1 Contrastive stress: weak and strong forms

Answers

1. is, does 2. has, did 3. hasn't 4. will 5. do, can

2 Vowel sounds: diphthongs

Answers

1. years
2. shade
3. coast
4. square
5. where/wear
6. below
7. weird
8. hair
9. blow your nose
10. this tastes great
11. it's really serious
12. the air fare

3 Problem sounds: /w/ and /j/

Model and practise the sounds. Ask students if they can hear the difference. Then model the expressions before asking students to practise saying them.